This innovative study moves briskl, ... comprehensively through three phases of the Third World's encounter with the Bible – precolonial, colonial and postcolonial. It recounts the remarkable story of how an inaccessible and marginal book in the ancient Churches of India, China and North Africa became an important tool in the hands of both colonizer and colonized; how it has been reclaimed and interrogated in the postcolonial world; and how it is now being reread by various indigenes, Native Americans, dalits and women.

Drawing on substantial exegetical examples, Sugirtharajah examines reading practices ranging from the vernacular to liberation and the newly emerging postcolonial criticism. His study emphasizes the often overlooked biblical reflections of people such as Equiano and Ramabai as well as better-known contemporaries like Gutiérrez and Tamez. Partly historical and partly hermeneutical, the volume will provide invaluable insights into the Bible in the Third World for students and interested general readers.

R. S. SUGIRTHARAJAH is Reader in Biblical Hermeneutics at the University of Birmingham. Dr Sugirtharajah is author of *Asian Biblical Hermeneutics and Postcolonialism* (1999) and has edited and contributed to a number of volumes including: *Dictionary of Third World Theologies* (2000), *Vernacular Hermeneutics* (1999), *Postcolonial Bible* (1998) and *Voices from the Margin* (1995 and 1991). He won the Catholic Press Association Book Award for *Voices from the Margin*.

THE BIBLE AND THE THIRD WORLD

Precolonial, Colonial and Postcolonial Encounters

R. S. SUGIRTHARAJAH

CAMBRIDGE
UNIVERSITY PRESS

PUBLISHED BY THE PRESS SYNDICATE OF THE UNIVERSITY OF CAMBRIDGE
The Pitt Building, Trumpington Street, Cambridge, United Kingdom

CAMBRIDGE UNIVERSITY PRESS
The Edinburgh Building, Cambridge CB2 2RU, UK
40 West 20th Street, New York, NY 10011–4211, USA
10 Stamford Road, Oakleigh, Melbourne 3166, Australia
Ruiz de Alarcón 13, 28014 Madrid, Spain
Dock House, The Waterfront, Cape Town 8001, South Africa

http://www.cambridge.org

First published 2001

Printed in the United Kingdom at the University Press, Cambridge

Typeset in Baskerville 11/12.5pt   System 3b2   [CE]

A catalogue record for this book is available from the British Library

Library of Congress cataloguing in publication data
Sugirtharajah, R. S. (Rasiah S.)
The Bible and the third world: precolonial, colonial and postcolonial encounters /
R. S. Sugirtharajah.
p.   cm.
Includes bibliographical references and index.
ISBN 0 521 77335 0 (hardback) ISBN 0 521 00524 8 (paperback)
1. Bible – Hermeneutics. 2. Christianity – Developing countries.
I. Title.
BS476.S85 2001
220′09172′4–dc21   00-065173 CIP

ISBN 0 521 77335 0 hardback
ISBN 0 521 00524 8 paperback

Contents

v

Acknowledgements

All those who are engaged in the task of producing books know that it is a collective venture. In relation to this book, there are many people to whom I would like to express my gratitude. Dan O'Connor, the gentle 'sahib', has been a great supporter and through the years has shown sustained interest in all my research projects. As the first reader of this work, he not only gave freely of his time and wisdom but also often made perceptive suggestions which considerably improved the tone of the text and prevented me from straying from the task at hand.

My thanks go to Kevin Taylor, the Senior Commissioning Editor of CUP, for his enthusiastic support for the project from its inception, for entrusting me with the venture and for many helpful suggestions along the way; to Jan Chapman for her meticulous and sensitive copy-editing; to Markus Vinzent, the head of the Department of Theology, for granting me an extended study leave, and for his personal interest and encouragement; to Ralph Broadbent for his willingness to sort out the computer complications that I often encountered; to Lorraine Smith for her support and scrupulous reading of various parts of the book; to the ever-friendly and resourceful staff at the Orchard Learning Centre – Meline Nielsen, Gordon Harris, Michael Gale, Robert Card, Janet Bushnell, Deborah Drury, Jane Saunders, Pauline Hartley, Gary Harper, Griselda Lartey, and Nigel Moseley, and especially to Nigel and Griselda for tracking down elusive material.

Finally my thanks also go to my wife Sharada, who, herself coming from a tradition which has a different perspective on texts, was often amused, annoyed and amazed at the way biblical hermeneutics operates, and who was, as ever, supportive of my work, even suspending her own research to enable me to finish mine on time. Her intellectual contribution and personal care were greater than she can imagine.

Introduction

Along with gunboats, opium, slaves and treaties, the Christian Bible became a defining symbol of European expansion. The underlying purpose of this volume is to trace how the Christian Bible, the ur text of European culture, as Stephen Prickett calls it, has been transmitted, received, appropriated and even subverted by Third World people. It narrates the arrival of the Bible in precolonial days, through to its appropriation in the postcolonial context, both by the colonizer and colonized.

Some of the organizing terms in the volume may cause uneasiness and anxiety, hence they need elaboration and explanation. Firstly, the use of 'Third World' in the title: ever since the term gained currency in the public domain, invigorating discussions have been going on regarding its value and limitation. It was introduced by the French economist and demographer, Alfred Sauvy. His intention was to bring out two aspects – the idea of exclusion, and the aspiration of Third World people. He saw in that class of commoners the Third Estate of the French Revolution, which not only suggested exclusion but also stood for the idea of revolutionary potential. However, Sauvy did not see the Third Estate as being in a numerical hierarchy, below the French aristocracy and the clergy, but as being 'excluded from its proper role in the world by two other worlds'.[1] His contention was that 'the Third World has, like the Third Estate, been ignored and despised and it too wants to be something'.[2]

[1] Kofi Buenor Hadjor, *Dictionary of Third World Terms* (London, Penguin Books, 1993), p. 3.
[2] Ibid.

At a time when the world is becoming increasingly globa-
lized, with the dismantling of the socialist experiment and the
apparent success of the market economy, a place for the Third
World may appear redundant. However, naming of the
peoples of Africa, Asia, Latin America, the Caribbean and the
Pacific has been problematic, and has gone through different
processes. In the earlier days, when Europeans were carving
up the continents of these peoples, words such as 'primitive',
'depraved races', 'savages', and 'inferior' were freely applied.
Later, after these countries gained independence, a new vocabulary was introduced – 'under-developed', 'least developed'
and 'low income group nations'. What such descriptions
suggested, at the worst, was racist and paternalist; they also
hinted that these countries had to be civilized and developed
in order to emulate and measure up to the expectations of the
West. At the height of the cold war, Mao Zedong, the late
Chinese leader, devised his own hierarchy of world order.
For him, the First World included the superpowers which
dominated international relations – the USA and Russia (at least
until now). The Second World consisted of the industrially
developed nations who were part of NATO and the Warsaw
Pact. The Third World consisted of economically worse-off
countries. In certain circles the term 'two-thirds' is mooted as
a possible option. The trouble with this term is that it gives
the impression that these people occupy and own a vast
amount of space, but it does not disclose the fact that they
neither own, control nor have access to its resources. More
importantly, the term does not sufficiently capture the helplessness or vulnerability of the people. Recently, without
rejecting the existence of the Third World, some have gone on
to postulate a Fourth World. When speaking about the indigenous people of the Americas, Gordon Brotherston revived
the *Mappa Mundi*'s description of the Americas as the Fourth
World, to describe the status and identity of Native Americans.[3] Similarly Christopher Rowland and Mark Corner

[3] See his *Book of the Fourth World* (Cambridge, Cambridge University Press, 1992),
pp. 1–6. According to *Mappa Mundi*, Asia was the first world, Europe the second and
Africa the third.

name the poor in the First World as the Fourth World.[4] Any definition has its limitations. For my part, I feel the term Third World is still serviceable because it encapsulates a particular way of existence and experience. It is a suitable semantic metaphor which conveys a relationship, especially the unequal relationship that exists between the strong and the weak. It refers to a people who have been left out and do not have the power to shape their future. It defines a relationship marked by power and mediated through old colonial ties, and currently through the economic and cultural presence of neocolonialism. Such iniquitous relationships exist both globally and locally. In this sense, there is already a Third World in the First World and a First World in the Third World. Ultimately, what is important is not the nomenclature, but the idea it conveys and the analysis it provides. I believe that the redefined term, Third World, does give an accurate picture. As Trinh T. Minh-ha points out, 'whether "Third World" sounds negative or positive also depends on *who* uses it'.[5]

Clearly this volume is not a systematic attempt to cover the entire Third World, nor does it offer a full history of the reception of the Bible. Instead, I envision this project as exploring particular ways in which the Bible has been received throughout the ages. This inevitably reflects my own area of interest and concern, my aim being to show how the Bible interfaces with different historical moments. I have chosen European colonization as a marker to delineate this relationship, and it requires explanation. I admit that this delineation is contestable. I am not saying that European colonization was the only intervention in the past. There were many others,[6] but they were not characterized by the kind of aggressive ethnocentric imposition of one's culture upon the 'other' as practised by European colonizers. In terms of world history, Western imperialism has been the most powerful ideological construc-

---

[4] Christopher Rowland and Mark Corner, *Liberating Exegesis: The Challenge of Liberation Theology to Biblical Studies* (London, SPCK, 1990), p. 157.

[5] Trinh T. Minh-ha, *Woman, Native, Other: Writing Postcoloniality and Feminism* (Bloomington, Indiana University Press, 1989), p. 97.

[6] For earlier forms of colonization see Marc Ferro, *Colonization: A Global History*, tr. K. D. Prithipaul (London, Routledge, 1997).

tion of the last four or five centuries. Osterhammel, who studied various types of colonialism, notes:

Ever since the Iberian and English colonial theorists of the sixteenth century, European expansion has been stylized grandiosely as the fulfilment of a universal mission: as a contribution to a divine plan for the salvation of the pagans, as a secular mandate to 'civilize' the 'barbarians' or 'savages', a 'white man's burden' that he [*sic*] is privileged to carry, etc. These attitudes were always premised on a belief in European cultural superiority.[7]

The impact of Western cultural colonialism upon the Other is the chief difference between earlier and modern European expansionism. Most significantly, Western civilization has outlasted the earlier colonialisms and etched itself more indelibly than the earlier ones on the memories, discourses, lives, histories and cultures of the people. To use Western imperialism as the focusing denominator for this study is not necessarily to reinscribe centre–margin binaries or totalize a particular historical experience. Rather, it is to suggest that a dialectical discursive relationship and tension exists between and within the colonized and colonizer.

A word about the method employed here: I have been influenced by the newly emerging postcolonial theory, and I have also enlisted insights from discourse analysis. Postcolonial discourse is not monolithic, and its diverse concerns and stances have not only opened up but also provided a valuable discursive tool to detect and critique colonial intentions embedded in texts and interpretations. How I employ the insights of postcolonialism and how they enter the debate will become clear as the reader progresses from chapter to chapter.

OVERVIEW AND ARGUMENTS

The volume contains three parts which are organized around different phases of colonialism. Part 1 which has a single chapter, 'Before the empire: the Bible as a marginal and a minority text', describes the first of the three stages – pre-

---

[7] Jürgen Osterhammel, *Colonialism: A Theoretical Overview*, tr. Shelly L. Frisch (Princeton, Markus Wiener Publishers, 1997), p. 16.

colonial, when the Bible arrived in Asia and Africa. It particularly concentrates on India, China and Romanized North Africa. It narrates the story of how the Christian Bible remained in venerable versions such as Latin and Syriac and was inaccessible to ordinary people, and how biblical materials were indirectly written in works ranging from liturgies and catechisms to theological treatises. Without the support of colonial apparatuses, the Bible remained a minor text in the precolonial phase; it found its place, among the many religious texts of other traditions, as one of the Books of the East and it did so without threatening, surpassing or subsuming them. It strove to carve a niche at a time when, within Christian tradition, other sites such as liturgy and sacraments were seen as the prime medium of God's revelation.

Part II, 'Colonial embrace', contains four chapters. The emergence and dominant presence of European colonialism provide a natural discursive backdrop to these studies. The first chapter, 'White men bearing gifts: diffusion of the Bible and scriptural imperialism', maps out how an inaccessible book in the precolonial phase has now become the most easily available one through the expansionist efforts of the British and Foreign Bible Society. It also maps out the main characteristics and effects of colonial interpretation. The next two chapters narrate the critical counter-discourse undertaken by colonized and colonizer. The principal aim of the former chapter, 'Reading back: resistance as a discursive practice', is to reiterate that the transmission of the Bible was not one-sided, but rather the colonized themselves actively serviced the very canonical texts newly introduced to them. Furthermore, the colonized profitably capitalized on both the language of evangelical Christianity with its appeal to the Bible, and on modernist values which the missionaries themselves had introduced. The chapter provides examples of the discourse of resistance undertaken by the colonized from different continents. It contains critical materials on Olaudah Equiano, William Apess, K. M. Banerjea, Pandita Ramabai, and African indigenous Churches, whose work on the Bible has been neglected, eclipsed and given no proper recognition by mainstream biblical scholarship nor by Third World theological institutions. Unfortunately, the interpretative practices of these people were not seen as sophisticated enough to be studied within the biblical disciplines and were relegated to church history, mission studies or practical theology. I hope that this chapter will serve not only as a reminder that the techniques employed by these people to read the Bible were as rich and subtle as the current ones, but also as a reminder that their very act of reading in the face of colonial oppression is worth emulating.

The chapter on John W. Colenso deals with an example of a missionary who broke ranks with his colleagues in order to side with the aspirations of the 'natives', and who complicated the missionary hermeneutics of the time by exposing its Eurocentricism. Colenso's hermeneutical activity was a controversial and a creative one for a colonizer to undertake during the colonial period. The chapter demonstrates how Colenso simultaneously disputed and dismantled the interpretative core of the missionaries, and used the very Zulu culture which they derided in order to pose new questions to the text and in turn be illuminated by them. In the controversy over his work on the Pentateuch, often his critical approach to the New Testament was overlooked – namely, his subjection of the New Testament documents to a scrutiny similar to that he meted out to the Hebrew Scriptures, and his unlocking of Paul's letter to the Romans with the help of Zulu cultural nuances. This chapter attempts to redress this omission. An important point worth reiterating is that the hermeneutical output of the colonized and a few colonizers should not be seized upon as noble examples of a radical unshackling of colonialism. Both were engaged in oppositional discourse, one employing the discourse of resistance and the other the discourse of dissidence. The discourses were laden with colonial language, and by nature and content were complicitous discourses undertaken by those who simultaneously condemned the evils of colonialism and complimented its virtues and its indispensability. The last chapter of this section ends with an important and often overlooked aspect of the reception of the Bible, namely its circulation and distribution. It looks at the role played by the cadre of colporteurs and Biblewomen, and at the type of Bible they tried to disseminate. Their story has been brushed aside, and is now recounted and given wider visibility.

Part III, 'Postcolonial reclamations', contains three chapters, each of which is concerned with interpretation undertaken in the aftermath of colonialism. The first of these chapters seeks to address the question of native interpretation. It seeks to provide illustrations of how Asians, Africans and Latin Americans overcame the strangeness and remoteness of biblical texts by galvanising their own cultural resources to illuminate biblical narratives. It makes visible the spectacular ways in which the vernacular has been creatively incorporated into current interpretative practices. It provides a definition of vernacular hermeneutics and illustrates it with examples from different contexts in which interpreters have drawn upon varying cultural resources, such as African trickster tales to Japanese Noh drama, to throw light on biblical narratives. It also deals with exegetical reworkings which are informed by a vernacular heritage and by the indigene's own identity. The chapter connects in part with the concerns of indigenization but also stands at a certain distance from them. While celebrating the arrival of the vernacular, it draws attention to the fact that the vernacular itself can become a conservative tool when it is used to emphasize purity over against plurality and diversity. This chapter itself is an enlarged version of a piece which appeared previously in another volume.

Chapter seven, 'Engaging liberation: texts as a vehicle of emancipation', examines one of the most influential biblical interpretations to emerge in our time – liberation hermeneutics. The chapter sets out the key tenets of liberation hermeneutics and the contexts in which it emerged, and it draws attention to the vibrant internal discussions which have altered the original terrain. It brings to the fore how biblical passages have been retrieved both by mainstream interpreters, such as Gustavo Gutiérrez and Elsa Tamez, and by various subaltern groups, such as Indian dalits (the self-designated name for those who were once called outcastes), women and indigenous peoples, and it shows how they have opened up fresh ways of interrogating and interpreting texts. The chapter demonstrates how biblical narratives have become an important means by which trained and ordinary people have been able to define and redefine their subaltern status, by choosing to situate themselves within biblical narratives in order to make sense of and attempt to control the circumstances in which they find themselves. It ends with a critique of liberation hermeneutics for its over-reliance on a modernistic agenda and underlines how such a mortgaging has effectively prevented it from facing up to new challenges.

The last chapter highlights the shift in Third World biblical scholarship, the emergence of a new critical category – postcolonial reading – and how it seeks to move beyond liberation hermeneutics, which was until now regarded as the most distinctive contribution of Third World biblical interpreters. This chapter captures the mood of postcolonial reading practice, identifies the different streams within the field, provides markers of its scriptural readings, locates the place of this new critical category among other intellectual currents of the time – namely, postmodernism, and other liberative discourses such as feminism – and demonstrates how it converges and diverges from them. The chapter seeks to understand the Bible in the postcolonial environment, but at the same time it wants to interrogate both the Bible and postcolonialism in light of each other. The chapter ends with a tentative support for the theory.

Although the volume is chronologically arranged and takes on a linear progression, each of the chapters stands on its own and can be read independently. Each chapter has its own unity, but is nonetheless connected with the Others.

Readers may be troubled by the gender-biased language in the volume. Most of this occurs in the colonial literature cited here. In these days of cleansing anything awkward, the temptation is to remove it. Instead, gender-biased language is left as it is, to indicate that language, too, provided an important tool in the imperial project of incorporating the other.

This volume does not present a complete picture. Scholars who are familiar with the landscape of Third World hermeneutics might like to challenge the choice of topics, interpretation and the over-all organization. What these chapters together seek to demonstrate is the diversity and the complex range of interpretations which unsettle, negotiate with and, at times, resist colonial forms of interpretations. I hope this volume will contribute to the dialogue that is occurring around us with regard to texts, multiplicity of interpretations and the art of reading.

PART I

Precolonial reception

CHAPTER I

Before the empire: the Bible as a marginal and a minority text

The *Way* had not, at all times and in all places, the selfsame name; the sages had not, at all times and in all places, the selfsame human body. (Heaven) caused a suitable religion to be instituted for every region and clime so that each one of the races of mankind might be saved.

Seventh-century Chinese Imperial Rescript

If all this be true, how is it that God waits over sixteen hundred years before giving us any knowledge of it; how is it that the Chinese are left out, and only the barbarians are mentioned? The Emperor K'and-hsi

As discussed in the introduction, there are three key junctures at which the Bible reached the Third World – precolonial, colonial and postcolonial. This chapter aims to describe the first phase of its arrival in Asia and Africa. In doing so, it will chart the reception and appropriation of the Bible in these continents.

Asia and Africa have close links with biblical Christianity. Africa's connection with the Bible is celebrated in famous courtly and common people who figure in the biblical narratives. These include royal personnages such as the Queen of Sheba; the Ethiopian Eunuch; Ebedmelech, another Ethiopian royal (Ebedmelech = son of a king), who helped Jeremiah out of a water tank; and other ordinary people such as Simon of Cyrene who bore the cross and came from North Africa (Luke 23.26).[1] Asia, too, has its claim to biblical connections. India is

[1] There was another Cyrenian called Lucius who was one of those who laid hands on Paul and Barnabas before they embarked on their journey (Acts 13.1–3). Among

13

mentioned at least twice in the Book of Esther (1.1; 8.9). In Maccabees there is a reference to an Indian mahout with Antiochus' war elephants (1 Macc. 6.8).[2] One often overlooks the fact that, of the twenty-seven books of the New Testament, nearly half were either written in Asia Minor or written as letters to Christian communities there. The popular perception is that Christianity arrived in Asia only a couple of centuries ago under the aegis of the European powers, when they were making political inroads into that region. John England, who has studied the expansion of Christianity in Asia, notes that the Christian presence began 'in the first-century spread of the Palestinian and Syrian Church eastward into Mesopotamia', while 'subsequent missions of the Churches of the East extended to at least twelve countries east of Persia by the eighth century. In some cases active churches continued in a number of countries for the first Roman Catholic missionaries to discover.'[3] In a recent study of the history of Asian Christianity, Samuel Hugh Moffett reminds us of some of these often forgotten facts. He points out that before Christianity moved into Europe, its

first centres were Asian. Asia produced the first known church building, the first New Testament translation, perhaps the first Christian king, the first Christian poets, and even arguably the first Christian state.[4]

---

other Africans was Apollos of Alexandria (Acts 18.24–19.1) who preached in Corinth (Europe) and Ephesus (Asia).

[2] 'And upon the elephants were wooden towers, strong and covered; they were fastened upon each beast by special harness, and upon each were four armed men who fought from there, and also its Indian driver' (1 Macc. 6.37). There were also other indirect references to India: Indian mercantile products such as textiles, linen and fragrances, birds such as peacocks and animals such as monkeys found their way to the court of King Solomon. See Zacharias P. Thundy, *Buddha and Christ: Nativity Stories and Indian Traditions* (Leiden, E. J. Brill, 1993), pp. 212–17. There is a distinct possibility of a Hindu god figuring in the Hebrew Scripture: when King Ahasuerus is enraged by the refusal of Queen Vashiti to grace the royal assembly, he calls the seven princes and one of them is Krishna (Esther 1.13, 14). I owe this reference to Ari L. Goldman; see his *The Search for God at Harvard* (New York, Ballantine Books, 1991), p. 84.

[3] John C. England, *The Hidden History of Christianity in Asia: The Churches of the East Before 1500* (Delhi, ISPCK, 1996), pp. 1–2.

[4] Samuel Hugh Moffett, *A History of Christianity in Asia*, vol. 1: *Beginnings to 1500*, revised and corrected edition (Maryknoll, NY, Orbis Books, 1998), p. xiii.

INDIA: LITURGICAL AND ICONIC USAGE

In the precolonial days, just before the advent of modern European colonization, the Bible was transmitted to Asia either through sea-routes or along the 'Silk road', together with commercial merchandise. It was mainly traders, travellers, monks and merchants who carried the 'pearl of the Gospel'. It was those who belonged to the Church of the East, often known as Nestorians,[5] who introduced the Christian Bible to Asia. The scope of this book does not warrant a detailed inquiry into the theological and other issues which led to the division of the Church into different groups. For our purposes, it is sufficient to say that the chief controversies centred around the Churches' Christological beliefs. Nestorius, the bishop of Constantinople, defined Christ as one person with two natures, but his ecclesiastical rivals from Alexandria claimed Christ as one person with one nature, both God and man.[6] The Bible that Nestorians brought with them was not the Western canon with its Latin version, but the Eastern Bible in the Syriac version known as the Peshitta.[7] Popularly, the Peshitta (Syriac, 'simple') was often perceived as a common or simple version or as aimed at simple people; alternatively, it was thought to refer to the style of translation. It was, in fact, simple in the sense that its text was free from obeli, asterisks and other marks, and from margins

---

[5] In this book the term Nestorians will be used rather than the Church of the East.

[6] For a detailed account of the creedal confusion and theological misunderstanding among Nestorians and against their rivals, see Moffett, *History of Christianity in Asia*, vol. I, pp. 175–80, 247–51.

[7] This version, which contains all canonical books of the Old Testament (except Chronicles), was translated straight from the Hebrew, and corresponded closely with the Massoretic text; parts of it had been influenced by LXX (Genesis, Isaiah, the minor prophets and Psalms). The Syriac New Testament, which was known as the 'queen' of all Bible versions, excluded 2 Peter, 2 and 3 John, Jude and Revelation and also John 7.53–8.11 and Luke 22.17–18. It superseded Tatian's *Diatessaron*. Since it has been cited by Ephrem, one of the fathers of the Church of the East in the fourth century, the version must have been in existence before that time. The five originally omitted were books included when the Philoxenian version, probably the first Syriac version which can be traced to a single translator, Bishop Philoxenus of Mabbug (485–523), appeared in 508 CE. It was Moses bar Kepha who first called it Peshitta. See Kurt Aland and Barbara Aland, *The Text of the New Testament: An Introduction to the Critical Editions and to the Theory and Practice of Modern Textual Criticism* (Grand Rapids, MI, William B. Eerdmans, 1987).

with various readings in Greek. The Peshitta was unencum-
bered with textual notations and glossorial expositions. 'The
Peshitto copies', in Isaac Hall's view, 'were free from all this
apparatus,' or 'simple' in this sense:

The name never could have meant 'for simple people', although
Harclenian, in contrast, was intended for, and was most profitably
used by scholars; or it could well have referred to the style of
translation. It was a 'clear text' edition, and 'simple' in that sense.[8]

The Peshitta was used by all Syrian Christians without
exception – Nestorians, Jacobites, Maronites, Chaldeans,
Melkites and St Thomas Christians of Malabar. It was this
version which was found in one of the Churches of the
Syrian Christians by Claudius Buchanan (1766–1815), the
provost of the Fort William College in Calcutta, who, using
the colonial authority of the time, surreptitiously spirited it
away from the hapless Indian Syrian priests.[9] However, the
Peshitta was not the first version of the Bible to reach the
sub-continent. There were copies of the Gospels and other
portions of the sacred writings already available in India.
Eusebius, in his *Ecclesiastical History*, speaks of the visit of
Pantaenus, a teacher in the catechetical school of Alexandria,
to India in 190 CE. On his arrival there he found that
Christians were acquainted with the Gospel of Matthew, a
copy of which had been left by the apostle Bartholomew, who
'had preached to them, and left with them the writing of
Matthew in the Hebrew language which they had preserved

---

[8] Isaac H. Hall, 'The Syriac Translations of the New Testament', in *The Syriac New Testament Translated into English from the Peshitto Version*, tr. James Murdock (Boston, MA, Scriptural Tract Repository, 1893), p. 490.

[9] Westcott in his *The Bible in the Church* informs his readers that it was presented to Buchanan by an Indian Syrian bishop; Brooke Foss Westcott, *The Bible in the Church: A Popular Account of the Collection and Reception of the Holy Scriptures in the Christian Churches* (London, Macmillan and Co., 1887), p. 233. For the rather dubious way in which Buchanan acquired manuscripts, either through bribery or using the power of the British government at that time, see Reinhold Wagner, 'The Malayalam Bible', *Indian Church History Review* 2:2 (1968), 119–45. The copy he acquired was written in the Estrangelo character, without points, but its date has not yet been accurately determined. The copy at Milan is probably the only complete ancient manuscript of the Syrian Bible in Europe which has the enlarged Syrian canon. But even this copy has only twenty-six books and does not include Revelation; Marshall Broomhall, *The Bible in China* (London, The British and Foreign Bible Society, 1934), pp. 185–6.

until that time'.[10] Jerome, too, attests that Pantaenus was sent to India by Demetrius, the then bishop of Alexandria, at the 'request of delegates of that nation'. There he 'found that Bartholomew, one of the twelve Apostles, had preached the advent of the Lord Jesus Christ according to the Gospel of Matthew, and on his return to Alexandria he brought this with him written in Hebrew characters'.[11] Copies of this were still in existence when Buchanan travelled down to Travancore in 1806 to collect ancient manuscripts, as part of his project of acquiring precious texts.

The Syriac version, especially of the New Testament, naturally reflected the theological position of the Nestorians. When the Portuguese arrived in India in the sixteenth century, they soon discovered to their astonishment a local Christian community totally different from themselves, and possessing a New Testament which was not completely identical to their own Latin version. They found a number of small variants reflecting the Nestorian theology. The Synod of Diamper[12] in its Actio III, Dec. 1–3 observes that

in Acts 20,28 the 'Nestorian heretics' changed in an impious way the words 'the Church of God' into 'the Church of Christ', to give another meaning to the passage . . . because the Nestorians 'incited by the devil' do not want to acknowledge that God has suffered for us, shedding his blood. In 1 John 3 they changed the words *caritatem Dei* to *caritatem Christi* not to say that Christ died for us. In Hebrew 2,9 they added the words *praeter Deum*, instead of *gratia Dei* because of their Nestorian heresy. In Luke 6,35 . . . they substituted *mutum date, et inde sperate*, to defend the practice of taking interest.[13]

In contrast with the Protestants' preoccupation with the Bible during the colonial phase, in the precolonial stage, especially in India, little use was made of it and it was rarely read as a book. Buchanan recalls in his memoirs the words of

---

[10] *The Ecclesiastical History of Eusebius*, tr. C. F. Cruse (London, George Bell and Sons, 1908), vol. V, chapter 10, p. 178.

[11] Jerome, 'Lives of Illustrious Men', chapter 36, *Nicene and Post-Nicene Fathers* vol. III (2nd series), p. 745.

[12] The Synod of Diamper was convened in 1599 to settle theological and ecclesiastical disputes between the St Thomas Christians and the Roman Catholics.

[13] J. P. M. van der Ploeg, *The Christians of St Thomas in South India and Their Syriac Manuscripts* (Bangalore, Dharmaram Publications, 1983), p. 55.

one of the elders of the Church, Abraham, who summed up the
position which the Bible held among Indian Syrian Christians:
'For years we have been quarrelling with the Romish Church
about supremacy, rites and ceremonies; but the Bible has been
out of the question.'[14] The faith of Syrian Christians was not
nourished by private reading or study of the Bible. It remained
for the people a numinous object denoting the nearness and
presence of God. A deep sense of reverence was accorded not
necessarily to its contents but to its mystical and magical
powers. The Bible must have had a powerful hold on the people
quite distinct from any possible practical benefit to be derived
from reading its detailed accounts of events and people and its
religious and moral content. It was privileged because of its
holiness and transcendental properties. Each of the churches of
the St Thomas Christians in Kerala had a Bible adorned with
gold, silver and precious stones. They were taken out occasionally in procession and people would kiss them; they rarely left
the confines of the church precinct since it was felt dishonour-
able to take the Bible, 'the foundation of the faith'[15] out of the
sanctuary. Furthermore, 'Priests used to bless the sick, read the
Gospel over them and attach to their bodies pieces of palm leaf
or paper on which were written versicles from the Sacred
Scripture.'[16]

The fact that the Bible came in a language unfamiliar to the
people further distanced it from the faithful. The ecclesiastical
lingua franca remained Syriac. In a precious colophon to his
commentary on the Epistle to the Romans, Isho'dad (425 CE)
wrote: 'This epistle has been translated from Greek into Syriac
by Mar Komai with the help of Daniel, the priest, the Indian',[17]

---

[14] Claudius Buchanan, *Christian Researches in Asia, to Which Are Prefixed a Memoir of the
Author, and an Introductory Sketch of Protestant Missions in India: With an Appendix Containing
a Summary of the Subsequent Progress of Missionary Operations in the East* (London, The
Society for the Promotion of Popular Instruction, 1840), p. 25.

[15] Placid Podipara, 'Hindu in Culture, Christian in Religion, Oriental in Worship', in
The St Thomas Christian Encyclopaedia of India, vol. II: *Apostle Thomas, Kerala, Malabar
Christianity*, ed. George Menachery (Trichur, St Thomas Christian Encyclopaedia of
India, 1973), p. 110.

[16] Ibid.

[17] Cited in John Stewart, *Nestorian Missionary Enterprise: The Story of a Church on Fire*
(Edinburgh, T. & T. Clark, 1928), p. 88.

indicating that the ecclesiastical language of Indian Christians at the beginning of the fifth century was Syriac, and not any of the many Indian languages.

A full translation of the Bible was never undertaken in Malayalam or in any other vernacular language until it was translated into Malayalam by Protestant missionaries in 1811. Unlike in the colonial period, when serious efforts were made to translate the Bible into various vernacular languages, the Syriac Bible remained untranslated. Two anecdotes from the memoir of Claudius Buchanan are relevant. The aforementioned Abraham told Buchanan: 'The Bible, Sir, is what we want, in the language of our mountains. With the Bible in his hand every man can become the Priest of his own family.'[18] The other was Buchanan's encounter with the Rajah of Tranvancore in 1806:

When I told the Rajah that the Syrian Christians were supposed to be of the same religion with the English, he said he thought that could not be the case, else he must have heard it before; if, however, it was so, he considered my desire to visit them as very reasonable. I assured his highness that their *shaster* and ours was the same; and showed him a Syriac New Testament, which I had at hand. The book being bound and gilt after the European manner, the Rajah shook his head, and said he was sure there was not a native in his dominions who could read that book.[19]

Even if the Bible was available in translation, it had only limited purposes. As the Synod of Diamper noted, a vast majority of Malabar Christians were ignorant. More significantly, they were proud of their own Syriac version, and distrusted any new textual intrusions. One of the priests told Buchanan:

But how shall we know that your standard copy is a true translation of our Bible? We cannot depart from our own Bible. It is the true word of God, without corruption – that book which was first used by the Christians at Antioch. What translations you have got in the West, we know not: but the true Bible of Antioch we have had in the mountains of Malabar for fourteen hundred years, or longer. Some of our copies

[18] Buchanan, *Christian Researches in Asia*, p. 25.
[19] Ibid., p. 75.

are from ancient times; so old and decayed, that they can scarce be preserved much longer.[20]

The Bible continued to be unavailable in Indian languages even during the time of the Dominican Martyrs of Thana (1321) and throughout the Jesuit mission of Francis Xavier.

The inaccessibility of the Bible to ordinary people was due to the paucity of copies as well as the language in which it was written. At the beginning of the nineteenth century no printed version was in circulation. A Syrian priest told Buchanan: 'The learning of the Bible is in a low state among us. Our copies are few in number; and that number is diminishing, instead of increasing; and writing out of a whole copy of the sacred scriptures is a great labour, where there is no profit and little piety.'[21] Before the mass production of the Bible, every copy had to be transcribed by hand. The Christian faith in Malabar survived, as Buchanan pointed out and as he as an evangelical Protestant understood it, because it 'enjoyed the advantage of the daily prayers, and daily portions of scriptures in their liturgy', and if these were not available, 'there would have been in the revolution of ages, no vestige of Christianity left among them'.[22] One of those liturgies which sustained the Malabar Christians was the *Liturgy of the Apostles Addai and Mari*, with its subtle allusions to the New Testament. This liturgy is still in use with little variation. Though it played a crucial role, one should not overstate the biblical elements in it. The liturgy omitted the Passion and Resurrection of Jesus and its oft-repeated theme was: 'Who didst appear in the body of our humanity, didst illuminate our soul by the light of Thy life-giving Gospel.'[23] George Nedungatt draws attention to the fact that when one speaks of the Bible and the liturgy celebrated in Syriac as 'sources of the spirituality of the Syro-Malabar Church', it should be with the proviso that these were conveyed and expounded 'in homilies, catechesis, symbols, etc.'.[24]

[20] Ibid., p. 25.   [21] Ibid., p. 76.   [22] Ibid., pp. 77–8.

[23] J. M. Neale and R. F. Littledale, *The Liturgies of SS. Mark, James, Clement, Chrysostom, and Basil, and the Church of Malabar* (London, Griffith Farran and Co., 1869), p. 158; see also, England, *Hidden History of Christianity in Asia*, p. 120.

[24] George Nedungatt, 'The Spirituality of the Syro-Malabar Church', in *East Syrian*

It is very difficult to assess the extent to which the Bible was used in the precolonial Indian Churches. In addition to its use in the liturgical readings, it provided the basis for the theological formation of Syrian priests. Later generations were raised on the Commentary of Ishod of Marv, a ninth-century Syrian synthesis of patristic biblical exegesis, including the Syriac version of the works of commentators like Chrysostom and Theodore of Mopsuestia. As part of their training, candidates for the priesthood were expected to memorize the Psalter and were required to copy out the Bible. At a time before printing was invented, and when education was not through visual but auditive means, it is tempting to assume that the biblical message could be disseminated through homilies, liturgies, catechesis and images. Even this presupposition, however, is too optimistic 'to be true of the past, seeing that preachers did not even have a translation of the Bible in the language of the ministry of the word, Malayalam.'[25] The situation was comparable to that of medieval England. The majority of Christians were little acquainted with Latin and there was no demand for a vernacular version in English. To exercise one's faith, to grow in spirituality, one did not need to have a copy of the Bible or even know how to read it, however useful this could be. A Bible-based spirituality is something recent and Protestant in its origin and orientation. Nedungatt recounts a recent incident which underlines the Bible's continuing subsidiary role in nurturing Syrian Christian spirituality. When Blessed Alphonsa, as recently as the 1930s, told her Clarist companions that they should come to know Jesus more personally by reading the Gospels, they were reportedly amazed and raised their eyebrows at the suggestion of reading as a means to know the Christ.[26] Now, a little more than a generation later, this idea of personal reading as a means to discern the divine truth is no longer a startling one.

To sum up this section, it is fair to claim that Syrian Christians seldom had any direct contact with the Bible, independent of corporate worship and ecclesiastical gatherings. Biblical teaching was conveyed through the enactment of liturgical rites.

CHINA: THE SURROGATE BIBLE – MONUMENTS AND MANUSCRIPTS

When Christianity arrived in China it was greeted as a 'scriptural religion'.[27] It was the Nestorians who introduced the Bible to China: the Syrian Nestorians arrived in China, carrying with them what they claimed to be the true scriptures. The leader of the Nestorians was the Persian bishop, Alopen. It is only his Chinese name that has survived. It looks like the translation of the Syrian name Yahb-Alaha, which is equivalent to the Greek Theodore and the Latin Deodatus. It is from the now famous Nestorian tablet of Hsi-an-fu, or Sing-an-fu, discovered about 1623, that we have come to know about Alopen and the Nestorians in China. The Monument tells of 'a highly virtuous man named A-lo-pen who, bringing sacred Books, arrived at the court of T'ai-Tsing' at a date which corresponds to 635 CE. The inscription is in Chinese with Syriac in the margin. At the foot of the main text the year 781 CE is given as the date of its erection. The composition and translation of the monument is attributed to one Adam (Ching-ching), who, according to Moffett, was one of the three important figures in the Nestorian Church in China at the time.[28] Alopen and his band came into China most probably from the Malabar coast of India. The twenty-seven standard works to which the Monument refers probably meant the Syriac New Testament (though it contained only twenty books), or the reference may even be to a translation of some Buddhist literature. If any translation of the Bible was made in Chinese at this time, there is no trace of it now.[29] It was nearly six hundred years before an indigenous version was produced, and this was not Chinese but Mongolian.[30]

---

[27] John Foster, *The Church of the Tang Dynasty* (London, SPCK, 1939), p. 43.

[28] Moffett, *History of Christianity in Asia*, I, p. 299.

[29] R. Kilgour, *The Bible Throughout the World: A Survey of Scripture Translations* (London, World Dominion Press, 1939), pp. 142–3.

[30] This was undertaken by the Roman Catholic missionary, John of Montecorvino, who translated the New Testament and the Psalms. He arrived in 1294, and in a letter to

In this phase, one cannot speak of the Bible, but only of the incorporation of biblical elements, selective portions of the New Testament, into Chinese writings. The Bible was yet to assume the pre-eminent position which came about following the Reformation and colonial times. The most important among these Chinese materials are the text of the Nestorian Monument and the manuscripts which have come to be known as the Bishop Alopen documents.[31] These manuscripts include *The Jesus-Messiah Sutra*; *Parable*, part II: *A Discourse on Monotheism*; *On the Oneness of the Lord of the Universe*; and *The Lord of the Universe's Discourse on Alms-giving*. The Monument and manuscripts reflect a substantial theology based on the Bible, with the exception of *Parable*, part II: *A Discourse on Monotheism* and *On the Oneness of the Lord of the Universe*.[32] These are apologetic tracts on monotheism, and contain no specific biblical references.

The Nestorian Monument text, besides reviewing the history of the Nestorians in China, contains several theological passages. It begins with a Christian affirmation of the Trinitarian formula, followed by the biblical story of creation and the fall of humankind, 'the Glad Tidings' of 'the birth of the Holy One' and how salvation was effected through 'the Messiah the Luminous Lord of the Universe who appeared upon earth as a man'.[33] It describes Jesus as the one who does good works,

Pope Gascon Clement V he wrote: 'I am now old and am become white, more from toils and troubles than from age, for I am fifty-years old. I have a competent knowledge of the Tartar language and character, which is the usual language of the Tartars, and I have now translated in that language and character the whole of New Testament and the Psalter, which I have written in their fairest language', Will H. Hudspeth, *The Bible and China* (London, The British and Foreign Bible Society, 1952), p. 10. The first translation of the entire Bible took another five hundred years, and interestingly it was not produced in China, but in India by John Marshman of Serampore, with the help of an Armenian called John Lasser. This version appeared in 1822 and was followed by Robert Morrison's the next year; see ibid.

[31] For discussion on date and authorship see P. Y. Saeki, *The Nestorian Documents and Relics in China* (Tokyo, The Academy of Oriental Culture, 1937), pp. 113–247.

[32] There are vague biblical allusions in *On the Oneness of the Lord of the Universe*. For instance verses 142–52 echo Matthew 7.24–7; and verse 154, 'If a man wants to see the manifestation of the one God, he has only to be pure in heart, for then he can see God', comes nearer to Matthew 5., 'Blessed are the pure in heart for they shall see God'; and verses 159–62 could be a seventh-century Chinese version of the Parable of the Wheat and the Tares. See Saeki, *Nestorian Documents and Relics in China*, p. 200.

[33] Ibid., pp. 54–5.

practises right faith, inaugurates life and destroys death. The section which maps salvation is remarkable because it is interspersed with Buddhist, Taoist and Confucian references, and significantly, although the Monument is surmounted by a cross, edits out the death of Christ:

Establishing His New Teaching of Non-assertion which operates silently through the Holy Spirit, another person of the Trinity, He formed in man the capacity for well-doing through the Right faith. Setting up the standard of the eight cardinal virtues, He purged away the dust from human nature and perfected a true character. Widely opening the Three Constant Gates, He brought Life to light and abolished Death. Hanging up the bright Sun, He swept away the abodes of darkness. All the evil devices of the devil were thereupon defeated and destroyed. He then took an oar in the Vessel of Mercy and ascended to the Place of Light. Thereby all rational beings were conveyed across the Gulf. His mighty work being thus completed, He returned at noon to His original position (in Heaven).[34]

Then the Monument text goes on to describe the ethical marks of the Christian life: no holding of male or female slaves; treating the noble and ordinary people with equal respect; no hoarding of property or wealth; setting a good example by fasting in order to subdue the mind; praying seven times a day; and offering a bloodless sacrifice once in seven days.[35] The Monument text ends with a reference to the good works done in the monasteries: 'The hungry came to be fed; the naked came to be clothed; the sick were cured and restored to health; and the dead were buried and made to rest in peace.'[36] This clearly echoes the phraseology and content of Luke 4, which in turn echoes Isaiah 61.1–4.

The Jesus-Messiah Sutra contains 206 verses and was probably one of the earliest attempts to communicate the Christian gospel outside the Mediterranean and Hellenistic cultures. It creatively fuses Mahayana terminology with Christian concepts. The text deals with some of the basic tenets of Christianity – the sovereignty of God and the sinfulness of humankind. The narrative begins in the manner of a Buddhist Sutra: 'At that time, preaching the laws of Hsu-po (i.e. Jehovah)

---

[34] Ibid., p. 55.   [35] Ibid., p. 56.   [36] Ibid., p. 64.

who is the Lord of Heaven, the Messiah spoke thus.' The opening lines speak of God and God's nature as the unmoved mover, and of the innate capacity of human beings to know God. Next comes the Fall and how human beings turned to idolatry. Sin came into the world 'because our ancestor committed the sin of disobedience in the "the Garden of seed-and-fruit bearing (trees)"' (v. 54),[37] and humankind turned to idolatry and made 'the images of camels, elephants, bulls, mules, horses, reindeer, deer, etc., with wood or clay'.[38] Sin is thus defined as a turning away from true worship to the adoration of idols. The remedy is to repent and commit oneself to the Lord of Heaven.

Then follows a summary of the law, based on selections from the Hebrew Scripture and the New Testament. There are ten vows and sixteen ethical precepts. These ten vows are the same as the Ten Commandments except that there is no mention of the Sabbath or idolatry. It is clear that the Christian gospel was seen as validating the ancient social customs of the Chinese – loyalty to the Emperor and fidelity to family. Service to God, service to the Emperor and to the parents were seen as inseparable: 'Of all these three things, the first thing is to obey the Lord of Heaven. The second is to obey the Sacred Superior. The third is to obey father and mother' (vv. 90–2).[39] To these, seven more vows were added from the Chinese precepts: show kindness to all living beings; serve father and mother; none should commit adultery; none should steal; none should covet another's money, property, rank, field, house or his man-servant or maid servant; none should forge false documents; and none should serve the Lord of Heaven at another's expense.[40] Added to these are important rules of life: not to take advantage of the defenceless; not to turn away from the poor; feed the hungry even though they are your adversaries; assist those who are labouring hard; clothe the naked; do not laugh at those who have chronic disease; care for the orphans and widows; do not quarrel or take each other to court. But above all, obey the Lord of Heaven.

[37] Ibid., p. 130.   [38] Ibid.   [39] Ibid., p. 134.   [40] Ibid., pp. 135–6.

The final section provides a concise history of the Jesus story. It begins with the fallen nature of humankind. Since all have sinned against the Lord of Heaven, the Lord of Heaven took pity on all and made a cool wind (Holy Spirit) to enter a virgin named, Mo-yen (Mary). He thus made clear his power, so that all might believe and 'return to good relations'. Mary bore a son named Ishu (Jesus) the Messiah. He was baptized by John and a voice sounded: 'The messiah is my son' (v. 173) Between the ages of twelve and thirty-three he 'sought for all people of evil life and made them return to the good life and the right way' (v. 177). After gathering the twelve, Jesus went on to heal the sick, the lame and the blind, to cure 'the deformed and strangely coloured people' (those afflicted with leprosy), and to cast out devils. But the literary men (i.e. scribes) were looking for every opportunity to destroy him, brought him before Pilate falsely accusing him, plotting his trial before Pilate. Eventually Jesus met his death on a tree, hanged between two high-waymen. There was darkness, the earth quaked, the graves opened and the dead were raised to life, as depicted in the Matthean passage (Matt. 27.51–3). The manuscript then breaks off in mid-sentence.

The Lord of the Universe's Discourse on Alms-giving contains references to passages in Genesis 1–3, Isaiah 53, Acts 1–2 and Matthew 5–7. Notably absent from the text of the Sermon on the Mount is the Lord's Prayer. The text, especially verses 30–62, covers more or less the whole of Matthew 7. The stress on Jesus' teaching may be a response to the Chinese preference for great teachers such as Confucius and Meniscus. Clearly, the Golden Rule presented a special problem to the translator: 'Whatsoever you would others do for you, others would also the same to be done by you. What others need to be done by you, you may naturally need to be done by them. Whatever others would do to you, you should again do to them as to reward and compensate them, (vv. 55, 56).[41] The document describes the

---

[41] Ibid., p. 210. Saeki attributes the poor translation of the verse to the author of the *Jesus-Messiah Sutra* not knowing the Confucian Golden Rule. Saeki does not agree with the suggestion that the negative form of the Chinese Rule would have confused the author. He draws attention to the existence of the negative form of the Golden

work of Christ as a 'sacrificing transformation', but, in keeping with the Nestorian belief, it makes clear that only his human nature suffered while his divine nature was unimpaired: 'For instance, it seems to be plain, therefore, that though the Messiah suffered death in His body of the "five attributes",[42] His life did not end therewith' (v. 100).[43] Unlike the *Jesus-Messiah Sutra*, this discourse mentions the resurrection of Jesus, the witness of the women disciples, Jesus' appearance to and his commissioning of the disciples. Just as Jesus in the Gospels offered a stark choice, the text urges the faithful to choose between God and mammon/idolatry:

All mankind should turn toward Heaven, and try to know the One (person of the Godhead), the Lord of Heaven and his determined will only . . . If there be any who go astray from the Way, they are those who are in fear of men or who give themselves up to the worship of the sun, the moon, and the stars and even the fire-gods. Those who are in fear of men, or who give themselves up to the devils and demons and the Yakchas and the Rakchasas etc., will fall into the hot Hell and have to remain there for ever. (vv. 242–5)

The document identifies the early disciples as poor and nondescript; it offers a reward to those who listen to the words of the good Sutra and put them into practice, and at the same time offers a warning to those who refuse to practise what is commanded: 'If there be any who neither delight (to hear these words) nor desire to listen to what is preached here they are in company with the devils. They shall be cast out into the Hell for ever' (v. 262).

It is obvious that the Bible as a sacred text was not a priority for the Nestorians or the Chinese Christians at this stage. Taken

Rule in the Jewish literature and the *Didache*, and, more importantly, to how the latter was used on many occasions by the Nestorian author; see pp. 236–8.

[42] The 'five attributes' are related to the five organs of sensation – eye, ear, nose, tongue and hands. Saeki writes: 'According to the Buddhist doctrine, the union of these five attributes dates from the quickening moment of birth and contributes to a personal being', ibid., p. 199.

[43] In describing the relationship between Jesus and Joseph of Arimathea (Matt. 27. 57–9), who asked for the body of Jesus, the text is careful in drawing attention only to the human aspect of this association: 'Now, when it was dark, there came a man who was a flesh-relation of "the five attributes" of the Messiah, and who was devoted to the Lord of the Universe and was called Yao-hsi (i.e. Joseph) at the change of name' (v. 115).

together, the Nestorian Monument text and the Alopen documents can be seen as a surrogate Bible. They are not a straightforward translation. The nearest to a translation we have is the Sermon on the Mount. Even here there is much summarizing and paraphrasing of scripture, with explanations, illustrations and moralizing. Yet beneath the makeshift metaphors, and the ornamental and flowery language, they do manage to convey the basic narrative facts of Jesus' life and some of the most essential doctrinal teachings of the Christian Church.

The appropriation of the Christian Scripture for Chinese culture involved a massive metaphorical and linguistic transformation. The line between inculturation, contextualization and distortion of the gospel is hard to define. For instance, the Nestorian Monument text freely uses terms, metaphors and similes from Buddhism, Confucianism and Taoism. Phrases like 'the eight cardinal virtues', 'hanging up . . . the Sun' and 'He took an oar in the vessel of mercy' are unmistakably Buddhist. The vessel of mercy could be a reference either to Amitabh Buddha's boat, which carries the saved to paradise, or to the Buddhist goddess of Mercy, Kuan-yin, who is herself regarded as a 'boat of mercy'. The 'new teaching of non-assertion' is a principle of Taoism but has a corresponding concept in Confucianism as well. 'How to rule both families and kingdoms' is from the Confucian teaching. The 'two principles of nature' yin and yang form the basic cosmology of Taoism and Confucianism.[44] The verse, 'Thereby all rational beings were conveyed across the Gulf', could have been from the Confucian Taoist book, *I Ching* (the *Book of Changes*).

Earlier mission historians, without the benefit of the Alopen documents, tended to be dismissive of the form of Christianity advocated by the Nestorians, for it lacked the basic tenets of orthodoxy and was replete with Confucian, Buddhist and Taoist concepts.[45] A closer reading of these texts reveals that

[44] See Moffett, *History of Christianity in Asia*, I, p. 311.
[45] For example James Legge accused the Nestorians of diluting the gospel message. See James Legge, *The Nestorian Monument of Hsî-an-Fû in Shen-Hsî, China* (London, Trubner and Co., 1888).

the type of Christian faith the early Nestorians communicated was much more complex than the 'hopeless syncreticism',[46] or neutered gospel, for which it was criticized. It is true that the Monument text does not contain what became the hallmark of evangelical Christianity a millennium later – the death of Christ and the supremacy of Christian Scripture. The Alopen documents, however, contain clear references to the trial, death and resurrection of Jesus.

On the advocacy of pluralism, the documents are ambivalent. On the one hand, *The Lord of the Universe's Discourse on Alms-giving* claims that 'the rest of the people (of Persia) all worship the Lord of the Universe and are united in declaring that I-shu (i.e. Jesus) is the Messiah' (v. 220).[47] On the other hand, we come across statements like, 'Every man talks in his vernacular speech, saying: we each have our own special Lord of Heaven. Each faith has its abiding merit',[48] and 'Those who have received the Lord of Heaven and His teachings must first teach other people to worship all Devas' (vv. 96, 97).[49]

Later Christian missionaries, in the colonial period, often dismissive of other cultures found Chinese philosophy and religions impregnable. One of the problems that Nestorians and later Roman Catholics and Protestants faced was how to present the gospel to a people who believed in the grandeur of their culture and the superiority of their way of life. What we see in these documents is the creative nature of the translating efforts of Nestorians. They used the Christian text as a spring-board rather than an immobilizing anchor. The documents demonstrate that translation was for them an independent transcreative act, an experience of freedom. Unlike the colonial preoccupation with exact philological equivalents, a way of assuming control, Nestorians were looking for parallel expressions in Chinese culture. In translation, inevitably, original texts lose their texture and tone, and in the process they gain a new texture and tone. This is what we see happening in the earlier Nestorian materials. The Christian text was forced to shed

---

[46] Foster, *The Church of the T'ang Dynasty,* p. 112.
[47] Saeki, *Nestorian Documents and Relics in China,* p. 226.
[48] Ibid., p. 127.   [49] Ibid., p. 134.

some of its theological claims and at the same time was infused
with images and concepts from the Chinese religious and
philosophical heritage. The sacred text of Christians became an
open text, subject to a variety of renditions.

AFRICA: LATIN BIBLE AND LOCAL CONTROVERSIES

The picture in Africa was slightly different. It is not easy to
determine how Christianity entered Africa. Possibly it took root
through Jewish residents of North Africa, and possibly also
through missionaries from Asia Minor. The Christianity which
came to Africa was initially hellenized and eventually adapted
itself to Egyptian language and culture. This adaptation was
facilitated by the infusion of native religion and rituals. It
contained elements from non-Christian religions. Augustine, in
one of his tracts, mentions that in the fifth century Christians
believed that God was Saturn re-christened. The Christianity
practised both by sophisticated thinkers like Tertullian and
ordinary people had as much in common with the practices of
their indigenous religion as with the new faith.[50]

With no well-marked literary tradition of her own, and no
indigenous writings to record her own ancient and rich folklore,
Africa in the early stages appropriated scripts from other lands.
The use of Coptic and Ethiopic in the north-east of the
continent is evidence for this. Ethiopic was introduced by
colonialists from Arabia. In later years of the second century
and the early years of the third, there not only existed Christian
congregations in North African cities but also far into the
desert. Tunisia produced three great Latin Church figures:
Tertullian (160–212 CE), Cyprian (200–58) and Augustine
(354–430). Though there were persecutions, Christian communities and congregations continued to grow. The numbers of
illustrious African bishops, articulate speakers and erudite
scholars who graced the ecumenical assemblies affirmed the
vibrancy of the African Church. Africa was the centre of great
biblical activity. Egypt became known for its translation work.

---

[50] See Susan Raven, *Rome in Africa* (London, Routledge, 1993), p. 168.

The Greek version of the Hebrew Bible – the Septuagint – was produced there. The Hebrew Law books were translated into Greek in the Egyptian city of Alexandria about 285–247 BCE. More than a thousand years before the English had their own vernacular Bible in the form of the Authorized Version, Africans had their own in Sahidic, an Egyptian language. It was this hive of translation activity which earned Africa the title, 'the cradle of Bible translation'.

Cities like Carthage, Hippo and Alexandria were known for their great deliberations on the Bible. Clement, Origen, Cyprian and Augustine were the pioneers in biblical exposition, and initiated a variety of reading methods. The most influential was Augustine's allegorical or spiritual interpretation, which he saw as an effective tool for a fallen humanity to discern God's signs and symbols. It was Tertullian who worked out the exegetical method, typology, which Maureen Tilley hails as 'the heart of the North African hermeneutics'.[51]

Despite fervent biblical activities, the use of the Bible in Africa in this phase remained elitist and confined to the Latinized classes. Augustine was a case in point. He belonged to the Latinized minority, who became increasingly isolated both linguistically and economically from the local peasant population. When Augustine tells in his *Confessions* of hearing a voice saying 'Take, read', the version he read was not in his native language, Berber. Though there were Berber congregations, they did not have any portion of the scripture translated into Berber until the nineteenth century.[52] The version Augustine used was the Latin version of the Alexandrian LXX, employed also by Tertullian and Cyprian, 'which was notoriously unclassical, and even ungrammatical in its language'.[53] In North Africa, Latin and not Greek was the official language. Though there were indigenous languages, Latin was the language of administration and culture and cultivated by the educated lay

---

[51] Maureen A. Tilley, *The Bible in Christian North Africa: The Donatist World* (Minneapolis, MN, Fortress Press, 1997), p. 26.
[52] Kilgour, *The Bible Throughout the World*, p. 35.
[53] David Norton, *A History of the Bible As Literature*, vol. I: *From Antiquity to 1700* (Cambridge, Cambridge University Press, 1993), p. 5.

people of the time. In spite of his African background, Augustine remained elitist; when he moved back to Carthage after his stay in Italy, he lived among those who were cultivated and Latinized, and thus removed from his own indigenous heritage. The fact that he could not connect with agricultural workers who spoke Punic, from whom the Donatists drew considerable support, was an indication of his remoteness from his own people. Later he urged his fellow-clergy to study the local language, Punic, so that they could make themselves understood by the local people. Although Augustine was a great exponent of the Bible,[54] he used his intellectual power and hermeneutical skills to side with the Established Church or imperial powers against those who wanted to be independent of Roman control. His ruthless handling of the Donatist controversy was illustrative of this. One of the reasons for his repudiation of the Donatists was because of his misunderstanding of what came to be known as one of the basic tenets of African exegesis, duality of reference or contrariness of signification, that is, what is censured in one context is condoned in another. He was both attracted to and repelled by it. Though he was appreciative of an ecclesiology propelled by such an exegesis, Augustine was, according to Pamela Bright, apprehensive of such an exegetical practice: 'He was alienated by an exegetical system that ignored (or seemed to ignore) so many of the tools of interpretation which Augustine himself had sharpened over the course of his own rhetorical training and which he now sought to make available for the interpretation of the biblical text.'[55] There was also an ambiguity in Augustine with regard to things African. In the initial stages, he was repelled by the African propensity for the supernatural, but over the years he gradually changed his view. On his return from Milan, he was rational in his approach, discounted the possibility of miraculous healing and went on to ridicule the naivety of the Donatists:

---

[54] For various uses of the Bible in Augustine's writings, see *Augustine and the Bible*, ed. and tr. Pamela Bright (Notre Dame, IN, University of Notre Dame Press, 1999).

[55] Pamela Bright, 'Biblical Ambiguity in African Exegesis', in *De Doctrina Christiana: A Classic of Western Culture*, ed. Duane W. H. Arnold and Pamela Bright (Notre Dame, IN, University of Notre Dame Press, 1995), p. 26.

'If anyone brings them a lump of earth from the East, they will worship it.' Two decades later, Augustine regales his readers with stories of resurrection, cures and signs performed by relics of saints and sacred objects.[56] On the whole, Augustine remained removed from his people, became increasingly Roman and was seen as out of touch with his own people. His combative nature and the energy with which he pursued his theological enemies on behalf of an institutionalized orthodox Christianity further alienated him. He utilized his exegetical skills to support the status quo and repudiated any dissenting voices. His writings were addressed mainly to the educated classes and senatorial families. As Frend has observed, Augustine 'represented the Church at the Imperial Court, and maintained the struggle against sundry intellectual disturbers of the peace, such as the Arians and the Pelagians'.[57]

Interestingly, one of the earliest controversies over the Bible took place in Africa. Church officials contrived with the power of the Roman Empire to persecute their own people who were trying to practise biblical principles in their lives. The conventional view is that the election of Majorinus to the bishopric as a rival to Caecilian sparked off the Donatist schism. Though there was some element of truth in this, the trouble had been brewing over the years. It originated when the Christian community was polarized over the issue of handing over the scriptures to the state authorities. When the 303 edict of the Emperor Diocletian, among other things, ordered the surrender of scriptures, the Church officials succumbed to the pressure whereas the congregations resisted. When another edict arrived which forced all to show loyalty to the emperor, Abitinians showed defiance, and as a result they were put in jail. While they were incarcerated in jail under inhuman conditions, the attempts of their friends to supply them with the basic necessities such as food and water were thwarted by the local bishops. Those who were in jail condemned the bishops and anyone who associated with them. For the Abitinians, even to

---

[56] See W. H. C. Frend, *The Donatist Church: A Movement of Protest in Roman North Africa* (Oxford, Clarendon Press, 1952), pp. 232–3.

[57] Ibid., p. 242.

amend a single letter of scripture was an act of villainy but to destroy the whole book at the behest of the civil, especially pagan, authorities deserved torture in hell. The author of the *Acts of the Abitinian Martyrs* wrote:

It is written in the Apocalypse, whoever adds to this book one part of a letter or one letter, to him will the Lord add innumerable afflictions. And whoever blots them out, so will the Lord blot out his share from the Book of Life (Rev. 22.18–19). If, therefore, a part of a letter added or a letter omitted cuts off a person at the roots from the Book of Life (cf. 2 Macc. 7.9) and if such constitutes a sacrilege, it is necessary that all those who handed over the divine testaments and the honored laws of the omnipotent God and of the Lord Jesus Christ to be burned in profane fires should be tormented in the eternal flames of Gehenna and inextinguishable fire. And, therefore, as we have already said, 'if anyone communicates with the traitors, that person will not have a share with us in the heavenly kingdom.'[58]

It was with this communication that the schism began. Over the next two hundred years the movement took different shapes as it responded to various political and social contexts. The Bible, too, which occupied and shaped the self-identity of the movement, went through its own vicissitudes. Maureen Tilley, in her study of the Donatists, addresses the significant role the Bible played in the movement: 'In the Church of the Donatists, the Bible became the storehouse for texts that made sense of their own world, that approved or disapproved both the characters who inhabited that world and the conduct enacted there.'[59] She identifies three major ways in which biblical materials were put to use in the martyr narratives: 'The verses and allusions helped Christians to make sense of the situation of persecution. They helped believers to recognize real heroes and true villains in the martyrs and their persecutors. Finally, they showed the faithful what to do in their own lives through the encouraging remarks and the commands issued in the stories.'[60] It was from two North African ancestors, Tertullian and

---

[58] 'The Acts of the Abitinian Martyrs', in *Donatist Martyr Stories:The Church in Conflict in Roman North Africa. Translated with Notes and Introduction*, tr. Maureen A. Tilley (Liverpool, Liverpool University Press, 1996), p. 46.

[59] Tilley, *The Bible in Christian North Africa*, p. 7.

[60] Ibid., p. 50.

Cyprian, that the Donatists drew their hermeneutical strength. From Cyprian they learnt what it was to be a pure Church uncontaminated by idolatry. From Tertullian they appropriated literal meanings of the texts, adopted a whole-Bible approach and inherited typological exegesis. The typological exegesis 'allowed the Donatists to give primacy to the literal words of the Bible while bringing the biblical world, its personal types, and its divine commands to each succeeding generation'.[61] Such a type of exegesis not only provided them with an identity but also allowed them to disparage those who tormented them. Thus they creatively reinvented themselves as the reincarnated Israel; they imagined themselves to be the latter-day Moses, Isaac, the prophets, Eleazar, the Maccabees and finally Christ; and their harassers were identified with the murderers of prophets and the pagan rulers Nebuchadnezzar and Antiochus. Tilley has identified four hallmarks of their exegesis:

first, a turn from the future as a source of hope to the past as a model for coping; *second*, a change in typological models from biblical figures who promoted a martyr's death to those who provided support in the struggle against assimilation; *third*, the adoption of the *collecta* or assembly of Israel as the model for the Church faithful to the observance of the Law of God; and *fourth*, the adoption of commands of separation as the essence of the Law of God and sine qua non of survival for the Church.[62]

It is evident that it was the biblical narratives which provided them with the means to make sense of their own, often dreadful, situation. They also provided the means to discern who the adversaries of the Donatists were, to determine those who were in and those who were out of favour, and, more importantly, they offered scriptural warrants for the movement's rules and discipline. Like the countless communities who were to come after them, some of whose hermeneutical endeavours will be recorded in this volume, the Bible not only offered the Donatists the spiritual and practical sustenance to survive under difficult conditions but, more significantly, authorized their opposition to established and institutionalized views. At a time when assimilation would have been an easy way out, the Bible offered

[61] Ibid., p. 176. [62] Ibid., p. 16.

Donatists a different moral and political option. The temptation is to see them as oppressed peasants fighting against a powerful enemy supported by the state apparatus. Tilley warns that such a notion would be too simplistic. What they achieved was to blaze a trail, a trend in biblical interpretation which later oppressed groups could use and emulate.

In spite of the imaginative use of the Bible by the Donatists and other African exegetical giants such as Augustine and company, on the whole, the access to the Bible in this phase was not direct, but mediated through its selected passages and personalities and encountered in liturgy, catechism, homilies and artifacts. Moreover, the highly innovative hermeneutical practices initiated by African thinkers and the exegetical tools sharpened by them remained elitist, and later their prolonged involvement in doctrinal controversies prevented the Bible from reaching the ordinary people. In any event, their hermeneutical outputs were aimed largely at the literate and urban class. It took centuries for these hermeneutical developments to penetrate to other parts of Africa, especially south of the Sahara.

CONCLUDING REFLECTIONS

There are some significant aspects of the place of the Bible in the precolonial phase. First, the introduction and propagation of the Bible took place at a time when Europe was yet to emerge as a cultural and political force. The Bible arrived in the East before Christendom and Europe came to be inextricably linked, and before Europe and Asia were thought of as distinct and segregated entities. Unlike the later missions, this phase of the expedition, especially in Asia, was undertaken by a Christian movement that had not succeeded in gaining state power and thus was not in a position to draw upon its military or bureaucratic resources. In contrast to the Byzantine and Latin Churches, the Nestorians had not enjoyed a privileged position in Persian society. Their ideas had not been informed by Catholic Europe or even Byzantium.[63] They were not even part

[63] See Dennis Hickley, *The First Christians in China: An Outline History and Some Considera-*

of the Mediterranean world. Their theology, liturgy speech and culture had been formed in Syria. According to Moffett, the Christianity that came to Asia was Asian in its origins, and 'chose to look neither to Rome nor to Constantinople as its centre. It was a Christianity that has for centuries remained unashamedly Asian.'[64] Nestorian Christians also differed in their missionary ambitions. While European Christians, who were to sweep through different continents a millennium later, made conversion of pagans their priority, Persian Christians did not consciously make conversion their chief aim.

Secondly, as the foregoing pages have made clear, the Bible remained a remote text for most of the faithful, and did not play a significant role in their lives, as it would in the next phase. It is likely, rather, that the Bible was known mainly through oral transmission, especially by way of liturgy, sermons, and so forth. It was not widely used and drifted further into the background whilst other, non-textual means came to be regarded as the prime media of God's revelation and presence.

The slogan, *sola Scriptura*, which placed the Bible as the prime source of salvation and grace, and which became the decisive hermeneutical principle in the succeeding stage, was yet to make its mark. In the early days, the Church never subscribed to the belief that the only means of knowing God's Word was through the written word. The Church had taught people to think about God, salvation and grace in different ways, and inculcated the faith directly through non-textual means. The Christian Church thrived by encouraging the veneration of saints and relics of apostles and saints; it encouraged pilgrimages to sacred places and gave importance to sacraments, festivals and the practice of miraculous healings. Communal piety and religion replaced the perspectives offered by texts or doctrines. Bartlett and Carlyle, in their study of the religious development of the period, conclude:

Even as an aid to the devout life, the Bible was becoming superseded by writings more expressive of the prevalent ideals of piety, especially

tions Concerning the Nestorians in China During the Tang Dynasty (London, The China Study Project, 1980), pp. 1–2.

[64] Moffett, *History of Christianity in Asia*, I, p. xiii.

of the ascetic type. Legends of the Saints and special manuals of
devotion and penitence more and more pushed even the New
Testament into the background, both in practice and in the spiritual
and disciplinary directions of spiritual advisers, as the fifth century,
which completed the dogmatic process, wore on. Further the conception of sacraments as the prime media of Salvation, media now
regarded in a semi-magical light, to no small degree assisted that
issue; and so helped incidently to render possible the dying art of
reading which use of the Bible ever tends to foster and keep alive.[65]

Thirdly, it is apparent that no translation of the complete
Bible was ever made available in the vernacular languages of
Africa and Asia. Access to the Bible was determined not only by
its availability, which was very limited at that time, but also by
the availability of translations that people could understand.
The languages in which it was available – Latin and Syriac –
were not indigenous to Africa and Asia. In Asia the Syriac
Peshitta assumed the role of an adjudicator and became the
yardstick by which to judge other available biblical literature.
John England, in his survey of the extant scriptural writings of
the time, points out that they were judged 'firmly within the
Peshitta tradition'.[66]

Fourthly, the Bible found its place among the many sacred
books; it did not threaten to subsume or surpass the religious
texts of other faith traditions, but coexisted with them as one
among many. Contrary to the excessive claims made for the
Bible during the colonial period, Nestorian Christians were
keen to show their neighbours that the biblical vision was not
incompatible with Buddhist, Confucian, Taoist or Hindu aspirations. Unlike the next phase, when missionaries, in their
attempts to propagate the gospel, had to invent alphabets with a
view to making the Bible available, Nestorians did not experience textual emptiness in India and China, but recognized an
environment replete with religions and textual traditions. Moreover, they encountered a religion which had already realized
the importance of texts for communicating religious truth. It
was not the Christian Church which first recognized the value

[65] J. Vernon Bartlett and A. J. Carlyle, *Christianity in History: A Study of Religious
    Development* (London, Macmillan and Co., 1917), p. 345.
[66] England, *Hidden History of Christianity in Asia*, p. 128.

of the written word for the propagation of faith. Buddhism, probably one of the oldest of missionary religions, had canonical scriptures in Pali three hundred years before the birth of Christianity. Like Latin in the medieval period in Europe, Pali was a major influential language in the East. When the Indian King Asoka embraced Buddhism in the third century BCE and installed it as a state religion, he made sure that his new-found faith also reached the other parts of Asia. He dispatched Mahinda, his alleged son, to Sri Lanka, and monks to South East Asia – countries which continue today to be Buddhist. The conversion of King Asoka and his proclamation of Buddhism as a state religion are, in Willard G. Oxtoby's view, comparable to the Emperor Constantine's conversion and governmental protection of Christianity.[67] While Theravada Buddhism took roots in the South East, another form, Mahayana, made its way from North West India to central Asia and then to China. Since Mahayana Buddhism was popular and lay-oriented, its texts were translated into local languages. The Chinese Buddhist canon, in size, outweighs the Quran, the Bible or the Talmud. In literary scale alone it is equivalent to the entire output of the Greek and Latin Church fathers.[68]

Linked with the idea of multiple texts was the apparent religious tolerance that marked the region. Rigid self-consciousness regarding one's religion was yet to make its mark. Marco Polo, in his travels, recounts an incident which encapsulated this relatively tolerant vision of the time in the behaviour of the Mongol Emperor, Kublai Khan, who observed all the principal feasts of the faiths known to him – Jewish, Christian, Islamic and Buddhist. When asked why he did so, his reply was:

There are four prophets who are worshipped and to whom all the world does reverence. The Christians say their God was Jesus Christ, the Sarcens the Mahomet, the Jews Moses, and the idolaters Sakyamuni Burkhan, who was the first to be represented as God in the form of an idol. And I do honour and reverence to all four, so that I may be

---

[67] Willard G. Oxtoby, '"Telling in Their Own Tongues": Old and Modern Bible Translations as Expressions of Ethnic Cultural Identity', *Concilium* 1 (1995), 35.
[68] Ibid.

sure of doing it to him who is greatest in heaven and the truest; and to him I pray for aid.[69]

Indian Syrian Christians not only lived amicably with their Hindu neighbours, but also shared the Hindu tolerance of other religions. This openness towards Hindu neighbours was treated as one of the 'errors' of the Syrian Christians by the Roman Catholics, and this was one of the charges levelled against them at the Synod of Diamper. They were indicted for holding on to one of the fundamental teachings of the Hindu *shastras*, that 'Each one can be saved in his own law, all laws are right.'[70] Faced with such a pluralistic vision and amidst this sense of tolerance and theologically propitious texts, the Bible's authority or superiority could not be asserted.

In concluding this chapter, let me make three points. First, in contrast to the next phase, the Bible did not come with monarchical authority in the precolonial phase.[71] The King James version, an icon of British culture, which helped to define the English language, and which would act as the supreme arbiter in matters of morality and theology, was authorized by His Majesty's government. It was published by 'authority' of monarchical power and was appointed to be read in churches, and, as we shall see in a later chapter, it was marketed as the book that 'our King reads'. Secondly, in this phase, the Bible occupied an ambiguous and a liminal space; bereft of any strong civil or ecclesiastical authority, it remained a minor concern. It survived and functioned beyond Christendom within small, marginal religious groups. Thirdly, its standing, either as a sacred text or as literature, was dubious. Augustine, with the benefit of the best literary education of his day, found the Bible 'quite unworthy of comparison with the stately prose

---

[69] Marco Polo, *The Travels of Marco Polo*, tr. Ronald Latham (London, The Folio Society, 1958), p. 98.

[70] Cited in A. M. Mundadan, *Indian Christians: Search for Identity and Struggle for Autonomy* (Bangalore, Dharmaram Publications, 1984), p. 27.

[71] There is a close affinity between English kings and English Bibles. When Miles Coverdale produced his first complete version in 1535, it was dedicated to King Henry VIII with the words, 'Set forth wyth the Kynges moost gracious licence'. See James Baikie, *The English Bible and its Story: Its Growth, its Translators and their Adventures* (London, Seeley, Service & Co. Limited, 1928), p. 208.

of Cicero';[72] as the emperor who was quoted in the epigram wondered, if it was so great, why had the Chinese not heard of it for centuries? It would be fair to say that the Bible did not have a great deal of influence on the general culture, and inevitably its impact was minimal.

[72] Augustine, *Confessions*, tr. R. S. Pine-Coffin (Harmondsworth, Penguin Books, 1961), p. 60.

PART II

Colonial embrace

CHAPTER 2

White men bearing gifts: diffusion of the Bible and scriptural imperialism

> It took God longer to write the Bible than it has taken Him to build the British Empire.   Wm Macdonald

> Christianity, or European influence, advances with sword or paper treaties in one hand, and the Bible or a case of gin in the other – as it appears to the native mind.   A. S. White

One of the pivotal moments in history was the unprecedented political, economic and cultural transformation that affected the peoples of Asia, Africa, Latin America and the Pacific as the result of European expansion. Each continent has its own date marking the start of European territorial colonization. The year 1492 is generally seen as the beginning of the conquest of Latin America; 1498 for Asia, and especially for India when the Portuguese adventurer Vasco da Gama reached Calicut on the south-west coast of India; and 1625 for the occupation of South Africa, pointing ahead to the scramble for that continent and its eventual partition and parcelling out among European nations. Scriptural imperialism began later, nearly two centuries after these territorial conquests. This chapter aims to map out the landscape of scriptural production and of the dissemination of the Bible leading to its circulation on a massive scale, through the agency of the British and Foreign Bible Society, and then to delineate some marks of colonial interpretation.

VENERABLE VERSIONS AND PAUCITY OF BIBLES

The map that I shall draw is the one created by the Bible Society itself to establish the perspective in which it set its own origination. The defining moment for scriptural imperialism was the formation of the British and Foreign Bible society in 1804 when it solemnly pledged to make physical dissemination of the Bible to all peoples its sole intention. The resolution moved by the Society's first general secretary, John Owen, encapsulated its aim:

A Society shall be formed, with this designation, The British and Foreign Bible Society; of which the sole object shall be to encourage a wider dispersion of the Holy Scriptures. This Society shall add its endeavours to those employed by other Societies for circulating the Scriptures through the British dominions, and shall also, according to its ability, extend its influence to other countries, whether Christian, Mahomedan, or Pagan.[1]

As we saw in the last chapter, the Bible had only a restricted circulation and use in precolonial days and hardly reached the ordinary people. This was all about to change due to the untiring efforts of the Bible Society. When European territorial rule started, neither the conquistadores, the Roman Catholic Church nor the great trading companies like the East India Company were keen advocates or avid readers of the Bible. The Roman Catholic Church at that time actively discouraged the Bible's reaching the ordinary people, the Church authorities being preoccupied with the aftermath of the Reformation and exhausting its hermeneutical energies on the Counter-Reformation. The Roman hierarchy traced some of its current troubles to the circulation of the Bible initiated by the Reformation.[2]

The vernacular, in the common parlance of the time, meant any modern European language, while an illiterate was perceived not as a person who could not read, but as a person who could not read Latin. The question as to whether European languages had the linguistic potential to convey the pristine purity of God's Word was an old one. It was an ignominy to be heaped later upon vernacular languages of the colonized by Europeans. As early as 1486, Berthold, the archbishop of Mentz, had wondered whether the 'German language is

[1] George Browne, *The History of the British and Foreign Bible Society: From Its Institution in 1804, to the Close of Its Jubilee in 1854* (London, Bagster and Sons, 1859), vol. I, p. 10.
[2] *The Bible in Many Tongues* (London, The Religious Tract Society, 1853), p. 85.

capable of expressing what great authors have written in Greek and Latin on the high mysteries of the Christian faith? . . . Certainly it is not, hence they invent new words, or use old ones in erroneous senses, a thing especially dangerous in sacred Scripture.'[3] A similar view was held with regard to the English language. The 1408 Oxford Convocation prohibited anyone from translating or even possessing the English version of the Bible without the licence of the bishop,[4] and no English translation appeared until Tyndale's version was printed in 1525. In 1530 King Henry VIII made it illegal for 'woomen or artificers, prentises journeymen serving men of the degrees of yeomen or undre, husbandmen [and] laborers', but noble women 'maie reade to themselves alone and not to others any [Texts] of the Byble or New Testament'.[5] Stephen Gardiner, a bishop of Henry VIII's reformed Church of England, wrote in 1547: 'Religion has continued in Latin fifteen hundred years. But as for the English tongue, itself has not continued in one form of understanding two hundred years; and without God's work and special miracle it shall hardly contain religion long, when it cannot last itself.'[6] This resistance to making the Bible available in vernacular languages pointed to the Church's linguistic conservativism. Giving vernacular versions to the common people was regarded as casting pearls before swine. The prevailing feeling, as David Lawton has observed, was based on the idea that: 'The Bible is old; truth is old; God is old; and so is Latin, whereas English is newfangled.'[7]

One of the fears the Church authorities had was that an easy access to the Bible would lead to misreading or irreverent

---

[3] Cited in *The Bible in Many Tongues*, p. 92. The archbishop went on to insist that any translation should be vetted by four doctors, and anyone who printed or circulated it without approval would be excommunicated, would forfeit their books and would be fined one hundred gold crowns.

[4] For the full text of the provincial council, see *Records of the English Bible: The Documents Relating to the Translation and Publication of the Bible in English, 1525–1611*, ed. Alfred W. Pollard (London, Oxford University Press, 1911), pp. 79–81.

[5] Cited in Jean-François Gilmont, 'Protestant Reformations and Reading', in *A History of Reading in the West*, ed. Guglielmo Cavallo and Roger Chartier (London, Polity Press, 1999), p. 221.

[6] Cited in David Lawton, *Faith, Text and History: The Bible in English* (Charlottesville, University Press of Virginia, 1990), p. 57.

[7] Ibid., p. 57.

interpretation. The Council of Trent was involved in initiating a series of hermeneutical schemes and censorship as a way of stopping the 'suspect and pernicious' vernacular translations contaminating the minds of the lay people. Among the measures the Council took were those of establishing the Latin Vulgate as the authentic version of the Bible and formally condemning and disallowing the use of the scripture in the vernacular:

As it is manifest by experience, that if the use of the holy writers is permitted in the vulgar tongue, more evil than good will arise, because of the temerity of man; it is for this reason all Bibles are prohibited, with all their parts, whether they be printed or written, in whatever vulgar language soever; as also are prohibited all summaries or abridgement of the Bibles, or of any books of the holy writings, although they should be only historical, and that in whatever vulgar tongue they may be written.[8]

The Council of Trent not only forbade any vernacular versions but also wanted to control interpretation and made sure that only the Church had the right to expound its true sense. A letter addressed to Pope Julius III by three bishops on 23 October 1533 indicated the perceived mood of the time. It is worth quoting their advice in full:

Finally, and we have reserved this advice for the last, because it is the most important that we are able in the circumstances to give to your holiness, you must watch with the utmost care, and effect by all means in your power, that only the smallest portion possible of the gospel (above all in the language of the people) be read in the countries subject to your dominion and which acknowledges your power. Let that little suffice which is read in the service of the mass, and let no one be permitted to read more. It is the fact that so long as men have remained content with this small portion of the Scriptures, so long your interests have prospered and your maxims have prevailed. On the contrary, your authority, both temporal and spiritual, has been continually declining [*sic*] from the moment that the common people have usurped a pretended right to read more. Above all, it is the book which, more than any other, has raised against us these agitations and storms which have driven us to the very brink of the pit: and it must be acknowledged that if any

---

[8]   *The Bible in Many Tongues*, pp. 93–4.

person examines it minutely, and then compares separately its contents with what is practised in our churches, he will find very great differences, and will see that our doctrines are not only quite different from what the Scripture teaches, but still further, are often entirely opposed to it. Therefore, from the moment that the people, excited by any one of our learned adversaries, shall have acquired this knowledge, the outcry against us will not cease till all is divulged, and we become the object of universal hatred. Therefore, those very few writings must be kept from notice, but yet with due caution and exact care, lest the measure should raise against us still greater uproar and disturbance.[9]

The dominant perception was that, for the laity to grow in spirituality and personal holiness, direct access to the Bible was not necessary. The role of the laity was simply to listen to the Word expounded for them by the clergy. Thus the Bible was subjected to a rigorous control. The Council also insisted that the written tradition received by the Church must be held in equal reverence to the Holy Writ. The Bible was thus made an adjunct and a complement to Church tradition and teaching.

Even the version approved by the Church was not easy to come by. In Italy, for example, there had been at least thirty-three editions of the Bible before 1579, but no single edition was published during the whole of the seventeenth century. In Spain, again, the printing of the Bible was prohibited during this period. Some editions of the New Testament in Spanish were printed in Venice and Amsterdam, but it was impossible to circulate them. As late as 1786 there was no single version of the whole Bible in Spanish. Portugal was equally bereft of the scriptures. A version printed in Lisbon was neither intended nor adapted for common use. When, in 1582, the Mogul Emperor Akbar requested a copy of the Bible, Jerome Xavier, the relative of Francis Xavier, composed a history of Christ – *Mirāt-ul Quds* (The Mirror of Holiness) or *Dāstan-i Masīh* (Life of Christ) – culling materials from the gospel narratives, which included the nativity and infancy of Christ, his miracles and teachings, his death and suffering, and his Resurrection and Ascension. The

[9] Ibid., pp. 96–7.

Mirāt-ul Quds also contained a fair share of old legends of the Catholic Church.[10]

The number of copies printed of each version was varied and limited. The Bible had not yet become a marketable commodity. In a petition sent to Sixtus IV in 1472, the printers complained of their poverty due to poor sales of books. They stated that books by classic authors had a print run of two hundred and seventy-five copies, whereas a theological work which included the Bible had only five hundred and fifty copies.[11] Even centuries later, copies that were available were too costly. When Mungo Park, the Scottish missionary, visited the Gambia, he came across Arabic versions of the Bible. A copy of the Pentateuch was equivalent to the prize of a prime slave which was about twenty guineas.[12] The situation in England was no more encouraging: even the 1611 King James Version, which in the course of the next two centuries would be triumphantly hailed as the book of the Empire, had its supply regulated and controlled. The five editions it went through before 1640 had only five thousand copies per edition, and the 1617 reprint did not even exhaust its print run.[13] More to the point, the King James Version was intended for public, not private, reading as the title page indicates it was 'appointed to be read in Churches'.

The Roman Catholic Church was aware of the importance of the Bible for the colonial project. The Jesuits received permission to engage in translation in 1615 but did not make use of it. Rather they spent their energies translating indigenous texts into European languages, or, to appeal to the Chinese literati, they rewrote versions of biblical stories to demonstrate conceptual and philosophical correspondences between biblical and Chinese traditions. In India, Constantine Beschi, employing the narrative principles of Tamil literature, produced

---

[10] Edward Maclagan, *The Jesuits and the Great Mogul* (London, Burns Oates and Washbourne, 1932), pp. 203–5.

[11] *The Bible in Many Tongues*, p. 89.

[12] Mungo Park, *Travels in the Interior Districts of Africa: Performed Under the Direction and Patronage of the African Association in the Years 1795, 1796 and 1797* (London, W. Blumer and Co., 1810), p. 468.

[13] *Records of the English Bible*, p. 67.

the first Christian Tamil epic, *Thembavani*, which had Joseph as its central figure. In Nicolas Standaert's view, there are a number of reasons for the absence of Bible translation and most of them can be traced to their European background: 'Catholic missionaries valued rational theology over narrative theology; popular preaching over exegesis; natural sciences over scriptural sciences.'[14] To this one could add one more, namely the colonial perception of the Other as incapable of comprehending the loftier truths lodged in the naked text of the Bible without proper and prior preparation. Abbé Dubois, the Roman Catholic missionary, suggested that what Indians, who were immersed in the grossest ignorance, needed was not the Bible but 'rather elementary works, such as catechisms, short and familiar instructions, plain explanations of the creed, of the ten commandments, simple lectures upon Christian duties, upon the principal virtues, upon charity, temperance, self-command, the forgiveness of injuries, &c. &c.'[15]

A pastoral application of biblical texts was seen as more important than the inherent authority of the texts themselves. Hence the Roman Catholic Church spent its energies on the production of indigenous liturgies, meditations, catechisms and homilies. The catechism for Vietnamese people produced by the French Jesuit Alexandre de Rhodes in the seventeenth century is an example of how narratives and texts were woven into his theological discourse.[16]

To sum up: prior to the formation of the British and Foreign Bible Society, both supply of and access to the Bible were severely limited. Vernacular versions were scarce and largely inaccessible to ordinary people. More significantly, being suspicious of impious reading, the Church assumed the sole responsibility for interpreting the Word.

---

[14] Nicolas Standaert, 'The Bible in Early Seventeenth-Century China', in *Bible in Modern China: The Literary and Intellectual Impact*, ed. Irene Eber, Sze-Kar Wan and Knut Walf (Sankt Augustine, Institut Monumenta Serica, 1999), p. 53.

[15] Abbé J. A. Dubois, *Letters on the State of Christianity in India* (New Delhi, Associated Publishing House, n.d.), p. 42.

[16] Peter C. Phan, *Mission and Catechesis: Alexandre de Rhodes and Inculturation in Seventeenth-Century Vietnam* (Maryknoll, NY, Orbis Books, 1998), *passim*.

CHEAP BIBLES AND SCRIPTURAL IMPERIALISM

Historically, the circulation of the Bible, and the mass campaign encouraging people to read it in the vernacular, originated with the Protestants. The basic Protestant beliefs include acknowledgement of the sufficiency of scripture, assertion of its authority over tradition, treating it as the incorruptible Word against human error and encouraging private reading over institutional mediation. The growth of Protestant Churches in the colonies has a familiar pattern. First, the denunciation of the natives' idolatrous practices, then preaching accompanied by the presentation and dissemination of the Bible as the answer to their miserable state, followed by the establishment of denominational churches, and the founding of educational and medical institutions. In this Protestant pursuit of the dissemination of the Bible, the British and Foreign Bible Society played a crucial role in putting 'into men's hands the open Bible . . . [bidding] them read it for themselves'.[17] The Society took the axiom seriously: 'Protestants without Bibles are soldiers without weapons, ready neither for conquest nor for defence.'[18]

The Bible Society itself had participated in its own myth-making process as the sole disseminator of the Bible by religiously repeating a heart-rending story about Mary Jones and her Bible. According to this, Mary Jones, a sixteen-year old from Wales, had a great love for the Word of God. She had to walk two miles to the nearest place where a copy of the Bible was available for her to read. She saved for years to buy herself a copy and travelled twenty-eight miles to Bala. There, to her utter disappointment, she discovered that every single copy had been sold. Moved by the simple piety of Mary, Thomas Charles, a minister, was able to give her a spare copy he had. When Charles narrated this story at a meeting of the Religious Tract Society – forerunner of the British and Foreign Bible Society – its secretary, Joseph Hughes, was said to have uttered these

---

[17] *Have Ye Never Read?: A Popular Report of the British and Foreign Bible Society 1912–1913* (London, The Bible House, 1913), p. 37.
[18] *The Bible in Many Tongues*, p. 141.

words: 'Surely a society might be formed for the purpose. But if for Wales, why not for the kingdom? Why not for the world?'[19]

George Browne, one of the secretaries of the Society who wrote a two-volume history of the Society on the occasion of its jubilee summed up its intention:

The Society is founded on the principle of reverence for the Holy Scriptures of the Old and New Testament, as containing a revelation from God to men – a heavenly message addressed to all, and of supreme importance to every one of the human family. It further assumes that these 'Oracles of God' are to be looked upon by those who are so happy as to possess them, not simply as a treasure to be enjoyed for their personal benefit, but as a trust to be used by them for the benefit of others. *Hence, the Society aims to make these Holy Writings known, in every nation and in every tongue, and, as far as may be, to render them the actual possession of every individual on the face of the whole earth: a magnificent object, surely all must admit, and as benevolent as it is grand!*[20] (italics mine)

The Society was born as a result of the evangelical and pious men and women who were enthused by the New Testament teaching. They saw the circulation of the Bible as an important divine calling. This was supported by a belief that the secret of England's greatness was its reading of the Bible. They also believed that it was the reading of the Bible which preserved England from any political upheaval, and that the Bible could be a vehicle for transmitting English values to the colonies. Like Macaulay's notorious Minute of 1835, there was a similar 'Bible Minute' of 1847 by the Marquess of Tweeddale, which extolled the benefits of introducing the Bible as the text for English classes in government schools in India. Despite popular protest in India, the Minute supported the recommendation of the Council of Education:

I can see no sufficient reason for objecting to the Bible being made available in our public schools under the rule laid down by the council. It is the only means I know of giving to the Natives a practical knowledge of the sciences from whence arise all those high qualities which they admire so much in the character of those whom providence had placed to rule over them . . . nor do I see how

---

[19] William Canton, *The Story of the Bible Society* (London, John Murray, 1904), p. 1.

[20] Browne, *History of the British and Foreign Bible Society*, I, p. 3; italics mine.

Native Society itself can safely and permanently advance, except upon this basis. I would therefore adopt the rule proposed by the council.[21]

The Society from the outset made it clear that it had different missiological aims from those of the existing foreign missionary organizations of the time, namely, sending missionaries was not part of its remit. Though most of the Society members served on the boards of various mission agencies, it was relentless in communicating to its supporters and adversaries alike that its simple aim was to promote the free circulation of the Bible. The ultimate purpose of the Society was not the transmission of the Christian faith but the circulation of Christian Scriptures. When Thomas Twining, in 1807, complained in a letter to the East India Company, that 'the universal dissemination of the Christian faith' could upset the fragile religious equilibrium in India, John Shore, Lord Teignmouth, the former Governor-General of India, and a supporter of the Society drew attention to the distinction between the British and Foreign Bible Society and other missionary societies:

There exists, Sir, in this country, as you very well know, a most venerable and useful Institution, 'The Society for Promoting Christian Knowledge'. This Society may be accurately enough represented within the limits prescribed by its charter, as having as its *object, the Dissemination of the Christian Faith*. The latitude of its designation, and the generality with which its object is expressed, allow to this Society, an unlimited choice of means. It may define, systematize, and classify, the several points of Christian Theology; it may issue Tracts on all and any matters of doctrines and discipline, at its discretion: it may employ Missionaries and catechists, erect Churches and Schools, and proceed *ad libitum*, for accomplishments of its purposes. And why? – For the reason above given: because its designation is *general* and its object *undefined*. Not so the British and Foreign Bible Society. It can do but *one* act for the propagation of Christianity, it can distribute but *one* Book, and that Book – the Bible. It can support no Missionaries, erect no Churches, endow no Schools, disseminate no Tracts; it cannot issue even a Dissertation to recommend the Bible, nor annex a single Note to explain it. Its designation and its object confine it to the

---

[21] *The Englishman*, IX (96), 15 April 1847.

circulation of the Scriptures; it can do nothing out of these limits; it can do nothing beyond them.[22]

David Brown, speaking at the Old Church at Calcutta on 1 January 1810, dispelled further any fears the traders might have had at that time, that conversion to Christianity by natives might thwart their mercantile enterprise. The Bible Society held no such threat. He said: 'I have, on a former occasion, mentioned the British and Foreign Bible Society, instituted in the year 1804, the exclusive object of which is to promote and assist the circulation of the Scriptures both at home and abroad . . .'[23]

The image the Society was keen to project was not of a sectarian group of men and women busily engaged in peddling some troublesome version of the gospel to convert the hapless urban poor at home or morally degenerate natives in the colonies, but that of a respectable business organization, involved simply in the innocuous task of publishing and circulating the Bible. John Owen compared the Bible Society with Lloyds of London: 'The line of business is, with few exceptions, as direct at the Bible committee as it is at Lloyds; and there is little reason to expect the peculiar tenets of Calvin or Socinus to enter into a debate for dispersing an edition of the Scripture, as there would be if the same men met to underwrite a policy of insurance.'[24]

Roger Martin, in his study of the evangelical revival of eighteenth-century England, concludes that the Bible Society was by far the 'largest and most ambitious of the great pan-evangelical organizations' of its time.[25] The statistics alone are staggering. For instance, organizationally its growth was exceptionally remarkable. It had an auxiliary in every English county. By 1832 it had thirty-five thousand committee members and a hundred thousand subscribers. A decade later, there were 859 Bible Society auxiliaries, two thousand Bible Associations and

[22] John Owen, *The History of the Origin and First Ten Years of the British and Foreign Bible Society* (London, Trilling and Hughes, 1816), vol. I, pp. 332–4.

[23] Ibid., II, p. 24.

[24] Roger H. Martin, *Evangelicals United: Ecumenical Stirrings in Pre-Victorian Britain, 1795–1830* (Metuchen, NJ, The Scarecrow Press, 1983), p. 88.

[25] Ibid., p. 91.

five hundred ladies' organizations. In close association with the parent Society, The Bible Society was formed in America and in Europe. In Russia alone there were over three hundred Bible Societies. Sheer size was not the only feature. Its impact on Church life was said to be incalculable. Attendances increased, and the Sabbath Day was now claimed to be a truly delightful experience. Importantly, it claimed to bring differing and often warring denominations together. One evangelical Anglican went so far as to claim that the Bible Society had inaugurated, 'a new era in the Christian world. They have roused the torpor of other religious institutions: they have thrown down the barriers which separated man from his brother, united in one body the energies of the pious and the wise.'[26]

The Society's literary production was equally phenomenal. In the first ten centuries of the Christian era, the scriptures were translated into some ten different languages: Greek, Syriac, Coptic, Latin, Ethiopic, Armenian, Gothic, Slavonic, Arabic and perhaps Anglo-Saxon. The total number of copies produced could have been about a thousand. In the two hundred and fifty years after the Reformation and the invention of the printing press, Bible translations were made into twenty-two European languages. In the first part of the nineteenth century, due to the tireless efforts of the Bible Society and its band of indomitable translators, the Bible was published in one hundred and sixty different languages or dialects.[27]

Scriptural imperialism had its roots in the image the Society invented for itself. It saw its mission in millennial terms and projected itself as the chosen agent of God to whose care the onerous task of transmitting God's Word had been entrusted. The oracles of God, which were first given into the custody of God's chosen, the Jews, had now been passed on to the Christians, especially the British, because the Jews had kept them to themselves and fenced them round. Now, among the nations, the mantle had fallen on the English, who had been endowed with the sword of the Spirit and the power to wield it. But among the missionary agencies, it was the Bible Society

[26] Ibid., p. 93.
[27] *The Bible in Many Tongues*, p. 146.

which was especially called. The Society's Annual Report for 1902 claimed:

May we not even say that, equally, our own revered Society stands as a monarch among the agencies to which God has entrusted the spreading of the truth. She is girded with His sword, and year by year, as her organization grows more perfect, she is able to wield the weapon to better advantage. She goes forth in the strength of the Lord . . .[28]

John Owen, speaking on the occasion of the formation of the Kentish Bible Society, claimed that it was under the 'supreme direction' of God that the Society had been established.[29] Later he went on to write that 'the Gospel of Salvation was a free, unmerited boon to mankind; let us therefore rejoice, that, under Providence, we are become the honoured instruments of its dispersion'.[30] God's calling and election had now been entrusted to the Society. Thus it saw its early task as taking back the Bible to where it had originally belonged. Browne hailed Asia as the birthplace of the Bible, where greater portions of it were originally written, and where the region provided the backdrop for many of its principal events. But over the years Asia had become a stranger to its hallowed treasure and was in desperate need of God's Word. Browne, using the same phrase that John Owen had employed – 'the honoured instrument' – saw the Society's task as 'carrying back the blessed Book to the countries whence it emanated'.[31]

The Society's intention of providing the Bible in the vernacular was another mark of scriptural imperialism. In colonialism's cultural conquest, vernacular Bibles, enabling the natives to read the Word of God in their own languages, could be seen as the sympathetic and acceptable face of its civilizing mission: it appeared to be a noble cause. But behind this noble claim, one came across constant complaints by the Society's translators who found that the indigenous languages not only had no suitable vocabulary but also lacked concepts to convey the ideas

---

[28] *The Book of God's Kingdom: A Popular Illustrated Report of the British and Foreign Bible Society 1901–1902* (London, The Bible House, 1902), p. 11.

[29] Owen, *Origin and First Ten Years of the British and Foreign Bible Society*, I, p. 285.

[30] Ibid., pp. 418–19.

[31] Browne, *History of the British and Foreign Bible Society*, II p. 98.

of the gospel. The Society saw its task as making the Bible available in the tongue in which a person was born. In this pursuit, the Society was upholding another Protestant principle – 'to supply every man with the Holy Scriptures in his own mother-tongue' – seriously.[32] Until this time, as we saw in the last chapter, the Bible had been for lay people an icon and a treasured relic, reserved for the priests and theologians to read. The only proper thing for the lay person to do was to kneel before it and kiss its jewelled covers. As far as the large majority of the faithful were concerned, the Book remained a holy object, unreadable and unread. When, in many of the liturgies, the Bible was read in a traditional venerable version, it was incomprehensible to ordinary worshippers. One of the Reports of the Society commented:

Thus the Roman Church reads it in Latin, the Greek Churches in ancient Greek, the Russian Church in Slavonic, and the Abyssinian Church in Ethiopic. But the Churches of the Reformation insist boldly that in their worship every man shall hear the Scripture in the tongue in which he was born.[33]

In translating biblical truths into vernacular languages, the Reports made clear the inadequacy of the local languages to convey the truth of God. The fact that the translators could not find verbal counterparts in indigenous languages was taken as proof that these languages were incapable of expressing the Christian message. The Reports were replete with examples of words missing from local languages to communicate the biblical truths. The Mosquito Indians in Nicaragua had no word for sin, Ibos had none for soul; and Nigerians had none for sacrifice, and so forth. When translating the Parable of the Prodigal Son into one of the languages of Indian tribals, the translators, with their characteristic Protestant disapproval of alcohol, ran into problems when they came to the verse that says 'began to be merry'. For the locals, feasting meant becoming intoxicated with native beer; it was not easy to find a word which did not suggest drunkenness. Fijians had no active transitive verb for forgive, so the sixth petition of the Lord's Prayer was rendered

---

[32] *Have Ye Never Read?*, p. 125.
[33] *Have Ye Never Read?*, p. 38.

as 'Be not angry with us on account of our sins, as we are not angry.'[34] A translator for the Bible Society, H. C. Withey, claimed that Ki-Mbundu, one of the strongest Bantu languages of South West Africa, had 'a full vocabulary for vices, but a limited one for virtues'.[35] Faced with such a problem, the report comments: 'Not only the heathen, but the speech of the heathen, must be Christianized. Their language itself needs to be born again. Their very words have to be converted from foul meanings and base uses and baptized into a Christian sense, before those words can convey the great truths and ideas of the Bible.'[36] The reborn vernacular language was seen as enabling the natives to enter the civilized world. When St Mark's Gospel was translated into Kopu, one of the languages of indigenous Chinese, A. G. Nicholls of China Inland Mission wrote: 'The arrival of this Gospel will transform the people.'[37]

The Bible was promoted as the only text among all the sacred writings of the world which could be made readable 'for men of every colour and in every country'. One of the Reports made clear to its supporters this view regarding other sacred writings: 'None of them professes to be a universal and ecumenical book. Only the Bible is the book of the whole human race.'[38] The Society claimed that 'it would be quite impossible for European boys to follow the ideas of the *Vedas* or the *Tripitaka*, however admirably translated. There is only one Book which rises above national and racial distinctions, and makes its appeal to the general heart of humanity.'[39] The Society certainly played a crucial role in translating the Bible into vernacular languages. Its translation activities prompted the revival of and, in some cases, the invention of alphabets for many

---

[34] *The Word Among the Nations: A Popular Illustrated Report of the British and Foreign Bible Society for the Year 1908–1909* (London, The Bible House, 1909), p. 13.

[35] *The Word Among the Nations*, p. 14.

[36] *The Book Above Every Book* (London, The Bible House, 1910), p. 22.

[37] *In the Vulgar Tongue: A Popular Illustrated Report of the British and Foreign Bible Society 1913–1914* (London, The Bible House, 1914), p. 22. Occasionally, the translators did acknowledge that the vernacular words conveyed the meaning most picturesquely. For instance, the word for love in Ambrym was 'the heart-calling of God', *The Word Among the Nations*, p. 15.

[38] *The Book Above Every Book*, pp. 30–1.

[39] *The Book Above Every Book*, p. 97.

languages, although for the Society the one concern was to transmit the Christian message.

Scriptural imperialism was furthered by the Society's ambition to print the Bible at affordable prices and place it within the reach of all people; it was also prepared to print and distribute Bibles at a loss. Its aim was to make the Bible the 'cheapest book' that had been published. The popular report for 1904–5 claimed: 'The Society exists to bring God's Book within the reach of all sorts and classes of men. That is to say, it must sell its editions at prices which Eastern peasants and ploughmen can afford to pay.'[40]

The Society's ambitious intentions were evident when it modelled itself on the lines of the British Empire. Its organizational patterns were based on the administrative structures of the Empire. The Society likened its Queen Victoria Street headquarters to 'our Downing Street', and its administrative jurisdiction was its realm. Like the British Empire, the Society's auxiliaries abroad were treated as embassies, and the head was called the agent just as the colonial administration had its government agents.[41] In one of its triumphalist moods, it claimed that its role extended more widely than that of the British Empire. Writing during the coronation of the King-Emperor, the 1902 Report states:

The work of our Society is indeed far more extensive even than that extensive Empire. For we serve the Lord Christ, and He alone is King of Kings, Lord of Lords. When He sends forth the Book of His Word upon earth, He alone can make good the claim of that Book that its leaves are for the healing of the nations without any exception whatever.[42]

The Society's object of mass circulation of the Bible was given a great boost by the transition that was taking place in the printing industry. The move from hand- to machine-printing at the beginning of the nineteenth-century had enabled the production of cheap Bibles. It could not have come at a more

---

[40] *Seed Corn for the World: A Popular Report of the British and Foreign Bible Society for the Year 1904–1905* (London, The Bible House, 1905), p. 91.
[41] *The Book of God's Kingdom*, pp. 20–1.
[42] Ibid., p. 7.

appropriate time. A new class of readers, too, was emerging in Britain. The new urban class – domestic workers, employees in trade and craft industries, and lower ranks in the army – enjoyed three necessary pre-conditions for reading: leisure, facilities like lending libraries and physical comforts like light, chairs and tables.[43] In the colonies, the educational efforts of the missionary agencies produced a new educated elite who were thirsting for Western knowledge and literature.

MARKS OF COLONIAL HERMENEUTICS

In the rest of the chapter I hope to highlight some of the marks and legacies of colonial interpretation. Colonialist reading includes interpretation that was undertaken during the colonial period and its aftermath. As a discourse it is neither monolithic nor static. It takes different contours as it moves through different phases of colonialism and neocolonialism. It is important to reiterate that colonial reading does not end with the demise of territorial colonialism. The current metropolitan interpretation, although historically distinct from the colonial project and not directly involved in it, still participates in it by organizing and reinforcing perceptions of colonialism. It exerts its colonial power by viewing the world from a single privileged point of view, namely white, male and Western, and it contributes to the complex of attitudes that made imperialism seem part of the order of things. One of its implicit presumptions is that, in order to qualify for inclusion, the hermeneutical output of Third World interpreters must conform to rules or criteria developed within the Western academic paradigm. The practice of referring to European or Western interpretation as *the* interpretation and routinely designating other regional discourses as Asian, African or Chinese is a sign of neocolonialism.

Colonial hermeneutics starts with the assumption that if a barbarous country like Britain can become civilized after turning to Christianity so can other nations. The editors of the

---

[43] See Reinhard Wittmann, 'Was There a Reading Revolution at the End of the Eighteenth Century?', in *A History of Reading in the West*, ed. Guglielmo Cavallo and Roger Chartier (London, Polity Press, 1999), p. 291.

Missionary Register, in their first issue in 1813, called upon their readers to take up their missionary vocation:

CHRISTIANS! the obligation, which lies upon you to join in this sacred cause, is infinite. Your own ancestors, in this very Island, once worshipped dumb idols: they offered human sacrifices; yea, their sons and their daughters unto devils: they knew not the truth: they had not heard of the name of Jesus: they lived, they died, without hope, and without God. Before the preaching of the Gospel of Christ, no Church here existed, but the temple of an Idol; no priesthood but that of Paganism; no God but the Sun, the Moon, or some hideous image. To the cruel rites of the Druidical Worship, succeeded the abominations of the Roman Idolatry. In Scotland stood the temple of Mars; in Cornwall the temple of Mercury; in Bangor, the temple of Minerva; at Malden, the temple of Victoria; in Bath, the temple of Apollo; at Leicester, the temple of Janus; at York, where St Peter's now stands, the temple of Bellona; in London, on the site of St Paul's Cathedral, the temple of Diana; at Westminister, where the Abbey rears its venerable pile, a temple of Apollo. But mark the contrast: you now are a favoured nation: your light is come: the glory of the Lord is risen upon you: all these heathen rites have ceased: the blood of the victim no longer flows: an established Christian Church lifts its venerable head: the pure Gospel is preached: ministers of the sanctuary, as heralds of salvation, proclaim mercy throughout the land – while civil and religious liberty have grown up under the benign influence of the Gospel, that sacred tree, the leaves of which are for the healing of the nations.[44]

This was a clarion call. The intention was to turn the former waywardness of the British and their present state of maritime power into an irresistible argument for the spread of the gospel.

Colonialists often discursively constructed contrastive paradigms such as Christian/savage, civilized/barbaric and orderly/ disorderly in order to define themselves, and also to explain the dominance and acceleration of colonial rule. Such contrastive pairings helped to condemn the other as inferior and also helped to determine the nature of their hold over the people they subjugated. The early missionary hermeneutics which abetted in this enterprise extrapolated this binary view to inject its own biblical values into the private and public lives of

---

[44] *The Missionary Register* 1.1813, pp. 7–8.

the colonized, and for the good of nations which were still living in a 'savage' state.

Inculcation

One of the earlier marks of colonial interpretation was the use of the Bible as a vehicle for inculcating European manners. Local customs were denigrated as barbaric compared with the civilized progress of biblical religion. The missionary literature never failed to testify to the significant cultural advancement brought about by the biblical message. One of the missionaries reported on the outward changes the Ugandan people experienced through the Bible:

Uganda today is no savage wilderness. It has its railways, its harnessed water-power, its post office and roads, its cultivated farms and neat homes. The Bible is the *sole* and *sufficient cause of this transformation.* There are other African tribes whose trade has gone without the Bible and degraded the people even as it has purchased their goods.[45]

Another missionary, from Tanjore in South India, wrote: 'Upon the whole, the moral conduct, upright dealing, decorous manners, and decent dress, of the native Protestants of Tanjore, demonstrate the powerful influence and peculiar excellence of the Christian religion. It ought, however, to be observed, that the Bible, when the reading of it becomes general, has nearly the same effect on the poor of every place.'[46] From South Africa, Robert Moffat noted that his translations of St Luke's Gospel had a similar behavioural impact in Botswana:

The same Gospel which had taught them that they were spiritually miserable, blind, and naked, discovered to them also that they needed reform externally, and thus prepared their minds to adopt those modes of comfort, cleanliness, and convenience which they had been accustomed to view only as the peculiarities of a strange people. Thus, by the slow but certain progress of Gospel principles, whole families became clothed and in their right mind.[47]

---

[45] Helen Barrett Montgomery, *The Bible and Missions* (West Medford, The Central Committee on the United Study of Foreign Missions, 1920), p. 180; italics mine.

[46] Owen, *Origin and First Ten Years of the British and Foreign Bible Society*, i, p. 323.

[47] Robert Moffat, *Missionary Labours and Scenes in Southern Africa* (London, John Snow, 1842), p. 505.

Any astute reader of the Bible at the time would immediately note that Moffat's reference to 'clothed and in their right mind' alludes to the demoniac in St Luke's Gospel (8.26–39) who was healed by Jesus. This was to testify that through the agency of the Bible the people who were once unruly, or even deemed to be mad, were now acquiring the benefits of Christian civilization. The internal transformations that were taking place had to be played out externally to signal the civilizing achievements of missionaries.

Encroachment

The second mark of colonial interpretation was the introduction to the 'other' of alien values, under the guise of biblicization. The idea was to repudiate initially the local culture for its inability to transmit Christian truths. Thus the indigenous culture had to be born again, baptized and christianized before it could become a conduit in expressing great truths of the biblical faith. In the process of achieving their goals, missionaries, if necessary, did not hesitate to alter or falsify local cultural values or wrench them from their roots. Norman Lewis provides a recent example of how missionaries propagated a sense of guilt, which was at the heart of missionary preaching, by injecting Christian values into native cultural norms, thus altering their way of perceiving things. The missionaries who worked in Central America among the Panare found that these people did not have Christian concepts such as sin, guilt, punishment or redemption; hence the question was how to preach the gospel to a people who did not understand these concepts. So something had to be concocted before repentance and salvation could be preached. The translators decided that the best way to go about it was to re-edit and rewrite the scriptures in such a way that the Panare were implicated in Christ's death. The New Tribes Mission's version of the Crucifixion rendered for the Indians was different to that of the biblical narration. The biblical record of Judas' betrayal, the involvement of the Roman officials, the Last Supper, the Trial of Jesus, the role of Pontius

Pilate and the crown of thorns were all excised. The new amended text read:

The Panare killed Jesus Christ because they were wicked. Let's kill Jesus Christ said Panare. The Panare seized Jesus Christ. The Panare killed in this way. They laid a cross on the ground. They fastened his hands and his feet against the wooden beams, with nails. They raised him straight up, nailed. The man died like that, nailed. Thus the Panare killed Jesus Christ.[48]

As Lewis commented, if this was not going to create a feeling of guilt, then nothing could.

The lack of lexical and conceptual Christian counterparts in indigenous languages and culture was seen as a proof that these languages and cultures were incapable of expressing the new and radical message of the Bible; hence the need to write such concepts into these languages and cultures. Instead of discerning the revelation of God afresh for the time, colonial hermeneutic was unthinkingly content with concepts and for-mulations suitable for the people of the Mediterranean world nearly two thousand years earlier, and re-applied them to Asian, African and Latin American contexts without recog-nizing the cultural and theological differences between the two.

Displacement

The third mark of colonial interpretation was the displacement of local culture. This approach is the opposite of the cultural encroachment that we witnessed in the previous paragraphs. Instead of a theologically and conceptually poverty-stricken culture, missionaries encountered local cultures brimming with egalitarian values. This they saw as a hindrance to their understanding of the 'progressive' nature of the gospel. Native customs and manners were seen as undermining the viability of Christian virtues and the colonial project. In Papua, the mis-sionaries saw the laid-back, no-rule, non-authoritarian lifestyle of Papuans as a sign of their primitiveness. Their communities lacked any central authority and well-defined purpose and

---

[48] I owe this reference to Robert Carroll. For the original citation see Norman Lewis, *The Missionaries* (London, Secker and Warburg, 1988), p. 210.

control. They did not have a chief with the power to awaken aspiration and encourage commitment. There were no courts, no judges, no penalties, no officers of law and order and no active sense of obligation, duty or rights. In such an atmosphere people were not only passive but also lacked the vocabulary to express their understanding of a purposeful life. For instance, in a no-rule, care-free atmosphere, the early biblical translators had difficulty in translating the sentence (in Jesus' parable) 'Compel them to come in.' So they had to rephrase it as: 'Urge them to enter in.' The writer of the 1914–15 Report of the British and Foreign Bible Society could now proudly inform the readers that law and order had been introduced to an unruly country as a result of the joint effort of British rule and the New Testament:

> However, moral ideas are now being introduced. Compulsion has come into the lives of the Papuans by the introduction of English law and justice. It is becoming easier to explain the New Testament by means of reference to the British Government. To-day a centralized authority exists, which can impose laws, and punish the breach of laws; there are magistrates and judges and policemen, and prisons. But all these things are foreign; the ideas they convey are foreign; and they have still to be translated into terms of native life and thought. A fresh world is being opened up to the Papuans, and a new life with a new sense of responsibility. They are being constrained into practical recognition of that Categorical Imperative which the New Testament translates in terms of love.[49]

In its attempt to restore 'order', missionary hermeneutics was sending a decisive signal to local people. The inherent cultural values were not acceptable and were inappropriate, and as such they were no match for the energy exuded by the biblical faith. Hence the cultural roots of natives had to be changed in order to accommodate the 'progressive' values of the gospel.

Analogies and implication

Another mark of colonial interpretation was the juxtaposition of biblical and secular history as a convenient weapon against

---

[49] *The Book and the Sword: A Popular Illustrated Report of the British and Foreign Bible Society for the Year 1914–1915* (London, The Bible House, 1915), p. 17.

those who dared to resist colonial intervention. Biblical narratives were reintroduced and opportunistically read back to justify the cruelty and suffering caused by violent invasion. Even Spanish Roman Catholic missionaries used the Bible to this end. In Latin America, in the sixteenth century, the Spanish legitimized the resultant miseries the natives faced as a punishment from God, and a necessary experience that the native Indians had to go through. They portrayed themselves as a divine instrument appointed to teach a valuable lesson. Fray Torbio de Benavente Motolinia juxtaposed the ten plagues God sent to Egypt with ten miseries that had happened in the lives of the indigenous people, to vindicate the Spanish dominance. Motolinia's ten 'native' plagues were: first, small pox from which the local people died like flies; second, the death of many in the conquest; third, the great famine that visited Mexico City after its fall; fourth, the death of the peasants and the blacks after the land was divided among the conquerors; fifth, the imposition of taxes; sixth, the death of countless Indians in the gold mines; seventh, the sacrifice of Indian lives in building the great city of Mexico; eighth, the forced recruitment of Indian slaves to work in the mines; ninth, the hardship faced in the mines; and last, the attacks by violent gangs of lawless Spaniards.[50]

The fusion of biblical and historical events was designed to implicate the natives in salvation history. Ironically their own history was read against them. It was an inverted reading in which God was seen as the one who wounded and inflicted punishment on hapless people, and the Spanish were portrayed as the saviours and liberators. By intertwining biblical and native history, the Conquistadors were depicted as benevolent invaders shielding and rescuing the Indians from cruelty. The European conquest was painted as mutually beneficial, but especially to the natives who had been liberated from misery.

[50] See Elsa Tamez, 'Quetzalcoatal Challenges the Christian Bible', unpublished paper, SBL Annual Conference (San Francisco, 1992), p. 4.

Textualization

Textualization of the Word of God, privileging it over the oral, is another characteristic of colonial hermeneutics. The firm belief of the missionaries was that no religious teaching was of any value unless it was found in written form. They recognized that the only access and entrance for converts was by means of the printed page. The British and Foreign Bible Society's Popular Report of 1933 was unequivocal about it:

Yet the missionary alone is not sufficient to establish the world-wide Kingdom of Christ. To the spoken must be added the written Word. The missionary who takes the Gospel to Africa, India, or China soon discovers that he cannot make progress beyond a certain point without putting that Gospel in a written form into the hands of the people. The converts must learn to read the sacred record as well as hear it expounded.[51]

The legacy of textualization is that the written word acted as the broker for God's revelation. To discern and experience God's purpose, one now had to privately analyse the printed word. In antiquity, and in cultures like Africa, Asia and Oceania, the Word of God need not be in written form to be efficacious. Its oral form, its recitation and memorization, and its public performance, through either visual or theatrical media, were seen as valid ways of expressing God's manifestation. When a translated copy of the New Testament was offered to Chief Namekei in the New Hebrides, his reaction was revealing. His immediate response encapsulated the oral/aural tension felt in certain communities: 'Can it speak? Make it speak to me! Let me hear it speak.' When parts of the book were read to him, his ecstasy was boundless: 'It does speak! It speaks my own language, too! Oh! give it to me.' He got hold of it, opened it and then closed it disappointed and said: 'I cannot make it speak! It will not speak to me!'[52] The written form of the Word of God, which was seen by missionaries as the ultimate measure of the Christian gospel, was ineffective as far the Chief was concerned, because his Aniwan New Testament

[51] *Tell the World* (London, The British and Foreign Bible Society, 1933), pp. 56–7.
[52] Montgomery, *The Bible and Missions*, pp. 126–7.

could not speak and it had no voice. Its inability to talk to him or talk with him distressed him. In Uganda, the common name given to an inquirer was 'reader', and the CMS (Church Missionary Society) missionary policy at that time was that no convert should be baptized until she or he possessed a copy of the New Testament.[53] In the words of Bishop J. J. Willis in Uganda: 'Two simple and very salutary rules have served to place the Bible in the forefront of all CMS work in Uganda. Every adult must learn to read before being baptized. Every candidate for confirmation must possess his own New Testament.'[54] That the Protestant Christians in Uganda were known as *abasomi*, meaning readers, was indicative of the importance accorded to literacy in Ugandan Christianity.

The assumption of the missionaries was that oral cultures were empty and were waiting to be filled with written texts. They saw their task as transforming oral cultures into literate ones. The missionaries were not preoccupied with the tricky dichotomy between orality and literacy, or the competing merits of oral recitation and silent reading. Their mission was premised, after all, upon a book, and they regarded the text as a prime transmitter of divine revelation. One consequence is that biblical interpretation has now become a private, solitary activity. In India, hermeneutics used to be a public activity undertaken by professional story-tellers and singers. Their mode of presentation, as Philip Lutgendorf has highlighted, included, 'simple recitation, recitation plus exposition and dramatic enactment'.[55] The legacy of colonial hermeneutics is that interpretation has become a literary activity confined to the urban educated class, and a private activity that effectively replaces the oral transmission of story.

A further implicit strategic aim of biblical literacy was to turn converts against their own textual traditions. The Society's Reports enthusiastically recounted instances of converts rejecting

---

[53] *Have Ye Never Read?*, p. 19.
[54] *Like Unto Leaven: A Popular Illustrated Report of the British and Foreign Bible Society for the Year 1923–1924*, (London, The Bible House, 1924), p. 47.
[55] Philip Lutgendorf, *The Life of a Text: Performing the Rāmcaritmānas of Tulsidas* (Berkeley, University of California Press, 1991), p. 39.

their own religious writings, and making a bonfire of their religious texts and artefacts as a sign of rejection of their old faith. The Society's Reports were quick to point out the New Testament precedent for such actions: 'Like the Ephesians in Paul's time, several families in Whang-hai made a bonfire of their ancestral tablets, their fetishes, their curios and their vanities.'[56]

Historicization of faith

Central to colonial hermeneutics was the affirmation of biblical religion as a historical faith. This heightened notion of historicity for Christian faith enabled colonial interpreters to portray non-biblical religions as the pagan 'other' of Christianity, needing deliverance. The sacred texts of other religions were treated as 'mythological absurdities and amatory trifles',[57] lacking any historical purpose or eschatological aims. These texts were portrayed as encouraging superstitious cults, containing morally degenerate materials rather than legitimate belief systems. The prophetic critique of these religions as idolatrous and the modernistic notion of biblical faith as the fulfilment of all the Near Eastern religions were uncritically transferred to other religious traditions. The lack of any historical consciousness was seen as a mark of their deficiency, replicating the orientalist view. W. B. Harris, comparing *Vedanta* with Christian faith, in a commentary on Romans written for the use of Indian students, tells his readers: 'These two types of religious experience, represented on the one hand by *Romans* and the other by Sankara, move in entirely opposite directions, meeting at no single point.' Then Harris goes on to show that biblical faith is personal as well as purposively historical, and how God will bring history to a triumphant end, while arguing that Hinduism is impersonal, that its conception of time and history are unreal and cyclical, and that Hindus are caught in the endless cycle of *karma-samsara*.[58]

---

[56] *The Book of God's Kingdom*, p. 52.
[57] Owen, *Origin and First Ten Years of the British and Foreign Bible Society*, 1, p. 335.
[58] W. B. Harris, *A Commentary on the Epistle of St Paul to the Romans*, The Christian Students' Library, 33 (Madras, The Christian Literature Society, 1964), p. 45.

Such exegetical comments reinforced the orientalist notion that Hinduism was doctrinally vague and had no clear eschato-logical direction, whereas biblical faith was doctrinally exact and had a purposive history. The writers of the commentary series, The Christian Students' Library, routinely reminded their readers that Hinduism lacked a sense of history:

In this regard a basic difference exists between the Jewish-Christian and Classical Hindu understanding of history. For biblical theology, history has ultimate significance because God acts in, with, and under historical events and so makes them vehicles of his revelation, thus creating life, faith and fellowship. For Classical Hinduism, history does not have ultimate significance.[59]

These commentaries constantly extolled the virtues of Christian salvation and simultaneously belittled Hindu under-standing of it. 'Like Gnosticism', writes Maxwell R. Robinson, 'Hinduism has no promise of universal redemption such as Christianity offers.'[60]

The other legacy of colonial hermeneutics was the replace-ment of the narrativel approach, which is widespread in Africa, Asia and Latin America, with the historical-critical mode of interpretation. Hindus tend to view texts as authorless narrative wholes, without any undue concern about their sources, or the situation in which they were written. The text is seen as a medium and not as a means to understand the truth. A narrative is seen as expressing emotive meaning, 'feelings, and attitudes rather than ideas, concepts, statements of universal truth'.[61] The text is seen for its beauty, grace and emotive power. The task of the commentator is seen not in terms of demonstrating his or her technical sophistry or of engaging in an archaeological reconstruction of the past, but in creating new stories. Indian textual critics do not struggle with the ur text of the *Ramayana*, but they come out with different versions or tellings to suit the situation. Historical scrutiny is replaced with recitation, repetition and memorization. By introducing

[59] Wolfgang M. W. Roth, *Old Testament Theology*, The Christian Students' Library, 41 (Madras, The Christian Literature Society, 1968), p. 8.
[60] Maxwell R. Robinson, *A Commentary on the Pastoral Epistles*, The Christian Students' Library, 27 (Madras, The Christian Literature Society, 1962), p. 168.
[61] V. K. Chari, *Sanskrit Criticism* (Delhi, Motilal Banarsidass Publishers, 1990), p. 9.

historical-critical methods, colonial hermeneutics effectively eclipsed allegorical, symbolic, figurative and metaphorical ways of appropriating the text. The narratival approach which is now in vogue in Western biblical circles vindicates the Indian approach to texts. Preoccupation with historical-critical questions sidelined some of the indigenous theoretical practices such as *dhvani, rasa* and *aucitya* in India, and *ki* in China.

In addition to biblical criticism, another legacy was the introduction of biblical theology. This theology was shaped by a mosaic of different influences – the Protestant Reformed tradition, the Enlightenment, and the neo-orthodoxy of Karl Barth and Emil Brunner. They dealt with European Protestant issues such as Law versus Grace, faith versus works, the Jesus of History versus the Jesus of Faith, and so forth. While castigating idol worship as a vain superstition, biblical theology introduced its own idol in the form of Rudolf Bultmann's demythologization. The evolution of demythologization coincided with the decline of religion, the rise of scientific consciousness and the emergence of secularization in the West. The whole project was seen as a transferable pedagogic strategy to illuminate the mental darkness of Asian, African and Latin American minds and their superstitious thinking. That the whole programme of demythologization was aimed at Europeans, who had lost a sense of awe and wonder and the feel for the numinous as the result of modernistic tendencies, went unnoticed.

In conclusion: a book which was so remote and inaccessible in the precolonial phase has now become an easily readable and affordable text to ordinary people. In making the Bible available the British and Foreign Bible Society played a critical role. When the Society made the Bible a readily accessible document, its aim was not to invite readers to discover the hitherto veiled meanings in the narratives but to make safe the essentials of orthodox Christianity. John Owen made it clear at the outset that the single purpose of the Society was to promote 'the cause of orthodox Christianity'.[62]

Colonial interpretation makes it abundantly clear that her-

---

[62] Owen, *Origin and First Ten Years of the British and Foreign Bible Society,* i, p. 265.

meneutical issues are not settled by simply referring to texts alone. They are decided largely by the interpretative concerns of those who employ them. Despite the declared reliance of Protestants on the Book alone, in the end, as the foregoing examples demonstrate, Western cultural practices were invoked to arrive at or impose a particular meaning. This, in a way, inaugurated one of the critical questions for modern hermeneutics – the link between interpretation and power; and the related and equally important question – the interface between indigenous and imported knowledge.

CHAPTER 3

Reading back: resistance as a discursive practice

In this modern world three nations above all others have known the Bible best: Germany, Great Britain, and the United States of America. Ernest Sutherland Bates

Have we a single chapter in the Bible written by an European? *Goodwill Toward Men*

When faced with colonial interpretation, the colonized resorted to two discursive practices – resistance and assimilation. Both provided a convenient entry for the colonized to engage in debate. Resistance has been theorized mostly in terms of opposition between Europe and its 'Other'. Edward Said amplifies the idea of resistance to include also political and scholarly activities. In his work *Culture and Imperialism*, he speaks of two types of resistance – territorial and cultural. He sees the armed struggle against the invader as primary, and the ideological as secondary.[1] Resistance, in his view, is a 'rediscovery and repatriation of what had been suppressed in the natives' past by the process of imperialism'.[2] Seen within the colonial context, resistance meant not simply a repudiation or rejection of Western rule or Western discursive practices. Rather, it was a profitable use of a paradigm provided by the colonizer, in that it was successfully turned against him. What the discourse of resistance achieved was to make certain that the debate was not weighted towards the colonizer. It helped to establish cultural differences and to affirm an identity within the discursive territory of the imperialists.

[1] Edward W. Said, *Culture and Imperialism* (London, Chatto & Windus, 1993), p. 252.
[2] Ibid., p. 253.

This resistance spilled over into the arena of colonial biblical interpretation. As the colonial situation differed from continent to continent, we see somewhat different appropriations of the Bible in North America, Europe, Asia and Africa. In this chapter I would like to highlight how the colonized appropriated the Bible in these continents. Ironically, our journey starts not in the colonies but in the metropolitan centre of the Empire – London.

AN EMANCIPATOR AS EMANCIPATOR OF TEXTS: OLAUDAH EQUIANO AND HIS TEXTUAL ALLUSIONS

Olaudah Equiano (1745–97) was a freed slave who lived in London. After gaining his freedom, he turned his attention to opposing slavery and in the process was drawn into both spiritual and hermeneutical quests. He became an outspoken opponent of the slave trade,[3] initially through letters to the newspapers, and later through his book, *The Interesting Narrative,* which he published in 1789. *The Interesting Narrative* (hereafter *Narrative*) went through nine editions during Equiano's lifetime and had important figures of the time among its subscribers – those who paid for copies before the publication of the book – among whom was John Wesley, earlier an Anglican missionary in America, later the founder of the Methodist movement. It was Wesley who introduced Equiano's *Narrative* to William Wilberforce, who played an important part in the movement for abolition of the slave trade in England.[4] Seen from within today's literary climate, Equiano's *Narrative* can be regarded as a postmodern pastiche. It contains anthropological details, travel adventures, spiritual quests, sermons, poems, anti-slavery discourses and economic treatises. What is crucial for our purpose is the extent to which the Bible and biblical passages occupied

---

[3] A less known fact in Equiano's career is his role in the working-class movement in the late eighteenth century. See Peter Linebaugh, *The London Hanged: Crime and Civil Society in the Eighteenth Century* (London: Allen Lane, 1991), pp. 415–16. I located this reference through Geraldine Murphy, 'Olaudah Equiano, Accidental Tourist', *Eighteenth-Century Studies* 27 (1994), 561.

[4] Vincent Carretta, 'Introduction', in Olaudah Equiano: *The Interesting Narrative and Other Writings,* ed. Vincent Carretta (London, Penguin, 1995), p. xxvii.

his *Narrative* and informed his writing. The earlier editions of the *Narrative* had a picture of Equiano holding a copy of the Bible in his hands, indicating the importance of the Book for him. Before we look at Equiano's use of the Bible, I include here a brief introduction to the man and his life.

Equiano was a native of Eboe (Igbo) in West Africa, now Nigeria. When he was eleven, he was kidnapped with his sister, though she soon disappears from the narrative frame. He was transferred from one owner to another as he sojourned in his own continent and before he was shipped to the 'New World'. There, as a slave, he worked for many years, mostly in vessels trading around the Caribbean and the North American area. While toiling in ships, it dawned on Equiano at a very early stage that his future survival and his freedom from his present misery depended on acquiring practical as well as literary skills. Therefore, he went about learning a variety of trading skills ranging from carpentry to navigation. He realized soon that learning to read and write were vital in the circles in which he moved. With the help of a series of instructors he rapidly acquired a command of the English language. His mastery of English soon brought him trouble, when his captain, James Doran, told him that he 'talked too much English'.[5] He was not only very erudite but also very enterprising, and he started to trade in goods such as glasses, tumblers, limes and mangoes. The money he acquired through his commercial efforts eventually bought him his freedom in 1766; he paid £40 for his release. Once he was free, he set off on a voyage of commerce and adventure to North America, the Caribbean, the Mediterranean and even towards the North Pole. By this time, the former victim was turning into an oppressor trading in slaves. He was converted to Methodism, married an English woman, Susannah Cullen from Cambridge, and settled in England. What is fascinating about his life is the fact that he had a double identity – enslaved and free person, African in origin but acculturated in British ways. This hybridized identity provided him with the unusual advantage of being able to speak from

[5] Ibid., p. 94.

both within and outside his own community. This was reflected in his use of the Bible.[6]

At a time when there was a fierce debate about the advisability of placing the Bible in the hands of slaves, Equiano was able to acquire a copy for himself. The stories of the Bible offered him the potential for understanding his life, and he used them also as a weapon to oppose the very institution of slavery which had denied him his humanity:

Now the Bible was my only companion and comfort; I prized it much, with many thanks to God that I could read it for myself, and was not left to be tossed about or led by man's devices and notions. The worth of a soul cannot be told – May the Lord give the reader an understanding in this. Whenever I looked in the Bible I saw things new, and many texts were immediately applied to me with great comfort; for I knew that to me was the word of salvation sent.[7]

Viewed from the standpoint of exegetical practices informed by Enlightenment principles, Equiano's employment of the Bible might look traditional, pious and uncritical. Some of the sentiments he expressed about the Bible went a long way towards confirming this. He accorded a supreme authority to biblical revelation: 'I [do not] believe in any other revelation than that of the Holy Scriptures.'[8] He advocated a total surrender of the will to God's Word and believed in predestination. He wrote: '[t]he only comfort I then experienced was in the reading of the Holy Scriptures, where I saw that "there is no new thing under the sun" Eccles[iastes] 1.9 and what was appointed for me I must submit to'.[9] But a closer reading of the *Narrative* will reveal a different Equiano, who was not only in control of the texts but also activated them in a purposeful way, often unsettling them to promote his ideas.

For Equiano, the Bible and his own life commingled and

---

[6] For biographical details see Carretta, 'Introduction', ibid., pp. ix–xxxviii; James Walvin, *An African's Life: The Life and Times of Olaudah Equiano 1745–1797* (London, Continuum, 2000); Angelo Costanzo, *Surprising Narrative: Olaudah Equiano and the Beginnings of Black Autobiography* (New York, Greenwood Press, 1987); for his spiritual quest see Adam Potkay, 'Olaudah Equiano and the Art of Spiritual Autobiography', *Eighteenth-Century Studies* 27 (1994), 678–92.

[7] Equiano, *The Interesting Narrative and other Writings*, p. 191.

[8] Ibid., p. 127.   [9] Ibid., p. 181.

there was a mutual interface and illumination between them.
The biblical history became a symbol or a mirror. He read the
cycle of salvation history – the patriarchal election, the enslavement and the emancipation – paralleling his own life and, by
extension, that of other Africans. It was the narrativel elements
in Genesis and Exodus and the salvific work narrated in the
New Testament which provided him with allegorical connota-
tions. His spiritual deliverance was seen as an allegory and he
read this back into the patriarchal narrative. Allegory, one of
the classical principles of interpretation, facilitated his appropriation of the Bible.

One can discern three stages in Equiano's life replicating the
events in biblical salvation history. The first stage was linked
with the patriarchs in their pastoral period 'before they reached
the Land of Promise'.[10] The African pedigree is traced to Afer
and Afra, the descendants of Abraham and his wife Keturah.[11]
The second stage was marked by his bondage which parallels
the enslavement of Israel in Egypt. This was underlined when
Equiano was strangely sold by his master, when he was expecting his freedom as a reward for his part in the Seven Years
War. He describes his feelings thus: 'At the sight of this land of
bondage, a fresh horror ran through all my frame, and chilled
me to the heart . . . I called upon God's thunder, and his
avenging power, to direct the stroke of death to me, rather than
permit me to become a slave, and to be sold from lord to
lord.'[12] The third stage in Equiano's life was associated with
freedom from slavery – both from physical captivity and spiritual alienation, which he called 'depravity': 'What am I, that
God should thus look on me, the vilest of sinners.'[13] Though
half-way through his narration Equiano gained his freedom
from bondage by the money he made, his freedom from the
figurative bondage of sin was achieved much later when he
gained the assurance of salvation effected by the 'crucified
Saviour bleeding on the cross on Mount Calvary'.[14] It was
marked by his reading of Acts 4.12: 'Neither is there salvation in

[10] Ibid., p. 43.   [11] Ibid., p. 44.   [12] Ibid., p. 98.
[13] Ibid., p. 191.   [14] Ibid., p. 190.

any other, for there is none other name under heaven given among men whereby we must be saved, but only Jesus Christ.'[15]

Besides positioning his life through the biblical narrative, Equiano was an active expositor too. There are three distinctive interpretative features which mark his use of the Bible. First, his use of allusions: Equiano's *Narrative* was strewn with biblical phrases, words and echoes. His utilization of allusions formed an important part of his narration and argument. Passages from the Bible appear in the *Narrative* without quotation marks, or textual references, and are left unidentified as scripture. Nevertheless they easily fitted in with the flow of his narration. On the face of it, these allusions to biblical materials may be seen as Equiano's wanting to take advantage of the authority linked to the Word of God; he seems to be evoking them to strike a hermeneutical chord with his readers, who were mainly Protestants and not only knew these words and phrases well but also held them in high veneration. A careful scrutiny will reveal, however, that his employment of allusion is rather more subtle than it appears.

To understand the subtlety of allusion and how it functions in a narrative, I would like to draw on the theoretical concepts worked out by Steven Marx.[16] Following Robert Atler's work, Steven Marx finds different patterns of allusion and shows how the trope of allusion is employed by authors. Among the various aspects of allusions identified by Marx, three are relevant to the present study. First, in Marx's view, allusion creates 'a feeling of intimacy and heightened communication between reader and author, reader and text, or reader and the interpretative community'.[17] Equiano, in his text, makes considerable use of biblical materials, especially biblical characters – Jacob, Moses, Michael and the Ethiopian. He identifies himself with these biblical personalities and portrays them in such a way that a ready link is established between him and the biblical figures. When Equiano worked in a Virginia plantation as a household servant, he described his state thus: 'I thought that these people

[15] Ibid., p. 192.
[16] Steven Marx, *Shakespeare and the Bible* (Oxford, Oxford University Press, 2000).
[17] Ibid., pp. 105–6.

were all made of wonders. In this place I was called Jacob.'[18]
The biblical literacy of his Protestant readership was very high;
they would have easily decoded what 'wonders' meant and why
Equiano referred to himself as Jacob. In the Hebrew Scriptures,
Egypt was where God performed and wrought many signs and
wonders. The Prophet Jeremiah records that God had 'shown
signs and wonders in the land of Egypt' (32.30; see also Ps.
106.7). The 'New World'/America, where Equiano marvelled
at the achievements of Europeans, was likened to Egypt. But
Equiano, identifying himself as Jacob, instantaneously signalled
another message. Equiano as Jacob, a metonym for Israel, now
in the land of plenty had been reduced to slavery. The land of
wonders (Egypt = New World/America), was turned into a
land of enslavement and misery for him. He alluded similarly to
other incidents in the biblical narrative. After a dark night of
the soul, when Equiano accepted Christ, he recorded: 'Then in
his name I set up his Ebenezer.'[19] Equiano uses the term
Ebenezer (in Hebrew = stone of help) figuratively. Ebenezer
was the name of the stone Samuel set up to commemorate
God's part in his victory at Mizpah over the Philistines (1 Sam.
7.12). Translated to Equiano's context, it meant that God had
triumphed over an unbeliever like Equiano. These allusions are
a way of prompting the reader to see the similarities and
differences between the biblical narratives and Equiano's own
history.

Secondly, in Marx's reckoning, an allusion also serves 'to
subvert the original meaning of an activated text by trying it in
a new context'.[20] In a number of cases, Equiano plucked out
biblical verses from their context and placed them strategically
in his *Narrative* to underscore an argument. Thus, he invoked a
verse from the prophet Micah (6.8) – 'to do justly, to love mercy,
and to walk humbly before God' – and applied it to eighteenth-
century England and to the slave trade, reminding white
Christians of their moral responsibility. Similarly, after seeing
for himself how freed slaves were being rehabilitated in

[18] Equiano, *The Interesting Narrative and other Writings*, p. 63.
[19] Ibid., p. 192.
[20] Marx, *Shakespeare and the Bible*, p. 114.

Philadelphia, he urged other slave owners to do the same with the words 'Go ye and do likewise', thus activating the saying of Jesus in the Samaritan parable. Here he unlooped a text from its intra-Jewish ethnic nexus and reconfigured it in the context of the plight of slaves. When one Drummond, a slave trader, told him how he cut off the leg of a slave who was trying to escape, it troubled Equiano. He wondered how as a Christian he could do this, and he reminded Drummond of the Matthean verse, 'do unto others as you would that others should do unto you'.[21] At a time when the idea of diverse races did not indicate human equality, Equiano appealed to Paul's speech at the Areopagus: 'God who hath made of one blood all nations of men for to dwell on the face of the earth' (Acts 17.26).[22] The Pauline speech which had the Jewish–Gentile issue as its focus was transferred to a racially charged eighteenth-century England to remind his Christian and white audiences of the powerful biblical argument that God had made people of all nations of one blood, thus making the case for a common humanity. His text is littered with passages from the Jewish wisdom tradition which show deep social concern: 'Those that honour their Maker have mercy on the poor' (Prov. 14.31) 'It is righteousness exalteth a nation; but sin is a reproach to any people' (Prov. 14.34).[23] In alluding to the Hebrew sages' deep commitment to the cause of the disadvantaged, Equiano implies that his white audience should emulate God's intentions for the oppressed and relieve them of their suffering. He also warns his readers what will happen to them if they fail in their duty to take care of the slaves. Once when he was disturbed by the ill-treatment of slaves, he went on to write that he had the fullest confidence that many of 'the sable race' would enjoy the pleasures of Heaven, whereas the oppressive whites would be cast into 'that doleful place' where they 'will cry, but will cry in vain, for a drop of water!'[24] Here 'the drop of water' was an obvious reference to the rich man in the Lucan parable (16.19–31), who was banished to hell for neglecting to look after Lazarus and in his tormented state cried out for water. It was a reminder to his

---

[21] Equiano, *The Interesting Narrative and other Writings*, p. 105.
[22] Ibid., p. 45.   [23] Ibid., p. 233.   [24] Ibid., p. 329.

white audience of the consequences they would have to face if they did not rightly deploy their earthly possessions, or failed to meet the needs of others. In appealing to these passages and applying them to the racial and economic condition of eighteenth-century England, Equiano was sending a message to his readers that the God of the Bible was a God who took sides and was biased towards the vulnerable.

Thirdly, according to Marx, an allusion provides 'authoritative evidence to support a given point, by echoing a memorable phrase',[25] thus giving it an edge. Equiano cleverly inserted a biblical phrase here or a familiar verse there to clinch an argument or score a point. For example, when his efforts to tutor an Indian prince in the ways of the Christian faith were thwarted by some of the messengers in the ship, Equiano likened their act to that of Satan (in the Lucan parable) who sowed tares, and he went on to call these people 'sons of Belial', a term used by Paul as a synonym for Satan in 2 Corinthians (2 Cor. 16.5).[26]

Besides his use of biblical allusions, a second distinctive feature of Equiano's interpretative practice involved a serious engagement with biblical texts. In his writings we see one of the earliest attempts to reread the letter to Philemon from a slave's point of view. His rereading was prompted by a Spanish-born Jesuit, Raymund Harris, in his book – *Scripture Researches on the Licitness of the Slave-Trade shewing its Conformity, with the Principles of Natural and Revealed Religion, Delineated in the Sacred Writings of the Word of God*. Equiano crossed swords with Harris's interpretation on a number of issues. When Harris claimed that slavery accorded well with the revealed religion and that St Paul was right when he made an earnest request to Philemon to take Onesimus back in his former capacity as a slave, Equiano outrightly dismissed Harris's claims as notoriously wresting Paul's words out of context. Equiano pointed out that when Paul urged Philemon to take Onesimus back, he was not expecting him to be taken back as 'a servant, but above a servant, a brother beloved'. More importantly, in other texts

[25] Marx, *Shakespeare and the Bible*, p. 114.
[26] Equiano, *The Interesting Narrative and other Writings*, p. 204.

when Paul spoke about the submission of slaves for the sake of conscience, he was at the same time scrupulous in reiterating the obligations of the masters. He exhorted the master 'to entertain such a measure of brotherly love towards his servant'.[27] Equiano went on to postulate that if Paul were to preach today, he would compel the contemporary slave masters, as he did with Philemon, to treat their quondam slaves not as servants, but as 'above servants – a brother beloved'. Furthermore, Equiano's contention was that Paul would not have expected Onesimus to be received by Philemon as his private property and a slave for perpetuity, because this was the very time that the early Christians were committed to a common ownership of property and had distributed their possessions among the needy. Equiano cited the verse from Acts which connoted socialism, 'and they had all things common amongst them',[28] to buttress his argument. He went on to maintain that if these words of Paul were to make any sense today, they would be 'subversive of African trade, and West India slavery'.[29] To challenge Harris's claim, Equiano summoned the doctrine of atonement. In his view, it was unwise to hold on to slaves because it was tantamount to dishonouring the basic tenets of the Christian faith, which claimed that people were bought with the inestimable price of Christ's blood and therefore should not end up 'as slaves and private property of their fellow-human beings'. His unequivocal message to Harris was: '[o]f this epistle [Philemon], which you cite strongly in favour of slavery, when the whole tenor of it is in behalf of the slave'.[30]

The third feature of Equiano's interpretative practice was to see a cultural and ritual correspondence between the Jewish and African ways of life. In doing so, he was able to challenge the popular images of Africa as a degraded tropical continent and its people as lazy and unintelligent. With the knowledge he had of his own people, and the new knowledge he had acquired of the Bible and its people, he was able to suggest parallels between the Jews of biblical times and contemporary Africans: 'We practised circumcision like the Jews, and made offerings and feasts on that occasion in the same manner as they did. Like them also, our children were named from some event, some circumstance, or fancied foreboding at the time of their birth.'[31] Furthermore, they had similar styles of governance with administration conducted by chiefs, wise men and elders.[32] Their rituals such as sacrificial rites, washing and purification were similar too. His claim was: 'I was wonderfully surprised to see the laws and rules of my country written almost exactly here.'[33]

One can see at least three reasons for Equiano's underscoring of the correspondences between biblical Jews and contemporary Africans. One reason was to assert the idea of mutual creation, that Africans and biblical Jews were more or less similar in their customs and habits and thereby their histories and destinies were intertwined. A second was pedagogical: he wanted to educate his fellow Africans who, like him, were in diaspora and felt inferior about their culture. He further reminded them that they had a heritage that went back to biblical times. His concern for his people was expressed thus: 'When they come among Europeans, they are ignorant of their language, religion, manners, and customs. Are any pains taken to teach them these?'[34] A third reason was to remind his white readers that their own cultural practices were found wanting and did not measure up to the required biblical standards. Equiano was amazed at the absence of the very practices enjoined in scripture among white people who made claims for the noble qualities of their culture – sacrifice, making offerings, eating with unwashed hands and touching the dead.[35] At a time when anthropologists and missionaries were critical of African and non-European cultures for a lack of sophistication, refinement and erudition, Equiano marshalled biblical norms to evaluate European culture and in the process punctured its weakness, pomposity and arrogance. In retrieving the Judaic parallels to African culture, Equiano was able to hammer home to his readers the noble aspects of Africans and their culture, and their close accord with biblical expectation and prescription.

---

[31] Ibid., p. 41.   [32] Ibid., p. 44.   [33] Ibid., p. 92.
[34] Ibid., p. 45.   [35] Ibid., p. 68.

The general tenor of Equiano's narrative was not vindictive but conciliatory and forgiving. He constantly sought reconciliation with British society, advocating ideas buttressed by both economic and biblical arguments. He appealed to the mind, morals and generosity of white people, constantly reminding them of the plight of the slaves, and their Christian duty to look after them: 'He that oppresseth the poor reproacheth his Maker: but he that honoreth him hath mercy on the poor' (Prov. 14.31).

He sought to achieve reconciliation in two ways. First, through interracial marriage: he saw mixed-race marriages as enhancing the harmony of blacks and whites. His own marriage to Susannah Cullen was a very successful one despite the horror in which such marriages and miscegenation were viewed at that time. To support interracial marriages, he seized upon the example of the biblical Moses 'that eminent, most wise, and inspired politician'[36] to drive home his point. Equiano contended that Moses not only encouraged strangers to marry Israelites, but himself set an example by marrying a foreigner, a marriage which was confirmed by the Lord. Equiano reminded his opponents of what happened to those who opposed this, how Aaron and Miriam were punished by God. Intermarriage, for Equiano, was a sign of 'national honour, national strength, and productive of national virtue'.[37]

Secondly, as a way of reconciliation and to rectify the horrors of slavery, he advocated free trade between Africa and Europe. He appealed to Adam Smith's *Wealth of Nations* and propounded the advantages of free trade over slavery. His plea was that, if a system of commerce was established in Africa, the demand for British goods would mostly increase, as the native inhabitants would adopt British fashions, manners and customs: 'A commercial intercourse with Africa opens an inexhaustible source of wealth to the manufacturing interests of Great Britain . . .'[38] In Swiftian vein he admitted that the only losers would be the manufacturers of neck-yokes, chains, collars, handcuffs, leg boots and drags (weights attached to legs to impede move-

---

[36] Ibid., p. 330.   [37] Ibid.   [38] Ibid., p. 234.

ment).[39] In effect, what he was advocating was that, instead of trading Africans as commodities, trading European goods in Africa would be of mutual benefit to both Africa and Europe.

There is no doubt that Equiano saw himself as a latter-day Moses and even expressed a hope 'to be an instrument, under God'.[40] He utilized his celebrity status and became a spokesperson for his community. His persuasive power and his hobnobbing with important and influential white people of the time did promote the cause. He was nostalgic about Africa and wistful about his uprooting from the continent of his birth, but his new religious allegiance, his material prosperity and his wide recognition revealed how acculturated he was as a British subject. It is important not to put Equiano on a pedestal, and portray him as a champion of the abolition of slavery. His understanding of slavery was circumscribed by the colonial mentality of the time, although it evolved over the years as he moved on from one stage of his life to another. He, too, became a slave owner and prided himself on being a model one. Like Moses, he, too, did not live to see the promised land. Slavery was abolished in the British colonies in 1838, more than forty years after his death, and in the United States another twenty-five years later.

Equiano's *Narrative* was written within but also against the colonial culture. He was very comfortable with its dominant values, but at the same time not afraid to confront them. In his *Narrative*, he was trying to point out what advantages Europeans, as refined people, possessed over those who were regarded as rude and uncultivated. He even went on to remind white people of their former state: 'Let the polished and haughty European recollect that *his* ancestors were once, like the Africans, uncivilised, and even barbarous. Did Nature make *them* inferior to their sons? and should *they too* have been made slaves?'[41] What was remarkable about him was that he was able to distance himself and at the same time affirm good things about the British. Interestingly, he appropriated a voice of resistance within the very culture which had incorporated him.

---

[39] Ibid.   [40] Ibid., p. 202.   [41] Ibid., p. 45.

We can see in this resistance an interactive relationship with the sacred texts. He took the most venerated icon of British culture – the King James Version – and made it his own by selecting from it, paraphrasing it and applying it to his own purposes. Unlike Protestant Christians of the time, who were subject to the text and were willing to be interrogated and absolved by it, Equiano was not afraid to take it, mould and appropriate it, significantly unhinging it from its original context and applying it to his own.

When Equiano, a product of oral culture, was introduced to the written text of the Christians, the Bible, his alienation from the literary culture was quite evident. His immediate worry was like that of Chief Namekei whom we encountered in the last chapter – whether the book would talk to him: 'I have often taken up a book, and have talked to it, and then put my ears to it, when alone, in the hope it would answer me; and I have been very much concerned when I found it remained silent.'[42] Unlike the chief, Equiano did not despair. Now, after his conversion to Christianity and, as importantly, crossing from oral to literary culture and being comfortable in it, Equiano was able to make the white man's book talk back in a black man's voice.[43]

CONFLUENCE OF HISTORIES: WILLIAM APESS AND
TEXTUAL RECLAMATIONS

William Apess (1798–1839) was a Native American whose use of the Bible is another example of resistant reading. He was a Pequot, and as a child he had a torrid time. He was indentured to white families and led a migratory life before he eventually turned to Christianity. He became a Methodist minister in the Protestant Methodist Church and ended up in Mashpee where

---

[42] Ibid., p. 68.
[43] For the trope of talking books in slave tradition see Henry Louis Gates, Jr, *The Signifying Monkey: A Theory of Afro-Afroamerican Literary Criticism* (Oxford, Oxford University Press, 1987), pp. 127–69, especially the chapter 'The Trope of the Talking Book'.

he was deeply engaged in local political struggles which attracted regional and national attention. He participated in what was known as the 'Mashpee Revolt', and he took part in drafting two petitions – one was for the right of the local people to manage their own affairs and the other was to remove the incumbent white minister and appoint Apess in his place. After a series of unsavoury incidents which involved the imprisonment of Apess, both petitions were granted. Following this period in the public gaze, Apess vanished from the scene until he met an unexpected death.[44]

Apess's hermeneutic has to be viewed in the context in which it was undertaken. This was a time when his people's existence was absent from official documents, and they were a despised community, seen by Europeans as the remnants of a dying population. At a time when invading Europeans claimed racial superiority, postulated that God had created separate races and placed the white children of Adam at the top of the created order, Apess contested this by tracing Native American lineage to the lost tribes of Israel. Like Equiano before him, Apess retrieved Jewish history and tried to implicate the Jews of old in the history of his own people. In his autobiography, *The Son of the Forest*, Apess wrote:

When I reflect upon the complicated ills to which my brethren have been subject, ever since history has recorded their existence – their wanderings, their perils, their privations, and their many sorrows, and the fierceness of that persecution which marked their dwellings and their persons for destruction – when I take into consideration the many usages and customs observed religiously by them, and which have so near and close resemblance to the manners, etc., of the ancient Israelites, and I am led to believe that they are none other than the descendants of Jacob and the long lost tribes of Israel.[45]

Apess went further and catalogued a series of similarities between Native Americans and the Jewish people. In his view,

[44] For a detailed account of Apess's life, see Barry O'Connell, 'Introduction', in *A Son of the Forest and other Writings by William Apess, a Pequot*, ed. Barry O'Connell (Amherst, The University of Massachusetts Press, 1992), pp. ix–xxii, and also Barry O'Connell, 'Introduction', in *On Our Own Ground: The Complete Writings of William Apess, a Pequot*, ed. Barry O'Connell (Amherst, The University of Massachusetts Press, 1992), pp. xiii–lxxvii.

[45] William Apess, *On Our Own Ground*, p. 53.

the two peoples did not differ much in their manners, customs, rites, ceremonies and languages. Just as the people of Judah were divided into twelve tribes and had a chief, so were Indian nations 'universally divided into tribes, under a sachem or a king, chosen by the people from the wisest and bravest among them'.[46] Like the Jews alluded to in Isaiah 49.6, Native Americans made marks on their hands and arms.[47] Their funeral customs were similar. Both showed respect to the graves of the dead and buried their families in one place. If someone died outside their home, their bones were brought and laid with those of their kith and kin. Apess reminded his readers of the patriarchal precedent for this practice. He cited the example of Joseph, who made the children of Israel take an oath that they would carry his bones from Egypt, and that of Moses, who fulfilled the oath when he carried Joseph's bones with him and buried them in Shechem (Gen. 49.29, 31; 50.25; Exod. 13.19; Josh. 24.32).[48] Their calendar, too, was similar. Both divided the year into spring, summer, autumn and winter and began the ecclesiastical year at the first appearance of the first new moon of the vernal equinox.[49] Both languages were guttural and similar in their roots and general construction.[50] In highlighting these similarities, Apess's main interpretative aim was to draw attention to the fact that Indians were 'indeed no other than the descendants of the ten lost tribes'.[51]

Apess used the Bible to reclaim an identity which was largely denied to his people. Unhappy with the use of the word 'Indian', which he amusingly thought originated from *in-gen-uity*, he scrutinized the Bible, found to his surprise that it was not mentioned there and came to the conclusion that it was a word 'imported' for the sole purpose of degrading Native Americans. He went on to propose 'Natives' as the proper name to distinguish Native Americans from the rest of the human family. His contention was that Native Americans were the 'only people under heaven who have a just title to their name, inasmuch as we are the only people who retain the original complexion of our father Adam'.[52]

---

[46] Ibid., p. 90. [47] Ibid., p. 84. [48] Ibid., pp. 92–3. [49] Ibid., p. 92.
[50] Ibid., pp. 56, 92. [51] Ibid., p. 114. [52] Ibid., p. 10.

In invoking the lost tribes of Israel, and identifying Native Americans as the genuine heirs of the biblical tribes, Apess's intention was to affirm a common pedigree for all humanity and equal status before God. A single parentage meant that every Native American was just as much a human person as an invading white, and as such deserved better treatment.

TEXTUAL CONVERSATIONS: K. N. BANERJEA AND HIS
VEDAS

K. N. Banerjea's (1813–85) attempt at intertextual reading of biblical narratives in conjunction with the Vedic texts falls into the category of assimilation as a mode of resistance. One of the 'star' converts of the Scottish missionary, Alexander Duff, he was a scholar in both Western and Oriental languages and literature. At a time when, in the enthusiasm for Western education, there was hostility towards Hinduism in nineteenth-century Bengal, Banerjea attempted to establish a credible relationship between the imported faith and the indigenous religion. His aim was to demonstrate that the biblical teachings were identical with the pure and undiluted form of the Vedic religion, and that the brahminical *shastras* conformed with biblical teachings. Initially, like all converts, he took a dim view of his own textual tradition and wrote vehemently against it, but after his retirement from teaching at Bishop's College, Calcutta, he revealed a completely different attitude to Hinduism and to its texts. His changed hermeneutical thrust shocked both his missionary admirers and fellow native Christians, and he naturally came under heavy criticism from both. He likened this to the hostility which Peter had experienced when he was 'impeached for consorting with men uncircumcised'.[53]

Faced with the intervention of Christianity and the despised status of his own tradition, Banerjea appropriated a version of Christianity which he presented as comfortable with Hinduism, and in the process he rescued both Hinduism and Christianity

[53] T. V. Philip, *Krishna Mohan Banerjea: Christian Apologist*, Confessing the Faith in India Series, no. 15 (Bangalore, The Christian Institute for the Study of Religion and Society, 1982), p. 121.

from missionary control. He set out to demonstrate that Christianity was the logical continuation of Vedic Hinduism and that Indian Christians were the rightful heirs of the faith of the ancient Indian rishis. He even went on to claim that if the authors of the Vedas were now to return to the earth 'they would at once recognize the Indian Christians, far more complacently as their own descendants, than any other body of educated natives'.[54]

It was in three of his later writings – *The Arian Witness*,[55] *Two Essays as Supplement to the Arian Witness*,[56] and *The Relation between Christianity and Hinduism*[57] – that Banerjea undertook his comparative textual work and tried to establish positive correspondences between the Vedic religion and biblical faith. Certain common themes ran through these writings. The idea of sacrifice was pivotal to his thinking, and this became increasingly nuanced and refined. In the first section of the *Arian Witness* Banerjea tried to demonstrate two things. The first was a historical connection between the brahmins and the biblical patriarchs. To make this plausible, he established textual evidence to prove to his satisfaction that Media, the place from where the biblical patriarch, Abraham, hailed, was the original 'seat of the Arians', the forbears of the present brahmins. The second was to highlight the striking philological resemblances between Hebrew and Sanskrit in order to establish that the term 'Arian' had its roots in the Semitic languages. He summoned various textual traditions from the *Rig Veda* to *Zend Avesta* to prove his point. After a detailed, often convoluted and densely argued case, he concluded that there was a common homeland – Media – 'the original home of the Arians'.[58] In his reckoning, the dispersion of the Arians took place after the

---

[54] K. M. Banerjea, *The Arian Witness: Or the Testimony of Arian Scriptures in Corroboration of Biblical History and the Rudiments of Christian Doctrine, Including Dissertations on the Original and Early Adventures of Indo-Arians* (Calcutta, Thacker, Spink & Co., 1875), p. 10.

[55] Banerjea, *Arian Witness*.

[56] K. M. Banerjea, *Two Essays as Supplements to the Arian Witness* (Calcutta, Thacker, Spink & Co., 1880).

[57] *The Relation between Christianity and Hinduism in which remarkable resemblances between Ancient Hinduism and Christianity are pointed out*, Oxford Mission Occasional Papers, no. 1 (1881).

[58] Banerjea, *Arian Witness*, p. 111.

Turanian invasion, resulting in some of them going westward to
Europe, and others eastward, finding their way to the banks of
the Indus and eventually crossing over into India.[59] The implication was that the arrival of Christianity in India could be seen
as a family reunion of Vedic Hindus and Christian brahmins.

After demonstrating a common background between Hindu
'Arians' and the biblical patriarchs, Banerjea undertook, in the
second section of the book, a comparative study of three
patriarchal narratives – the Creation, the Fall and the Flood. As
to Creation, Banerjea's view was that both the Vedic writers
and Moses, whatever might have been their sources of information, had 'described the condition of our globe, before the
existing arrangement was formed, very much in the same
way'.[60] In the tenth Mandala of the *Rig Veda*, Hymn 129,
Banerjea saw a parallel narrative to the Pentateuchal creation
story. He was quick to point out, however, that although there
were resemblances, in one respect the biblical narrative differed
from the Vedic account. The latter failed to acknowledge that
God called the world into being out of nothing:

The Mosaic idea of God as the original Creator of the Universe,
without the assistance of any pre-existing materials, appears to have
been unknown, or if it was suggested anywhere by report or tradition,
to have been misunderstood, or in communities which had constructed systems of faith, laid on other foundation than the Word of
God.[61]

As regards the Fall, Banerjea drew attention to a similar story in
the Serpent Section of the *Mahabharata*, where a curse was
pronounced against the serpent. Similarly, he traced a flood
story in the Arian legends. He identified seven principal points
in the Mosaic narrative – the increase of human wickedness
which occasioned the deluge; the singling out of Noah as the
righteous man of his generation; instructions for the building of
the Ark to a prescribed measurement; the number of people
and the pairs of living creatures who entered the ark, and the
provision for them; the resting of the ark at Mount Ararat;
Noah sending out birds to find out whether the waters had

---

[59] Ibid., pp. 111–12.   [60] Ibid., p. 122.   [61] Ibid., p. 120.

dried up; and Noah building up the altar and making a burnt offering. Then he proceeded to demonstrate how a similar story in *Satapatha Brahmana*, where Manu was saved by a fish, concurred with the basic contents of the biblical narrative. For Banerjea, the names of Manu and Noah had the same etymological root: '"Manu" must have been the Indo-Arian ideal of Noah.'[62] In the last chapter, Banerjea concluded that both men, Noah and Manu, offered sacrifice after the Flood, and it was this which was common to both narratives. For him the act of sacrifice was the first act of religion.

Banerjea expanded further his idea of sacrifice in the other two writings, trying to establish that the concept of sacrifice was common to both the Bible and the Vedas:

This is curiously coincident with the Biblical account of Abel's offering in the Ante-Diluvian world. Noah's offering in the Post-Diluvian world equally corresponds to the *paka* offering of Manu, the surviving man after the flood in Vedic legends. In the whole description of the patriarchal dispensation, the Veda seems to follow the lines of the Bible – the only difference being in the greater clearness and still greater firmness and certainty of decision with which monotheism is upheld in the Jewish Scriptures. Almost in all other respects, the Vedas represent with equal clearness the ideals of the patriarchal dispensation in the ages of Noah, of Abraham, of Melchisedic, of Job and of similar characters noticed in the Bible – when religious devotion was manifested by sacrifices and offerings as types of the Divine Saviour, the Lamb slain from the foundation of the world.[63]

After having established sacrifice as a theme common to both textual traditions, Banerjea went on to demonstrate that the Vedic understanding of salvation by the self-sacrifice of Prajapati, the Lord and Saviour of Creation who had given himself up as an offering for this purpose, finds a remarkable correspondence with the biblical doctrine of salvation in the form of the sacrifice of Christ:

Christ is the true *Prajapati* – the true Purusha begotten in the beginning before all worlds, and Himself both God and man. The doctrines of saving sacrifice, the 'primary religious rites' of the Rig Veda – of the double character priest and victim, variously called

[62] Ibid., p. 158.
[63] Banerjea, *Two Essays*, pp. 69–70.

Prajapati, Purusha, and *Viswakarma* – of the Ark by which we escape the waves of this sinful world – these doctrines, I say, which had appeared in our Vedas amid much rubbish, and things worse than rubbish, may be viewed as fragments of diamonds sparkling amid dust and mud, testifying to some invisible fabric of which they were component parts, and bearing witness like planets over a dark horizon to the absent sun of whom their refulgence was but a feeble reflection.[64]

To clinch his argument he drew attention to the fact that the meaning of *Prajapati* accords with the person and work of the historical Jesus. *Prajapati* means not only Lord of the Creatures but also supporter, feeder and deliverer of his creatures. Banerjea claimed that Jesus in Hebrew meant exactly the same:

And that name was given Him because He would *save* His people from their sins. In the prophecy cited by St Matthew, He is described as *Heigoumenos* [*sic*], a leader or ruler, who 'shall feed (*poimanei*) my people Israel'. He is therefore to His people what a shepherd is to his flock – both leader, ruler, and feeder. The same is the import of *pati*; the name *Prajapati,* therefore, singularly corresponds to the name Jesus.[65]

Banerjea's intention was to prove that Christianity, far from being a foreign religion, was the fulfilment of the Vedas. Since there was a close relationship between Hinduism and Christianity, Banerjea went on to claim that Queen Victoria, as the defender of faith, was virtually the protector of the primitive principles of Hinduism. In a public address at Christ Church in Calcutta, he told the audience:

A proper understanding of the relation between the two systems, involved in the propositions which I have enunciated, may lead to a better understanding between the rulers and the ruled, between men of the West and men of the East. It will at least prove that the 'Defender of the Faith' is virtually the protector of the primitive principles of Hinduism.[66]

In his reclamation of the Vedas, Banerjea was successful in altering the status of the Vedic texts. Firstly, they had been re-elevated to their rightful place as sacred writings. By seeing them as repositories of gems of the Christian mysteries, they

---

[64] Philip, *Krishna Mohan Banerjea,* p. 196.
[65] Ibid., p. 194.   [66] Ibid., p. 182.

were now seen not as the heathen Veda of inveterate and idolatrous Hindus, but as textual treasures which 'taught doctrines and practices that approached to the Gospel'.[67] Further, by juxtaposing the Vedic texts with Persian, Greek and Assyrian writings, he not only delineated the interconnections between them but also helped to acquire a global status for the ancient writings of India:

We can no longer consider it as a mere jargon of fairy tales but must place it side by side with other records of Asia . . . When, however, you, find the intimate connection of the Rig Veda with Zend Avesta, and realize the fact of Indian life on Iranian land, you feel yourself relieved from an intolerable incubus, retarding your search for Truth. The embargo which had prohibited inquiries into Vedic facts out of the limits of India is now removed, and now you feel yourself free to investigate the wide extent of the references contained in the Rig Veda.[68]

Secondly, though the Vedas gained a venerated status, they were seen as proleptic and incomplete. Banerjea envisaged them as laconic, containing only the rudiments of faith and, as such, latent and underdeveloped ideas needing fulfilment. In his reckoning, Hindu texts were admirable drafts of the Bible, unfinished in themselves but anticipatory of the final truth, though at the same time theologically suggestive and stimulating. The Vedas for him 'foreshew the Epiphany of Christ', and he saw no 'national humiliation, in acknowledging the historical "Jesus" of the New Testament' who corresponded 'to the ideal Prajapati of the Veda, and strengthened the cornerstone of the Vedic system'.[69] For him the ancient writings of the Rishis were fragments of the whole, and the biblical revelation was in historical continuity with the Vedic faith. Banerjea challenged those who were reluctant to utilize the Vedas for theological purposes. His point was that, if both physical and medical sciences had profitably utilized for the material improvement of Indians the theories of gravitation and blood circulation suggested in the Vedas, Indians should not be

---

[67] Ibid., p. 195.
[68] Banerjea, *Two Essays*, p. 32.
[69] Philip, *Krishna Mohan Banerjea*, p. 197.

reluctant to use the concealed gems in the Vedas for their spiritual advancement. He once wrote:

If such things are proper in the sciences of Astronomy and Medicine, and they are not only proper but necessary for the safety of life and for the true knowledge of the solar system, then, I ask, why should not a like course be pursued in the case of Theology which is far more momentous for the best interests of humanity?[70]

For him, it was modernity in the form of the Christian Bible which had provided the heremeneutical key to unlock the 'sealed manuscripts of the Vedas'.[71] An obsolete text was now being resuscitated by the intervention of a Western Asian text which came to Bengal via Europe. The place of Vedic Prajapati, whose throne was vacant since no Hindu god could occupy it, was now, according to Banerjea, being filled by the historical Jesus. Banerjea reminded both Hindus and Christians that: 'No one now can claim that crown and that throne . . . so rightfully as the historical Jesus, who in name and character, as we have seen, closely resembles our primitive "*Prajapati*".'[72]

Banerjea invested heavily in inter-textual reading; he showed how a person transformed by an imported text might then make sense of his own indigenous text and in turn transform it sensitively. Unwilling to surrender his own *shastras*, he coopted them into the Christian corpus and made them speak the language of the Christian vocabulary. In the process he made Christianity his own, thus subverting the missionary version.

Like Equiano and Apess, Banerjea selected from the biblical narratives to validate his project. The difference was that, unlike the other two who were trying to identify with the history of the patriarchs, Banerjea was focusing on the notion of biblical ritual – on sacrifice as a validating principle. In selecting texts from the high Sanskritic culture, he privileged it as the sole repository of Hindu tradition. This projection into the past was necessitated by the nationalist ideology of the time to reveal the greatness of Indian culture. With the emergence of dalit voices, Banerjea's 'Arian' theory may not have the purchase it had in

---

[70] Ibid., p. 199.
[71] *Relation between Christianity and Hinduism*, p. 199.
[72] Philip, *Krishna Mohan Banerjea*, p. 197.

colonial India. Much water has passed under the Howrah Bridge since he mooted the idea. Currently, the reclamation of Indian history based on the Aryan theory is undergoing radical modifications.[73] In the light of these contestations, Banerjea's appropriation of a glorified Aryan past could be seen as racialist and casteist. His hermeneutical efforts have to be seen in the light of the politics of identity and construction of the self in colonial India.

TEXTUAL MANAGEMENT: PANDITA RAMABAI AND HER BIBLE

Pandita Ramabai (1858–1922) was one of the prominent figures whose activities generated a great deal of interest both inside and outside colonial India. Her complex religious identity enhanced her attraction. As a brahmin turned Christian, she provoked both celebration and denunciation. Before her acceptance of Christ, she was seen by her community as a model Hindu woman, and she was praised for her Sanskrit knowledge, in recognition of which she was given the title *pandita* (learned one). Her call for women's education, especially the training of women medical doctors, was received with enthusiasm. But her conversion to Christianity came as a shock to Hindus, and it alienated her from the Hindu community. The Christian Church, on the other hand, which was in expansionist mood in colonial India, saw in her conversion a jewel in their proselytization crown. But she had a series of theological skirmishes with the ecclesiastical authorities which turned her into a crown of thorns for Christian orthodoxy. Her books, *Stree Dharma Neeti* (Morals for Women) (1882) and *High Caste Hindu Woman* (1888), were runaway bestsellers of the time and produced enough money for her to visit England and the United States. Later in her life she settled in Pune and ran a home for widows – Sharada Sadan. Her achievements have

---

[73] See Romila Thapar, 'Some Appropriations of the Theory of Aryan Race Relating to the Beginnings of Indian History', in *Invoking the Past: The Uses of History in South Asia*, ed. Daud Ali (New Delhi, Oxford University Press, 1999), pp.15–35; and Thomas Trautmann, *Aryans in British India* (New Delhi, Oxford University Press, 1997).

yielded a fair share of both reverential biographies[74] and critical works confirming her contribution to Christian theology and Hindu philosophy,[75] to feminist causes[76] and to her ambivalent relations with the authorities in colonial India and late Victorian England.[77] What I hope to do here is to bring to the fore an often overlooked aspect of her work – her contribution to biblical hermeneutics, especially her efforts at translation, which I see as an example of resistance hermeneutics.

Ramabai's views on the Bible emerge especially from the epistolary conversation she had with various Anglicans – Sister Geraldine of the Community of St Mary the Virgin, Miss Beale, principal of Cheltenham Ladies College, and Canon William Butler. In her dealings with the institutional Church authorities she soon realized that central to her spiritual direction and religious independence was the management of the Bible, and the freedom to interpret it in order to establish her identity. Having come from a Hindu background, where scriptures did not belong to the entire community and the reading of the Vedas was forbidden to certain sections, especially women in her time, Ramabai soon recognized the importance of the written word for Protestant Christianity, and how individually accessing and interpreting it was strategically significant.

She found the doctrinal teachings of the Anglican Church cumbersome and unhelpful and saw them as the Church's way of controlling its believers. She was sceptical about the

---

[74] These were mainly written by missionaries; they portray her as a prime example of the civilizing influence of Christianity and often use her criticism of her own tradition as offering insights into brahman decadence. For example; see Nicol Macnicol, *Pandita Ramabai* (London, SCM Press, 1927); J. Chappell and H. S. Dyer, *Pandita Ramabai: A Great Life in Indian Missions* (London, Pickering and Inglis, n.d.).

[75] A. B. Shah, *The Letters and Correspondence of Pandita Ramabai* (Bombay, Maharashtra State Board for Literature and Culture, 1977); S. M. Adhav, *Pandita Ramabai*, Confessing the Faith in India, no. 13 (Bangalore, The Christian Institute for Study of Religion and Society, 1979).

[76] Uma Chakravarti, *Rewriting History: The Life and Times of Pandita Ramabai* (New Delhi, Kali for Women, 1998).

[77] Antoinette Burton, 'Colonial Encounters in Late-Victorian England: Pandita Ramabai at Cheltenham and Wantage', *Feminist Review* 49 (1995), 29–49, and Leslie A. Flemming, 'Between Two Worlds: Self-Construction and Self-Identity in the Writings of Three Nineteenth-Century Indian Christian Women', in *Women as Subjects: South Asian Histories*, ed. Nita Kumar (Charlottesville, University Press of Virginia, 1994), pp. 81–107.

doctrinal developments of the post-biblical period as having no biblical validation. She found the virgin birth, the doctrine of the Trinity and the Athanasian Creed difficult to accept, and, more to the point, in her opinion they did not have any scriptural warrant. In one of her theological disputes with her Anglican supporters, she asked: 'Is Christianity the teaching of Christ or the teaching of a certain body of men?'[78] After having made great efforts to free herself 'from the yoke of the Indian priestly tribe', she was not now willing to place herself 'under another similar yoke by accepting everything which comes from the priests as authorised command of the Most High'.[79] Her point was that as a Christian she must be allowed to think for herself. Faced with the heavy arm of ecclesiastical and doctrinal imposition, she judiciously decided to derive her authority from the very book of the Church – the Bible – and denied any mediatory role to priests and ecclesiastical authorities: 'I am not bound to believe in comments. I believe in the Word of God only and in the testimony of His prophets. I am a disciple of Christ – though one of the least – and not of the commentators.'[80]

In her endless theological clashes with conservative Anglicans, Ramabai insisted on her own hermeneutics and placed paramount importance on the teachings of Jesus. In one of her letters, she wrote: 'Take away all outward shows of your words and grand ceremonies and teach simply the words of Christ as they fell from His lips, without making any comments and you will see what power they have of enchanting the people's hearts.'[81] One passage which especially appealed to her was the Lord's Prayer. She wrote:

When I was not a Christian and never dreamed of believing in this religion, even then I felt the great and deep meaning of the Lord's Prayer. How many words are used, how many grand things are told by other people when they pray or when they write books, when they preach sermons, but the true life and spirit do not seem to come in them. On the other hand, think of the Lord's Prayer. Is there anything left that we need to ask in it? Can there be any other words in the

[78] Shah, *Letters and Correspondence of Pandita Ramabai*, p. 151.
[79] Ibid., p. 59.   [80] Ibid., p. 150.   [81] Ibid., p. 24.

whole world's literature so full of life and spirit yet so few and simple? The answer is 'No.'[82]

Ramabai was empowered by the Bible and at the same time distanced herself from some of its elements. She underplayed the miraculous deeds recorded in the biblical narratives. 'I cannot induce myself entirely to believe the miracles of the Bible', she wrote once.[83] She interpreted miracles as parables. For instance, she read the healing of the blind in Mark 8 as being symbolically enacted in her own life – blinded by the old faith and seeing afresh through the new-found faith.[84]

A further demonstration of her desire for textual control can be seen in her advocacy of a new Marathi version of the Bible. Her aim was to bring out a translation that was well-suited to the people with whom she was working, rather than depending on the versions produced by the British and Foreign Bible Society. In one of the circulars she wrote to the Bible Society about its translation, she made it clear that, as a reader of their Marathi version for twenty years, she did not dislike it, but it was rendered in high-flown Marathi studded with Sanskrit, Arabic and Persian words and was useful only to scholars. For the Biblewomen, catechists and native preachers, who had only an elementary knowledge, such a version was tedious and difficult to read. Her aim was to make the vernacular Bible simple so that all people, especially women, children and simple people, would understand it. She wrote in the same circular: 'The common men, women and children, especially those living in villages, should have the Bible given them in the language which they will easily understand.'[85]

In her view the existing vernacular translation was crude and unsatisfactory; it was produced under the superintendence of missionary translators and Hindu pundits. The former, she claimed were unaccustomed to or had an unfavourable attitude towards Indians and their culture. The latter lacked the sophistication to understand the nuances of the philology of biblical languages and Christian theology. Her remedy was not to direct Indian translators to lexicons and concordances, which

---

[82] Ibid.   [83] Ibid., p. 155.   [84] Ibid., pp. 156, 139.
[85] Adhav, *Pandita Ramabai*, p. 201.

she felt might bamboozle them, but to make them consult as many translations as possible so they could arrive at a satisfactory meaning, rather than 'altogether depending upon the opinion of small communities of translators of the Bible in each vernacular'.[86]

The second motive for a new Marathi translation was that Ramabai felt that the current versions were tainted both with 'idolatrous' Hindu concepts and also with the modernist vice of higher criticism. She produced a list of words from missionary translations which, in her opinion, unwittingly marred the Marathi version by a subtle introduction of Vedantic philosophy.[87] For instance, she pointed out that the translation of one of the Beatitudes – 'Blessed are the meek' into 'Meritorious are the meek' (Matt. 5.3) – would in her view 'lead the Hindu to think that the meek by virtue of their humility earn the right to the Kingdom of Heaven', and she went on to caution: 'It is dangerous and sinful to use them, [i.e. Hindu concepts] if done knowingly, as they make wrong impressions on the minds of non-Christian hearers.'[88]

Ramabai also resisted the application of higher criticism to translation work. She had no patience with the hermeneutical subtleties of higher criticism; she saw it as being engaged in the 'arbitrary use of certain meanings and pronunciations of the Hebrew and Chaldee words as given', thus 'setting at nought the opinions of hundreds of scholars' associated with the Authorized Version and its interpretation.[89] Instead of the usefulness of higher criticism for such questions as authorship, literary sources and historical authenticity of the narratives, she advocated lower criticism focusing on texts, their texture and theological tone. Being a Sanskrit scholar and well versed in the Hindu *Puranas*, what was crucial for her were the different retellings of the same story rather than an accurate reproduction of them. Hindu hermeneuts do not engage in a fierce battle over the textual veracity of the many tellings of the *Ramayana* and the *Mahabharata* which proliferate both in the sub-continent and beyond. She was trying to introduce the same hermeneutical

[86] Ibid., p. 204.   [87] Ibid., 207–12.   [88] Ibid., p. 208.   [89] Ibid., p. 213.

emphasis in her approach to the biblical narratives. For her, the Authorized and the Revised Versions of the Bible were different ways of telling the Christian story. Her claim was that if the Authorized Version and the English and American Revised Versions were able to render the meaning without the benefit of higher criticism, there was no need to introduce this to the Marathi version.[90] She was resistant to the modernist notion of restoring the original. She saw translation as a search for the essence of a text, rather than dependence upon it. Her aim was far from literal rendition. Her ambition was 'not only to translate correctly the words but the "*thoughts* expressed in the Holy Scriptures"'.[91] She articulated her resistance in Christian apologetic language:

The Gospel of Jesus Christ was used to save many, many of us from hopeless idolatry and dark sin, and we do not now need higher criticism. I entreat all those who are considering higher criticism to give your time and prayerful labour to the teaching and preaching of the simple Gospel to our people, and not to take the trouble to introduce higher criticism into your theological schools and Sunday schools.[92]

The factual and historical questions which higher criticism was engaged in solving, in Ramabai's view, would not 'make a single convert to Christ'.[93] She learnt Greek and Hebrew to provide an authentic translation of the Bible which her girls would then print in the press at Mukti. It was said that she was able to see the last proofs of her translation before her death.

Ramabai turned to the Bible because she saw it as the repository of the life and work of Jesus, and for this reason she venerated it. She dissociated it from all the post-biblical accretions which surrounded his personality. She declared a fascination for Jesus, but not for the heavy doctrinal Christ of traditional and colonial Christianity. She expressed her doubts over the miraculous birth of Jesus and belief in a resurrected

---

[90] Despite the presence of Robertson Smith, the Revised Version committee took a dim view of higher criticism, and embraced 'wholeheartedly' lower criticism. See Peter J. Thuesen, *In Discordance with the Scriptures: American Protestant Battles Over Translating the Bible* (New York, Oxford University Press, 1999), p. 45.

[91] Adhav, *Pandita Ramabai*, p. 204.

[92] Ibid., pp. 214–15.   [93] Ibid., p. 214.

Messiah: 'I have no doubt that Jesus is raised by God from the dead; but I doubt the resurrection of his earthly body.'[94] The Christ that Ramabai embraced was not the all-conquering colonial hero preached by missionaries or the abstract Christ of Church doctrines, but the Christ she had come to know initially through the Bramo Samaj. The Bramo Samaj was the nineteenth-century movement in Bengal trying to reform Hinduism from within by incorporating Western, Christian and indigenous elements into its framework. The image of Christ they projected was a de-Judaized, universal, Oriental teacher who revealed God and dispensed moral teachings and guiding principles which were interpretable to suit different contexts.[95] Ramabai was a member of the Prarthana Samaj, an organization akin to the Brahmo Samaj, and was well acquainted with the Brahmo religion. In a letter to Canon Butler, with whom she was engaged in debate, she said that her reason for conversion to Christianity was not because she was impressed with the unselfish service of the sisters and missionaries, but because of the stimulation generated by the Brahmo Samaj's thinking on Christ:

I was indeed impressed with the holy life of the Sisters, and their sublime unselfishness, and am so impressed to this moment, but I must say for the sake of truth that their life was not the cause of my accepting the faith of Christ. It was Father Goreh's letter that proved that the faith which I professed (I mean the Brahmo faith) was not taught by our Veda as I had thought, but it was the Christian faith which was brought before me by my friends disguised under the name of Brahmo religion. Well, I thought if Christ is the source of this sublime faith, why should not I confess Him openly to be my Lord and my Divine teacher?[96]

Her acceptance of Christ did not lead Ramabai to a complete rupture with her own tradition, as the colonial missionaries wanted. She saw her conversion as a fulfilment of her spiritual quest. What attracted her to Christ was his teaching and exemplary behaviour, especially his putting into practice what

---

[94] Shah, *Letters and Correspondence of Pandita Ramabai*, p. 160.
[95] For an extract on the Brahmo Samaj's understanding of Christ, see Adhav, *Pandita Ramabai*, pp. 8–10.
[96] Shah, *Letters and Correspondence of Pandita Ramabai*, p. 74.

he preached. For her, this was the significant difference between the religion she had left behind and the new faith she embraced. 'Hindu religion gave me teaching but not an example', she claimed once. She focused mainly on the teaching, and on the figure of Jesus as exemplary. She was especially concerned with following Jesus' teaching as reported in the Gospels. Eventually it was this form of the praxis of Christian religion which made the difference to her: 'The Hindu religion brings the Supreme Being, the Holy God to the level of a creature like myself but Christianity lifts man up to God. What is the lifting up of a man to God can be better understood by reading and imitating the life of Christ than by describing it in my defective words.'[97] She formulated her own creed strictly based on the teaching of Christ.[98] She believed that this creed, together with good works, especially as expounded in the Gospels of Matthew and John, and desisting from sin were sufficient for salvation.

As her spiritual life matured, Ramabai's sense of a relationship with Jesus gradually became more important to her than interpreting the biblical text. Though she was never a serious contemplative and spent most of her time in social work, in her later life her spiritual bond with Jesus grew deeper and deeper. Like most Indian Christian converts of an earlier generation, what ultimately mattered to her was the personal experience of Christ, and biblical texts increasingly occupied a secondary place.[99] She wrote: 'This has been my experience for the last four years and it is a great joy for me to find out daily what a truly wonderful saviour is the Lord Jesus Christ.'[100]

Ramabai mobilized the Bible as a way of resisting the Church authorities and securing her identity, and, more significantly, to make it accessible to the people of her community. Antoinette Burton considers that Ramabai's conflicts with the Church authorities are more than her articulated attack on the

---

[97] Ibid., p. 151.
[98] For her creed, see ibid., pp. 156–8.
[99] For the peripheral role of the Bible and the importance of the experience of Jesus for theological enterprise among the Indians, see, R. S. Sugirtharajah, 'The Bible and Its Asian Readers', *Biblical Interpretation: A Journal of Contemporary Approaches* 1:1 (1993), 55–7.
[100] Shah, *Letters and Correspondence of Pandita Ramabai*, p. 322.

Church: 'Rather it suggests that she used the clashes over religious orthodoxy as an opportunity to contest the terms of Western Christian colonial reform and to free herself from authorities, both religious and cultural, through which her English friends were trying to discipline her.'[101]

Ramabai has a secure but little-known place in Christian hermeneutics. The recent emergence of dalit voices in the Indian theological landscape tends to marginalize her work as representative of the oppressive brahminical tradition. Western Christian feminists are largely and uncharacteristically unaware of her existence. When Western Christian feminists celebrated the centenary of Elizabeth Cady Stanton's work on biblical hermeneutics and rememorialized the forgotten voices of women biblical critics, Ramabai, who went beyond mere feminist concerns to include the needs of children and the poor in her translation, was conspicuous by her absence.[102]

AFRICAN EMANCIPATORY MOVEMENTS AND THEIR BIBLES

The transmission of the Bible in Africa, as in the other continents, was not a one-sided affair. Africans were not mute and hapless recipients of the missionary imposition of the Bible. Vittorio Lanternari identifies two kinds of appropriation of the Bible in the face of imperialist imposition – resistance and assimilation.[103] The former is employed by indigenous emancipatory movements, and the latter by local integrative movements. Both types of movement were subjected to and unsettled by dispossession. In one case it was land that was stolen, and in the other, culture. One of the communities which felt the brunt of land loss was the native South African. The Native Land Act of 1913 deprived them of any reasonable living-space in their own country and, far worse, they were denied any access to farming land, when 15 per cent of land was cultivable. This Act

---

[101] Burton, 'Colonial Encounters in Late-Victorian England', pp. 43–4.

[102] See for example, *Searching the Scriptures*, vol. 1: *A Feminist Introduction*, ed. Elisabeth Schüssler Fiorenza (New York, Crossroad, 1993).

[103] Vittorio Lanternari, 'Revolution and/or Integration in African Socio-Religious Movements', in *Religion, Rebellion, Revolution: An Interdisciplinary and Cross-Cultural Collection of Essays*, ed. Bruce Lincoln (London, Macmillan, 1985), pp. 129–56.

meant that one million Europeans had a far larger share than the five million Africans, who were restricted to the barren so-called Bantu lands or reserves. It was this segregative policy which really shook the heart of the native community and led them to say accusingly, 'At first we had the land, and you had the Bible. Now we have the Bible, and you have the land.'[104] Those communities which faced disruption due to imperial exploitation – land expropriation, segregation, repatriation and forceful conscription – discovered, nevertheless, a revolutionary potential in the Bible. They recovered episodes from the Hebrew Scriptures which identified with nationalistic, anti-foreign and revolutionary causes. In the New Testament, they drew upon the insurrectionary nature of the Apocalypse and reconfigured the Christian concept of the Kingdom as recon-quering and recovering the land from the whites. In other words, they selected the biblical insights which easily resonated with their liberatory hopes in the face of colonial onslaught. The Bantu Churches fell within this category. For these Churches, the Hebrew Scriptures formed the foundation of their belief, and Moses was a pivotal figure in the Bible as the liberator, with John the Baptist added from the New Testament as the ideal diviner-prophet. Bengt Sundkler, who has studied the movement, observes: 'Obviously the Old Testament forms the foundation of the belief of these Churches.'[105] For them the truth is found in the books of Deuteronomy and Leviticus and in the role of Moses: 'Moses is the central figure in their Bible; Moses as leader, liberator; Moses overcoming the dangerous waters of the Red Sea; Moses fixing detailed prescriptions of taboos (food and sex).'[106]

Conformity with the Bantu heritage was taken as a yardstick by which to judge the Bible. Any biblical injunction or regula-tion which contradicted the Bantu culture was rejected. For instance, biblical teaching which denounced the practice of polygamy was viewed with suspicion. Thus, Isaiah Shembe, one of the key Bantu prophets, declared that 'European monogamy

[104] Bengt G. M. Sundkler, *Bantu Prophets in South Africa* (London, Lutterworth Press, 1948), p. 33.
[105] Ibid., p. 277.   [106] Ibid.

was St Paul's invention: it was Paul's legislation and not God's. Had not God said: "*Zalani nande* (Be fruitful and multiply)"?[107] Scripture, which had little to do with the African way of life, was found wanting, or was viewed as having nothing to offer to the indigenous context. The Hebrew Scriptures were privileged by these Churches because they validated some of the Bantu customs:

The sacrificial system of the Semites offers striking resemblances to that of the Bantu; some of the tabus are closely similar; the agricultural feasts have their parallels; much of the old law as found in Exodus regarding servants, cattle, the *lex talionis*, and the attitude to other tribes, can be paralleled in Bantu life. The supreme authority of tradition and custom is common to both. Circumcision is universal among northern Bantu tribes, and its significance as admitting to full membership of the tribe (and therefore in Africa to a relationship with the tribal spirits) is in line with Jewish thought.[108]

When the Hebrew Scriptures and the New Testament prescribe conflicting standards, 'the Old Testament standard is generally accepted'.[109]

Among the New Testament figures it was not Jesus, but John the Baptist who was preferred. This was not only because he was identified with the Old Testament figure of Elijah but, more importantly, because he was seen as the one who promoted 'much that is valuable in the old order of African life: purification rites, ancestral cult'.[110]

For the integrative groups who were torn between their own ancestral cultures, which they regarded as socially alienating and anachronistic, and the imported modern culture which came with the Europeans, the Bible provided a model for solving their identity crisis. Unlike in South Africa, dispossession of land was not a crucial question, nor was there any forced repatriation of people. There were no settler problems and they did not face territorial segregation but only social segregation. Exploitation was indirect. The local people were

---

[107] Ibid.
[108] Godfrey E. Phillips, *The Old Testament in the World Church: With Special Reference to Younger Churches* (London, Lutterworth Press, 1942), p. 7.
[109] Ibid., p. 6.
[110] Sundkler, *Bantu Prophets in South Africa*, p. 277.

compelled to grow on their own land crops and produce which were financially beneficial to the invaders, crops which were intended for European trade – coffee, cacao, peanuts, palm oil and copra. But this indirect exploitation deprived the chiefs of their power and authority. For rural people it was a clash with a stronger, technologically advanced and culturally disruptive foreign power. They selected and reinterpreted mystical, spiritual and redemptory contents in the New Testament in order to meet the void created by the clash of cultures. They mobilized biblical accounts of healings, miracles, exorcisms, spiritual power and spirit possession. The New Testament model of Jesus as a healer appealed to them. Textual evidence is hard to find and we are obliged to depend on reports of oral discourse. The Harrist and Aladura movements, which appropriated the Bible in order to readjust and redefine themselves, fell within this category.

CONCLUDING REFLECTIONS

The Bible in the colonial context was a cultural weapon which both the colonized and the colonizer employed to enhance their positions. While the missionaries saw the Bible as sufficient for dealing with all the ills of the natives and used it as a tool for civilizing and rescuing them from their moral degradation, the colonized, on the other hand, employed it as a weapon of reprisal. Rather than seeing it as unsettling their way of life, the invaded turned it to their advantage. They learned to master it in order to survive or resist the new social, political and economic situation. The selection of texts and their interpretation stunningly invert and undermine the complex theological and ideological edifice the colonialists erected with the help of Christianity. All their readings happen within a matrix of colonial reality and presence. Their individual and personal engagement with the text overrides any other possible interpretation. They are the specific interpretations of individuals and groups rather than any sort of approximation to the intention of the biblical writers.

Although these readings emerge from different contexts, in

some ways they connect with each other. When Equiano, Apess and Banerjea turned to the Bible, their aim was to achieve two things. One was to trace the origins of all human beings to a biblical ancestry, and to prove that the racial and religious diversities of the human population were due to geographic movement and migration. The second was to recover an alternative textual tradition, to defend oneself against foreign onslaught. In most cases, it was the biblical narratives which provided such a defence, but in the case of Banerjea, it was the interaction of these with the indigenous textual tradition which offered a safeguard against any intrusion.

Finally, it should be stressed that none of these interpreters entertained any revolutionary intent or worked for the ending of the Empire, though Banerjea's work pointed clearly in that direction. They were astute observers of their society and knew the impact colonialism was having on it. They often colluded with it, though were not entirely mesmerized by its benefits. In the face of colonial atrocities, it was both Christian and non-Christian texts that provided them with the much-needed support to maintain their dignity and identity. They altered, negotiated and appropriated biblical texts to create a discourse of resistant reading and to reconstruct their identity. Their intention was never to reject the Bible, but to reconstitute it as a more inclusive, amenable and attractive text.

CHAPTER 4

The colonialist as a contentious reader: Colenso and his hermeneutics

A bishop there was of Natal
who took a Zulu for a pal
Said the Kafir 'look 'ere
Ain't the Pentateuch queer?'
And Converted the Lord of Natal

A nineteenth-century popular verse

The cultural and hermeneutical interaction between the colonizer and the colonized is a complex one. In examining this interaction, colonial discourses often tend to explore the ambivalence and anxiety of the colonized. The last chapter was an example of this. An under-examined aspect of this encounter is the nature of the response of the colonizer. However imperialist and hegemonic the colonizer's role may be, his perception is often sharpened and interrogated by the experience of the colonized Other. Ashis Nandy, the Indian social scientist, in his study of the impact of colonialism on the colonizer, has identified four such reactions: sanctification of institutionalized violence; production of a false sense of cultural homogeneity in colonizing societies; encouragement of religious and ethical theories as part of the colonial project; and imputation of permanence and omnipotency to the colonizer. A rare fifth case involves opting out of the colonial framework and positioning oneself against the hegemonic and expanding discourse of the time.[1] This chapter will consider an example of this last reaction – a model of dissent, exercised in this case by a

[1] Ashis Nandy, *The Intimate Enemy: Loss and Recovery of Self Under Colonialism* (Delhi, Oxford University Press, 1991), pp. 32–7.

missionary bishop who engaged in an imaginative hermeneutical and political enterprise, modified and controlled by a colonial mode of thinking.

The bishop in question was John William Colenso (1814–83) who went to Natal, South Africa, with enthusiastic backing from the Society for the Propagation of the Gospel (SPG).[2] He was both a biblical critic and a critic of British colonial policy – an uncommon combination for a bishop of the Established Church. His career was bedevilled by constant battles with both the ecclesiastical authorities and some colonial administrators. In him we see one of those rare colonialists who was able to free himself from and rise above crude colonial ideas and intentions. His ability to converse in Zulu and the insights he had gained into the customs and way of life of the Zulus strengthened his intuitive sympathy for them. He was able to recognize the uneasiness of Africans in the face of the double onslaught of both theological and territorial colonialism. In his early days in Africa he was able to witness for himself the type of Christianity the missionaries were trying to establish on the continent. Their hell-fire preaching instilled fears in Africans, and the biblical stories they propagated sounded morally and historically preposterous to them. Later in life he was able to see for himself the brutality and duplicity of British colonialism in its dealings with the Zulus, and he was inevitably drawn into championing their cause.

This chapter will look at Colenso's critique of the colonial-

---

[2] There were a few missionaries like Colenso who sided with the colonized against the colonizers and employed the Bible in a radically different way from the then reigning notions of missionary hermeneutics. James Long (1814–87), who worked in Bengal, India, was one such missionary. He, like Colenso, was involved in the local struggle and sided with the Indigo workers, but unlike Colenso who benefited from the newly emerging 'higher criticism' and resorted to a relentless critical reading of the Bible, Long adapted a narrativel mode of interpretation. In keeping with the orientalist notion of India's preference for symbolic language, Long tried to communicate biblical insights through parables and proverbs, which he reckoned would 'excite interest and arrest attention'. His work on this subject includes: *Scripture Truth in Oriental Dress* (1871); *Bible Teaching and Preaching for the Millions by Emblems and Proverbs* (1874); *How I Taught the Bible to Bengali Peasant Boys* (n.p.; n.d.). Since I had difficulty in obtaining these works, I have not been able to pursue this further at this stage. Geoffrey Oddie's *Missionaries, Rebellion and Proto-Nationalism: James Long of Bengal 1814–87* (London, Curzon, 1999) has references to Long's hermeneutics, though this was not the main focus of Oddie's book.

hermeneutics of power through his problematization of biblical texts, and his mobilization of Zulu cultural resources to illuminate these texts. His employment of the Bible went against the accepted modes of interpretation of the time and, more importantly, drew on the very Zulu culture and insights which were despised at that time, but came to be seen by him as a vital key in opening up the biblical narratives. By way of conclusion, I will try to locate Colenso in both the interpretative and the colonial context.

The aim here is not to invest Colenso with monumental qualities and see him as a trail-blazer of biblical criticism or as a radical political activist who shook the very foundations of colonialism. It is important to note that he was a person of his period. While he was critical of scriptural literalness and theological obscurantism and disapproved of certain predatory aspects of colonialism, Colenso took for granted and accepted colonial notions of the time. He was part of the Victorian flow of men and women, high ideals and mercantile capitalism which were to invade, and to have a tremendous impact on, the lives of people outside Western culture. He was convinced of the superiority of the Christian faith and consistently maintained that the expansion of British imperial interest was divinely ordained by God to benefit the 'heathen'. In his public talk on 'Mission to the Zulus in Natal and Zululand', he claimed:

And it seems to be in the order of providence that the Briton, more than any other, should go out into other lands from his own beautiful, but crowded, island home, and take possession of different regions of the earth, where he will be brought at once into connection with races on a lower level of civilization.[3]

It is interesting that in spite of opting to be within the colonizing ideology Colenso tried to unsettle its unsavoury assumptions from within.

---

[3] Reproduced in John William Colenso, *Bringing Forth Light: Five Tracts on Bishop Colenso's Zulu Mission*, ed. Ruth Edgecombe (Pietermaritzburg, University of Natal, 1982), p. 221.

OUT OF THE MOUTHS OF THE HEATHEN

Interestingly, Colenso did not begin his career as a theologian but as a teacher of mathematics, which he studied at St John's College, Cambridge. In the 1840s he produced a series of widely used texts on this subject. However, it was his persistent preoccupation with Christian theology, the Bible and especially the then nascent biblical criticism and his commitment to the Zulu cause which attracted the attention of nineteenth-century England.

In the highly charged circles of the Victorian Church it was his critical study of the Old Testament, *The Pentateuch and the Book of Joshua*, which caused the controversy which led to his trial and excommunication. This was a seven-volume work spanning seventeen years (1862 to 1879), and containing more than 3,500 pages. Equally provocative and theologically challenging, however, was his commentary on Romans, published in 1861, before his work on the Hexateuch. In Romans Colenso investigated two of the most cherished doctrines of contemporary evangelical Christianity – atonement and eternal punishment. In Colenso's view, these caused a double theological jeopardy in the propagation of the gospel, communicating a wrong image of God, and failing to acknowledge any goodness in the heathen. He reformulated his basic ideas on this in the form of sermons which he delivered at Pietermaritzburg. His Natal sermons are rich hermeneutical resources but rarely studied by scholars. We see Colenso not only subjecting the New Testament writings to severe scrutiny, as he did with the Old Testament, but also communicating his ideas through a popular medium which could reach a wider audience.

Colenso's dissident reading has to be seen within the context of the hermeneutic of the day. Unlike his fellow British or German biblical critics, Colenso grounded his critical and comparative work in the African context, claiming that his Western counterparts

[H]ave not been engaged personally in such work, but have written from a very different point of view, in the midst of a state of advanced civilization and settled Christianity. Hence they have usually passed by altogether, or only touched very lightly upon, many points, which are of great importance to Missionaries, but which seemed to be of no immediate practical interest for themselves or to their readers.[4]

It was the Zulus with whom Colenso worked who prompted him to rethink his presuppositions and caused considerable concern to his Christian conscience. The natives were not dumb listeners but active participants in Colenso's search. William Ngidi acted as his translator and was his *agent provocateur*. Ngidi's probing questions led Colenso to rearticulate his attitude to Africa and his understanding of the Bible and Christian faith. Colenso was forced to reconsider two hermeneutical issues – the historical accuracy of the Bible and its teaching on morality – which he admitted that he and others like him conveniently overlooked when they were engaged in parochial work in England.[5] In narrating the questioning of Ngidi, Colenso recalled:

While translating the story of the Flood, I have had a simple-minded, but intelligent, native, – one with the docility of a child, but the reasoning powers of mature age, – look up, and ask, 'Is all that true? Do you really believe that all this happened thus, – that all the beasts, and birds, and creeping things, upon the earth, large and small, from hot countries and cold, came thus in pairs, and entered into the ark with Noah? And did Noah gather food for them *all*, for the beasts and birds of prey, as well as the rest? My heart answered in the words of the Prophet, 'Shall a man speak lies in the Name of the Lord? Zech. xiii.3. I dared not do so.'[6]

William Ngidi not only showed scepticism about the historicity of the Bible, but was equally if not more concerned with its moral content. He could not reconcile the idea of God as merciful with depictions of God inflicting punishment on hapless people, as in the biblical narrative. Ngidi raised two vital ethical issues – the biblical treatment of servants, and biblical warnings of eternal punishment for the unrepentant

---

[4] John William Colenso, *St Paul's Epistle to the Romans: Newly Translated and Explained from a Missionary Point of View* (Cambridge, Macmillan and Co., 1861), p. v.

[5] John William Colenso, *The Pentateuch and Book of Joshua Critically Examined* (London, Longman, Green, Longman, Roberts, & Green, 1862), part I, pp. vi–vii.

[6] Ibid., p. vii; see also John William Colenso, *Ten Weeks in Natal: A Journal of a First Tour of Visitation Among the Colonialists* (Cambridge, Macmillan & Co., 1855), p. 143.

heathen. When reading passages such as Exodus 21.4 and 20.21, which speak about treating servants as money, Ngidi was appalled at the supposedly gracious God's clear disrespect for the feelings of the enslaved. Colenso noted the revulsion of his Zulu interpreter:

His whole soul revolted against the notion, that the Great and Blessed God, the Merciful Father of all mankind, would speak of a servant or maid as mere 'money', and allow a horrible crime to go unpunished, because the victim of the brutal usage had survived a few hours. My heart and conscience at the time fully sympathised with his.[7]

Zulus like Ngidi could not believe that a loving God could cause pain to his unrepentant people. When reading Romans, they kept asking Colenso, 'Are you sure of this?'; 'Do you know this is to be true?'; 'Do you really believe that?'[8] Colenso himself had witnessed preaching of this type and he showed considerable uneasiness at the way the British and Foreign Bible Society and its colporteurs were trying to introduce the Book as a book of terror, and referring to a God about to strike anyone who failed to follow its teaching. In his *Ten Weeks in Natal*, he recounted his experience of a colporteur giving an account to his employees of Africans who were 'careless and negligent of divine things'. The colporteur thundered: 'They would *perish like those heathen*; and their children, about whom they thought so much, would twine about them, like creepers on a gnarled oak, and they would burn, – burn – burn on, for ever.'[9] The searching questions of the Zulus and the condemnatory preaching of his fellow missionaries were terrible blows to Colenso's Christian conscience. He could not face the suggestion that the Christian God could allow servants to be spoken of in terms of mere money and could acquit a master of murder should his servant survive his master's assault for a few hours. Nor could he come to terms with a repressive God who would punish people for not heeding his ways. Colenso's view was that such a presentation would not make the task of evangelism easy,

---

[7] Colenso, *The Pentateuch*, I, p. 9.
[8] Colenso, *St Paul's Epistle to the Romans*, p. 218.
[9] Ibid., p. 211; Colenso, *Ten Weeks in Natal*, pp. 251–2.

because evangelism 'either among the ignorant Zulu or the learned Hindoo, shall no longer be impeded by the necessity of our laying down, at the very outset, stories like these for their reception, which they can often match out of their own traditions, and reacquiring them, upon pain of eternal misery, to "believe" in them all "unfeignedly" . . .'[10]

This uneasiness led Colenso to pose a question which other missionaries of the time dared not ask. It struck at the very source of missionary propaganda, the Bible, and re-positioned its claim to theological worthiness: 'How is it possible to teach the Zulus to cast off their superstitious belief in witchcraft, if they are required to believe that all the stories of sorcery and demonology which they find in the Bible – the witch of Endor, the appearance of Satan in the court of heaven – are infallibly and divinely true – that God's own voice pronounced on Sinai.'[11]

CLEANSING THE CONTRADICTIONS

Employing what was at that time known as higher criticism, Colenso dealt with the moral repulsiveness of some scriptural narratives by showing them to be historically unreliable. In the process, he transformed the image of God from a bloodthirsty and vengeful tyrant into a modern benevolent paternal figure of love and care. Colenso set out to achieve this in two ways. One was to dispute the accuracy of certain biblical narratives, and the other was to recover what he claimed was the Bible's pure essence.

At a time when the dominant missionary preaching presented the Bible as an historical and infallible document containing all things necessary for salvation, Colenso found the Hebrew Scriptures 'a book full of perplexities and contradictions'.[12] For him it was 'an imperfect agency',[13] full of

[10] Colenso, *The Pentateuch*, I, p. 149.
[11] Colenso, *Bringing Forth Light*, p. 232.
[12] John William Colenso, *Natal Sermons: A Series of Discourses Preached in the Cathedral Church of St Peter's Maritzburg* (London, N. Trubner & Co., 1866), series I, pp. 17–18.
[13] Colenso, *The Pentateuch*, I, p. 154.

'inconsistencies, and impossibilities'.[14] It had been set up as an idol, against God's will, for people 'to bow down to it and worship it'.[15] He did not spare the New Testament either. For him, the Gospels were of a 'legendary character'[16] and were not 'historically true'[17] and contained 'fictitious accounts' of Jesus before and after his death.[18] He found that the narratives about Jesus' temptations were 'mythical or legendary additions',[19] and the Resurrection accounts 'legendary'.[20] Paul and the other apostles were mistaken as to the time, mode and form of Jesus' second coming.[21] To put it bluntly, for Colenso a belief in the historical truth of all parts of the Bible was 'utterly untenable'.[22]

In his relentless application of critical methods Colenso was trying to show by 'means of a number of prominent instances'[23] that the books of the Bible contained remarkable contradictions, and that they could not be regarded as true narratives of actual, historical matters of fact. For Colenso, being credible to his converts was more vital than the credibility or accuracy of the Bible. To be honest with his converts who found certain biblical passages morally repugnant, he used the then available biblical criticism to prove the unreliability of these passages and to discredit their authenticity. One such example was his reading of the Israelite massacre of the Midianites. He found the exaggerated figures of the murdered victims and the looting of cities recorded in the Book of Numbers imprecise and untrustworthy. Since the figures did not add up, his conclusion was:

[h]ow thankful we must be, that we are no longer obliged to believe, as a matter of fact, of vital consequence to our eternal hope, the story

---

[14] John William Colenso, *The Pentateuch and Book of Joshua Critically Examined* (London, Longman, Green, Longman, Roberts, & Green, 1863), part II, p. 173.

[15] Ibid., p. 381.

[16] John William Colenso, *Natal Sermons: Second Series of Discourses Preached in the Cathedral Church of St Peter's Maritzburg* (London, N. Trubner & Co., 1868), p. 127.

[17] Colenso, *Natal Sermons*, I, p. 196.

[18] Colenso, *Natal Sermons*, II, p. 127.

[19] Colenso, *Natal Sermons*, I, p. 313.

[20] Colenso, *Natal Sermons*, II, p. 114.

[21] Colenso, *Natal Sermons*, I, p. 77.

[22] John William Colenso, *The Pentateuch and Book of Joshua Critically Examined* (London, Longman, Green, Longman, Roberts, & Green, 1864), part IV, p. xxxvii.

[23] Colenso, *The Pentateuch*, I, p. 17.

related in Num. 31, where we are told that a force of 12,000 Israelites slew *all* the males of the Midianites, took captive *all* the females and children . . . *all* their cattle and flocks . . . and *all* their goods, and burnt *all* their cities . . . and by command of Moses, butchered in cold blood all the women and children.[24]

Colenso went on to say that the 'tragedy of Cawnpore, where 300 were butchered, would sink into nothing, compared with such a massacre, if, indeed, we were required to believe it'.[25]

Like other reformers, Colenso believed that by retrieving the 'primitive truth', a truth which had been 'corrupted and deformed by age', and had 'been choked-up, and covered-over with rubbish and decaying matter',[26] he could make the Bible a humane book which would appeal to the Zulus. The 'primitive truth', for Colenso, was the fatherly love of God, which was available to all people. He asserted that, in spite of the contradictory passages which spoke of damnation, the central message which ran through the Bible was that the God of the Bible was a God who loved and cared for people:

And, if words seem, at first sight, to contradict other words in the Bible, and other facts in the Scripture history, we must seek for the truth which underlies the whole, and connects all together, as different branches of the same root. The root is the fatherly Love of God to His creatures, which leads Him at one time to bless His children, at another to chasten them, at one moment to reveal to them the signs of His Favour, at another to cut them off for a time in displeasure, to banish them, it may be, into outer darkness, and yet suffers Him never to forget them, or cast them off altogether.[27]

For Colenso, moral and contextual needs took priority over dogmas traditionally taught by the Church. One of the dogmas which he found unappealing and damaging to the cause of Christianity was the Calvinistic doctrine of the depravity of man and the eternal punishment of the unconverted heathen. He challenged the view, central to evangelical Christianity of the time, that all unrepentant people, including children, would

[24] Ibid., pp. 143–4.
[25] Ibid., p. 144. The Cawanpore tragedy Colenso refers to is that of the revolt of Indian sepoys in 1857.
[26] Colenso, *Natal Sermons*, I, p. 13.
[27] Colenso, *St Paul's Epistle to the Romans*, p. 261.

face eternal torment. For him, such a theological assertion went against the spirit of the gospel, and, more importantly, this dogma did not make any distinction 'between those who have done things worthy of many stripes and those who have done things worthy of few – between the profligate sensualist and the ill-trained child'. He went on further to question how 'some few individuals, called by the name of Christians, but living comfortably all the while, notwithstanding their professed belief that myriads of their fellow-men are, every moment, passing into perdition, will, by some special act of Divine favour, be so fortunate as to be excepted from it'.[28]

His remedy was to reread Romans. This Epistle, he considered, was well suited to answer and contradict evangelical doctrines of predestination and eternal damnation. He was unequivocal about his claim: 'I need hardly say that the whole Epistle to the Romans is one of the strongest possible protests against such a notion.'[29] He declared: 'I can no longer maintain, or give utterance to, the doctrine of the endlessness of 'future punishments' – I dare not dogmatise at all on the matter. . .'[30]

In rereading Romans, Colenso went against the conventional evangelical idea of atonement. First, he challenged the theory of penal substitution which proposed the notion that Christ sacrificed himself to appease a wrathful God and God's righteous anger against sin. In going through Romans he was able to say confidently that 'once for all let it be stated distinctly, there is not a single passage in the whole of the New Testament, which supports the dogma of modern theology, that our Lord died for our sins, in the sense of dying *instead of* us, dying *in our place*, or dying so as to *bear the punishment* or *penalty* of our sins'.[31] Negatively, what occurred on the Cross was not appeasement but a blow to sin and its extinction; positively, it was reconciliation between God and humanity.

He also, further, found the traditional explanation for the rejection of the heathen to be unbiblical. The prevalent exegetical explanation of the time was to seize upon the example in Romans 9 of the potter who rejected one jar and accepted

---

[28] Ibid., p. 210.   [29] Ibid., pp. 210–11.
[30] Ibid., p. 197.   [31] Ibid., p. 115.

another. But Colenso, basing his interpretation on Jeremiah, argued that it was the same lump of clay that the potter used in making the two jars, one after the other, as a sign of God's equal treatment of people. There was no question of the potter abandoning one jar and selecting another, and thus there was no question of eternal rejection or election. Colenso was quick to point out that the Epistle did not propose universal salvation, but spoke of the hope that all will be saved.[32]

Going against the homiletical grain of the time, Colenso spoke of Christ redeeming all people everywhere whether they had heard his name or not. All people were justified in Christ. The Gospel was preached to the heathen not to admonish them but to set before them an instance of God's love. He wrote:

As regards their state in the eternal world, Ishmael and Esau and their descendants (among whom we may reckon the Zulus and Kafirs) stand on the same level, and will be judged with the same righteous judgement, as others more highly favoured in this world with the means of grace and the hope of glory, as their brethren in the Jewish Church of old, or in the Christian now.[33]

Colenso castigated his fellow missionaries who complained bitterly of the hardness of heart of the heathen, and said that it was impossible to awaken them to a sense of sin, when the missionaries themselves were at fault in preaching a false message of indiscriminate wrath and divine vengeance rather than proclaiming the gospel as a 'redeeming Love, offering a way of escape'.[34] Colenso was advocating a homiletics which emphasized the gospel as an invitation and not an admonition, and which projected 'the fatherly love of God' and the corresponding lighter side of the heathen.

One may conjecture another reason for Colenso wanting to do away with the traditional understanding of the atoning sacrifice of Christ. This was the time when colonial anthropologists were discovering indigenous sacrificial rites and ceremonies related to various African people. Such practices not only called into question the uniqueness of Christ's sacrificial death but also caused severe discomfort among Christian apolo-

---

[32] Ibid., p. 241.   [33] Ibid., p. 234.   [34] Ibid., p. 218.

gists. It was not easy to sustain the specialness of the Christian sacrifice in the way it was presented.[35]

Particularly striking was the way Colenso was trying to subvert the dominant notion of revelation. Unlike Christian theologians of the time who held on to a view of revelation which restricted it to the Bible and the Christian faith, Colenso had a broader vision which accommodated other religious traditions and texts. While most missionaries demanded adherence to and belief in the biblical texts as the only vehicle of God's message, he suggested that God was revealed to all humanity and that revelation was not confined to 'one nation, or to one set of books'.[36] The prospect of revelation in other religious texts did not for him pose any threat to biblical authority. Colenso used and freely appealed to other religious texts. To show that God's gracious love was documented in the texts of other faith traditions, he went on to say in one of his Natal sermons that,

There were multitudes who lived the life of God on earth before there was a Bible: there are multitudes now, who I doubt not, walk with God, even in heathen lands, though they have no Bible. The Galla of N. E. Africa, who could write this prayer – 'Good God of this earth, my Lord! Thou art above me, I am below Thee! Calling upon Thee I pass the day, calling upon Thee I pass the night! If I do not pray to Thee from my heart, Thou hearest me not! If I pray to Thee with my heart, Thou knowest it, and art gracious unto me. O Lord, who hast no Lord, there is no strength but in Thee! Under thy hand I pass the day; under Thy hand I pass the night! Thou art my Mother, Thou art my Father!' – or the Indian who said, 'He is my God, who maketh all things perfect: I believe that God made man, and he maketh everything: He is my Friend. O God, Thou art, as it were, exceeding riches; Thy regulations are without compare; Thy servant prayeth for true patience, and that he may be devoted unto Thee.'[37]

He sought to place the Bible in a wider, universal, comparative context, an endeavour which had little place in either the colonial missionary hermeneutics of the time or among Euro-

---

[35] Boyd Hilton, *The Age of Atonement: The Influence of Evangelicalism on Social and Economic Thought 1785–1865* (Oxford, Clarendon Press, 1991), p. 282.
[36] Colenso, *The Pentateuch*, IV, p. xxxv.
[37] Colenso, *Natal Sermons*, I, pp. 68–9.

pean biblical scholars. His mammoth work on the Hexateuch, especially his concluding remarks, were filled with comparative and intertextual references to ancient Egyptian, Persian, Greek, Chinese, Hindu, Buddhist and Sikh writings. His view was that the same divine spirit which inspired the most sublime passages of the Bible was also at work in other religious traditions. He wrote:

But then, too, they must be taught to recognize the voice of God's Spirit, in whatever way, by whatever ministry, He vouchsafes to speak to the children of men; and to realize the solid comfort of the thought, that, – not in the Bible only, but also out of the Bible, – not to us Christians only, but to our fellow-men of all climes and countries, ages and religions, – the same Gracious Teacher is revealing, in different measures, according to His own good pleasure, the hidden things of God.[38]

He further argued that the same Divine Spirit taught the 'Hindu Philosopher to say, "He thought, I will make worlds, and they were there", and taught also the Zulu first to say, though, as it were, with childish lips, "Unkulunkulu – the Great-Great-One – made all things, made all men." '[39] Colenso found that Hindus and Zulus, among others, had received the same inspired revelation of a universal religion that appeared in its most authentic form in the biblical tradition.

His universalism was undergirded by two factors. First, it was largely influenced by his wife's friend, F. D. Maurice, who in his 1846 Boyle Lectures advocated a Christian inclusivism which acknowledged religious truths in other religions. Secondly, it was based on a liberal humanism which assumed a vast underlying reserve of feeling and experience common to all humankind who have the same capacity to reason, to love and receive the word of God. Colenso asserted that 'all *human* beings in all conditions and circumstances – high or low – rich or poor – educated Englishman, or wild barbarian kafir'[40] had the capacity. He said: 'It comes with that power to all alike – to the learned and unlearned, to the wise and unwise, to the civilized

---

[38] Colenso, *The Pentateuch*, I, p. 154.   [39] Ibid., IV, p. 117.
[40] Colenso, *Ten Weeks in Natal*, p. 101.

man and the savage, wherever the eye of the soul is not altogether blinded and darkened.'[41]

For Colenso, the Bible was constituted of different classes of data, and not all had the same authoritative value. Using moral judgement and commonsense as hermeneutical keys, he developed a hierarchy of profitable and suitable passages which could be read in congregations. Subjecting the Bible to the New Testament test of letter and spirit, Colenso worked a two-pronged theory of truth. According to him, a text had an inner or spiritual, and an external or outer meaning. If on scientific grounds it became impossible to believe in the historical authenticity of particular biblical narratives, these were to be regarded as the disposable outer husks of spiritual truth. He recommended the dismissal of scores of verses and even chapters containing genealogies and lists of places.[42] He would also leave out texts which would have been profitable at the time in which they were written but had no relevance to the present. Here he included passages which validated slavery or legitimized the execution of witches.[43] He also felt that it was wrong to use Romans 13, which advocated obedience to constituted authority as 'expressing the whole of the Apostle's mind on the subject', and suggested that Paul himself would have modified his thinking to suit special circumstances.[44] In expurgating various passages, Colenso did not in any way deny their importance, but showed them as being comparatively less authoritative than other passages. Then there were textual segments which conveyed moral and religious truths which were eternal and universal, and which could be safely proclaimed 'at all times and to all persons, as the Word of God'.[45] For Colenso, such truths were summed up in the phrases which became the hallmark of nineteenth-century liberal Christianity – the fatherhood of God and the brotherhood of man: 'I have done my best to show that the central truths of Christianity – *the Fatherhood of God, the Brotherhood of Man* – . . . are unaffected by

---

[41] Colenso, *Natal Sermons*, I, p. 28.
[42] Colenso, *The Pentateuch*, IV, p. 298.   [43] Ibid., II, p. 170.
[44] Colenso, *St Paul's Epistle to the Romans*, p. 271.
[45] Colenso, *The Pentateuch*, IV, p. 298.

these results of scientific enquiry, or rather are confirmed by the witness of which the Pentateuch, when stripped of its fictitious character, gives of the working of the one Divine Spirit in all ages.'[46] In one of his sermons, he went on to assert:

Here then are the chief archives of that Divine Religion, which, when purged of its human accretions and reduced once more to its essential principles, as Christ taught it – the Fatherhood of God, the Brotherhood of Man, the manifestation of the Divine in the Human through the Incarnation of the Living Word, through the indwelling Presence of the Spirit, bearing witness with our spirits that we are all in very deed the sons of God – will embrace, as we trust, at length, the whole human race.[47]

His method was to extract this core message from the Bible, and in turn employ the same message as a critique of the Bible. The Fatherhood of God and brotherhood of man provided him with such a criterion which he could use as a measure to evaluate the deficiencies of the biblical narrative and its later accretions.

After he had cleansed the Bible of its unacceptable aspects, Colenso was able to say:

And I trust that, as Ministers of God's Truth and God's Message of Love to mankind, we shall be able before long to meet the Mohomedan and Brahmin and Buddhist, as well as the untutored savage of South Africa and the South Pacific, on other and better terms than we now do, – being no longer obliged to maintain every part of the Bible as an infallible record of past history, and every word as the sacred utterance of the Spirt of God.[48]

Though Colenso carried on a relentless assault on the status of the Bible throughout as an exclusive repository of revealed truth and for its historical accuracy, it still remained for him the 'mightiest instrument' for awakening in people's minds God's gracious and merciful dealings with humanity. For him, it was only through this infallible book in spite of its human elements, errors and ignorance, that God was revealed. He professed a firm commitment to the moral grandeur and spiritual beauty of

---

[46] John William Colenso, *The Pentateuch and Book of Joshua Critically Examined*, (London, Longmans, Green & Co., 1871), part IV, p. xv.
[47] John William Colenso, *Natal Sermons, Series III* (n.p.; n.d.), p. 190.
[48] Colenso, *The Pentateuch*, I, p. 150.

the biblical faith. 'In spite of its apparent contradictions', the Bible was 'full of the Glory and Goodness of God'.[49] This was Colenso's consistent message, and it came through very forcefully in all of his writings.When criticism has done its work, the scriptures remain still the oracles of God: 'They teach us about God, and His doings; they speak messages from God to the soul; they are still profitable for doctrine, reproof, correction, instruction in righteousness: they are a gracious gift of God's Providence, that we "through patience and comfort of the Scriptures might have hope".'[50] Whatever his opponent might say, he was not seeking to destroy the Bible but was trying to understand, redefine, limit and expand its scope.

EXEGETICAL CONTESTATION

Colenso undertook his textual criticism at a time when the historical-critical approach was making a great impact on the life of Western Christians. What allegorical interpretation did for the early Church fathers, historical criticism did for Christians in Victorian times – it helped to remap the biblical teaching to the changed world-view and made it possible to provide moral precepts and practical guidelines for people. The type of critical engagement Colenso was involved in – detailed linguistic analysis, and critical and logical scrutiny of the text – was described at the time as higher criticism, a term hardly found in Colenso's writings. He often termed his method scientific criticism. The aim of higher criticism was to determine date, authorship, source, literary forms and the integrity of various books. Colenso had more in mind than simple technical criticism or detailed philological analysis. His aim was to make the Bible theologically credible and an attractive document to non-believers. For him the new tool was not merely an instrument for solving academic questions but one of immense missiological practicality.

This is not the occasion for comprehensive and detailed

---

[49] Ibid. vi, p. 644.
[50] Colenso, *Natal Sermons*, i, p. 53.

analysis of Colenso's exegetical practices. There is a competent body of work dealing with this.[51] In the current mood of biblical scholarship, where the emphasis is on the literary and the narrativel, where theories and methods are subordinated to readers' own processes of understanding, Colenso's exegetical practices may look restrictive, although at a time when biblical literalness held sway, they seemed to be emancipatory. What is clear is that he brought the whole weight of the Enlightenment idea of rationalism to bear upon the Bible. Being a mathematician, he felt that if the figures and numbers in the biblical accounts did not add up, they had to be discarded even if they were part of the scriptures. Sometimes his calculations revealed an impish sense of British humour. For instance, he studied the size of the court of the tabernacle and calculated that, if old men, women and children were left out, there would have been 603,550 men eligible to attend, and if they all turned up to hear Moses, the assembled crowd would have reached thirty miles into the desert.[52] Similarly, if there were only three priests – Aaron and his two sons – who were officiating in the desert, and if there were two hundred and fifty births a day and they had to perform five hundred sacrifices to meet the prescribed requirement, it could not have been done in a single day and would have taken them forty-two hours.[53]

Unfortunately, it was this kind of scholarly prank which made him notorious and, to many, a maverick, and obscured the significance of his innovative approach. In his exegetical practices we see an early attempt at what has now come to be known as cultural exegesis. One of the exegetical practices which went against current modes of interpretation was Colenso's invocation of the Zulus and their culture. He made use of Zulu concepts – *uGovanta* and *uNembeza* – to illuminate the Pauline description of the double nature in humankind – the willingness to do good and the capacity to err: 'Among the Zulus there is a distinct recognition of the double nature of man. They speak of the *uGovanta*, which prompts him to steal

[51] See John Rogerson, *Old Testament Criticism in the Nineteeth Century: England and Germany* (London, SPCK, 1984), pp. 220–37.
[52] Colenso, *The Pentateuch*, I, p. 33.   [53] Ibid., pp. 123–4.

and lie, commit murder and adultery, and the *uNembeza*, which "bids him", as a native would say, "leave all that".[54] When missionaries were casting aspersions upon the Zulus, Colenso was trying to establish that essentially there were no differences between the English and the Zulus – both were capable of good as well as evil. In his *Ten Weeks in Natal*, he noted that the only act of violence he came across personally was committed 'not by the fierce, untutored, heathen savage, but by educated Christian English men'.[55] There was no case for condemning them. The moral debasement of the Zulus was due to their ignorance in not knowing the true Law. The sins committed were not wilful sins but sins committed in ignorance. Unlike the missionaries who doomed them to eternal perdition, 'God winks' at them, 'till His word is brought home to them.'[56] In the past, under the Mosaic law, certain things were permitted – polygamy, slavery, concubinage, butchery of innocent persons captured in war. These were not seen as transgressions or sin, though now condemned by the gospel. Similarly, many things which were practised by heathens, 'however offensive in the eyes of a white man and a Christian, are not transgressions of God's known law'.[57] By identifying *uNembeza* as a central moral force and *uGovanta* as a destructive force in Zulu culture, Colenso was trying to convey that, as with Jews and Christians, Zulus, too, wrestled with good and evil and had a moral narrative of their own.

One can detect three exegetical ambitions in Colenso's writings. First, he wanted to reverse and rectify the uncharitable judgements that the missionaries had passed in their 'arrogant self-confidence upon our heathen-fellow men'.[58] At a time when anthropologists and missionaries were openly debating whether these 'naked savages' who existed outside the theological framework of Judaeo-Christianity had the power to comprehend anything, let alone the nuances of the gospel message, Colenso affirmed that they were 'capable of receiving

[54] Colenso, *St Paul's Epistle to the Romans*, p. 176.
[55] Colenso, *Ten Weeks in Natal*, pp. 88–9.
[56] Colenso, *St Paul's Epistle to the Romans*, p. 53.
[57] Ibid., p. 106.   [58] Ibid.

at once and cherishing that advanced Christianity'.[59] When
biblical scholars and missionary practitioners readily discerned
parallels between the Graeco-Roman religions and the religions
of the heathen, Colenso was concerned to distance himself from
such practices. In exegeting Romans 1.24, he placed Paul in his
first-century context, saying that he was speaking of 'heathens
especially in his own time',[60] and his use of an aorist was an
indication that he was not referring to individual cases, or
'speaking of all heathen indiscriminately',[61] therefore it had no
relevance to contemporary Africans. He dissociated himself
from those who took advantage of Darwin's theory and tried to
place Africans in some lower form of existence. In his address to
the Marylebone Literary Society, Colenso conveyed to his audience: '[W]hatever the first men may have been, from whatever
source they may have sprung, we know in ourselves that a life
beats within us – as spiritual life – which raises above the brute,
which is the image and reflection of the life that is in God.'[62]

Distancing himself from the missionary homiletical practice
of seeing heathens as primitives, Colenso likened them to the
Jews of old. Like Jews, the fathers of the Kafir race, whom
Colenso believed to be descendants of Abraham, possessed the
knowledge of 'one Supreme Creator'.[63] In the Pentateuch he
discerned correspondences between Israelites and Zulus. He
saw Zulus as the Jews of Natal and used them as a yardstick to
verify and validate cultural patterns and historical accounts of
the Jews. Just as the Jews were called Hebrews because they
were the people who crossed the river Jordan, Zulus were called
abawelayo, the 'people who have crossed' their native land or
migrated from time to time driven by fear or for some other
reason.[64] The Zulu way of life, the pastoral lifestyle, patriarchal
households, sacrifices, seasonal festivals and the ritual calendar
all perpetuated a religious way of life which was like that of
ancient Israel. Colenso wrote: 'The Zulu keeps his annual

---

[59] Colenso, *Ten Weeks in Natal*, pp. 23–4.
[60] Colenso, *St Paul's Epistle to the Romans*, p. 50.
[61] Ibid., p. 54.
[62] Colenso, *Bringing Forth Light*, p. 210.
[63] Colenso, *St Paul's Epistle to the Romans*, p. 58.
[64] Colenso, *The Pentateuch*, II, p. 351.

Feasts, and observes the New Moon as the old Hebrew did.'[65] He even used the size of a Zulu hut to raise a suspicion over the number of tents Israel needed to have in the wilderness.[66] The colony of Natal, its size and population, provided a basis to assess the Land of Canaan, its size and population.[67] In tracing the emergence of the name Jehovah among the Israelites, Colenso likened it to the Zulu name for the creator, *Unkulunkulu*, and how it came about; he went on to postulate: 'Is it not *possible*, then, that the Name Jehovah may have been first employed by Samuel in order to make more distinctly the difference between the Elohim of the Hebrews and the Elohim of the nations round them?'[68] These observations, Colenso claimed, 'an English student would scarcely think of looking at'.[69] In the words of Colenso, the Zulu 'mode of life and habits, even the nature of their country, so nearly correspond to those of the ancient Israelites, that very same scenes are brought continually, as it were, before our eyes, and *vividly realized in a practical point of view*'.[70] What is interesting is the fact that that Colenso overturned normal hermeneutical procedures. He discerned parallels between the customs of contemporary 'savages' and the supposedly cultured biblical Jews. At a time when the natives were despised for their uncivilized manners and customs, Colenso used them as a benchmark to evaluate the biblical Jews, who were hailed as the epitome of advanced culture. Although the Bible had been used and will continue to be used to appraise African culture and its thought patterns, Colenso at least tried to initiate a process of reading the Bible in terms of African life.

Let me digress here: interestingly, in his commentary on Romans, Colenso did not identify the Jews with the Zulus. Instead, he sees them as the Calvinists of Paul's time: 'The Jews were the Calvinists of those days, and believed themselves as God's chosen people, sure of the kingdom.'[71] Just like the Jews of old, the Calvinists (read British Christians) were trying not only to impose their customs and laws but also to exclude Zulus

---

[65] Ibid., IV, p. 117.   [66] Ibid., I, p. 46.   [67] Ibid., p. 83.
[68] Ibid., II, p. 262.   [69] Ibid., I, p. xxi.   [70] Ibid.
[71] Colenso, *St Paul's Epistle to the Romans*, p. 235.

from God's Kingdom. Zulus, this time, are seen as Greeks and
Gentiles. Colenso went on to warn British Christians that they
had no privileged access to salvation:

All will be judged according to their works, and according to the Light
vouchsafed to them. With reference to the Light, which we, Christians
from England, have received, it might be said, in like manner,
'England has God loved, and Africa has He hated'. Yet not all English
Christians are children of the Light, nor are all African heathens
children of Satan; but those, who have received most, shall have most
required of them.[72]

The identification of British Christians with the Jews of old and
Zulus with the Greeks was significant. The implied message was
that, although salvation was open to all, the British were the
first in line for it and then came Zulus and others. In spite of his
openness, Colenso still operated on a Christian and a Euro-
centric world-view.

Colenso's second exegetical aim was to make known not only
the truth in the Bible but also the truth about the Bible,
however unpalatable it might be. For him, what was ultimately
at stake was the morality both of the biblical God and of biblical
interpretation. In his view, neither the Bible nor the authorities
of the Church ought to persuade a person to believe anything
which contradicted 'the moral law, that sense of righteousness,
and purity, and truth, and love, which God's own finger has
written upon his heart. The voice of that inner witness is closer
to him than any that can reach him from without, and ought to
reign supreme in his whole being.'[73] This meant not only that
any morally questionable passages had to be exposed and made
known to congregations but also that it was 'equally wrong and
sinful to teach them the scripture stories of creation and the
Fall, and the Deluge', as 'infallible records of historical fact'.[74]
What was important for Colenso was the credibility of the
interpreter. He went on to say that one cannot expect the
congregation to 'look to us for comfort and help' in their
religious perplexities if they cannot place entire confidence in
'our honesty of purpose' and good faith.[75] He saw this as an

[72] Ibid., p. 234.   [73] Ibid., p. 210.
[74] Ibid., IV, p. xxxviii.   [75] Ibid., I, p. xxvi.

important hermeneutical duty: 'Our duty, surely is to follow the Truth, wherever it leads us, and leave the consequences in the hands of God.'[76] He further claimed: 'I believe that I am doing the best service to the cause of true Religion by showing that we are *not* obliged to receive as the Infallible "Word of God" these statements, which conflict with certain conclusions of Science, and by asserting that the "Word of God" is wholly independent of the amount of credence which we give to these ancient narratives.'[77]

For Colenso, thirdly, exegesis was an exegesis of practical engagement. In one of his Natal sermons he said:

We know that our salvation cannot possibly consist in implicitly believing the historical certainty of this or that miraculous narrative, or in the unquestioning reception of this or that particular dogma – but in a 'faith that worketh in us by love' to God and to our fellow men – in 'doing the Will of our Father in Heaven' – in listening to the Living Word, which speaks with us in God's name continually, in the Bible and out of the Bible, in the teaching of our Lord and his apostles, or in the secrets of our own hearts, and in the daily intercourse of life.[78]

He went on to reiterate: 'It is the religion taught in the life and death of Jesus, and practised by those who try to live in his spirit and tread in his steps.'[79]

True to his words, Colenso was fully involved in the Zulu struggle against colonial greed and atrocities. His conscious advocacy in the case of Zulu chiefs – Langaliblee and Ceteshwayo[80] – is well documented. For him the truth of biblical religion had to be enacted in life and demonstrated in concrete terms. This meant demonstrating biblical virtues such as love,

[76] Ibid., p. x.
[77] John William Colenso, *The Pentateuch and Book of Joshua Critically Examined* (London, Longman, Green, Longman, Roberts, & Green, 1863), part III, pp. xli–xlii.
[78] Colenso, *Natal Sermons*, I, p. 197.
[79] John William Colenso, *The Pentateuch and Book of Joshua Critically Examined* (London, Longmans, Green & Co., 1879), part VII, p. 528.
[80] For details see George W. Cox, *The Life of John William Colenso D.D Bishop of Natal*, (London, Ridgway, 1888), vols. I and II; Jeff Guy, *The Heretic: A Study of the Life of John William Colenso 1814–1883* (Johannesburg, Raven Press, 1983); John Wolffe, 'Rethinking the Missionary Position: Bishop Colenso of Natal', in *Religion in Victorian Britain*, vol. V: *Culture and Empire*, ed. John Wolffe (Manchester, Manchester University Press, 1997), pp. 136–75.

mercy and justice. For one of the last sermons Colenso preached against colonial high-handedness in dealing with the Zulus he chose the text from Micah. In speaking out against the actions of the colonial government, Colenso reminded the congregation that what they ought to confess was not their private sins, but their 'national and public faults and transgressions'. He further castigated the colonial authorities for their 'brute force, proud prestige and crafty policy'. He hit them hard where it hurt them most by telling them that, by their failure to show love, mercy and justice, they pandered to their basic instincts and thereby reduced themselves to the level of heathens. He ended his sermon with a hell-fire warning such as he himself had earlier deprecated. He warned that if the pillage continued 'then indeed there will be reason to fear that some further calamity may yet fall on us, and perhaps, overwhelm us – by assegai, famine, or pestilence – in what way we cannot tell, but so that we shall know the hand that smites us'.[81] Unlike the liberation theologians, who a hundred years later would choose the Exodus as their model, Colenso opted for a verse from the prophet Micah as a scriptural basis for his theology. The Exodus for him was a *'pure fiction'*[82] and unhistorical. For him essentially the faith was not faith in an 'orthodox form of words' but a faith that 'worketh by love'.[83]

THE SACRED TEXT IMPROVED AND RESTORED

Colenso's exegetical engagements were undertaken at a time when there were contradictory perceptions of the Bible. This was the era when the Victorians believed in the verbal accuracy and inspirationalist idea of the Bible, and, when, at the same time, severe critical examination of the Bible was being undertaken. Some Christians of the time believed in its incontestable accuracy, were convinced of the universal Deluge and accepted

---

[81] John William Colenso, 'What doth the Lord Require of us?', a sermon preached in the Cathedral Church of St Peter's, Maritzburg on Wednesday, 12 March 1879, p. 23 (reprinted in *Natalia* 6, 1976).

[82] Colenso, *The Pentateuch*, II, p. 372.

[83] Colenso, *Natal Sermons*, I, p. 120.

Adam and Eve as actual historical figures. The older pre-modern ways of dating biblical events, such as the seventeenth-century calculation establishing the Creation in 4004 BCE, were still in vogue,[84] and nineteenth-century editions of the Authorized Version still printed such dates in the margin.[85] The Words of an ecclesiastical authority of the time summed up the mood:

The Bible is none other than the voice of Him that sitteth upon the throne. Every book of it, every chapter of it, every verse of it, every word of it, every syllable of it (where are we to stop?), every letter of it, is the direct utterance of the Most High. The Bible is none other than the Word of God, not some part of it more, or some part of it less, but all alike the utterance of Him who sitteth on the throne, faultless, unerring, supreme.[86]

Viewed against such a rigid attitude to the Bible, two contradictory images of Colenso as a hermeneut emerge – one modern and the other conservative. What we see in his hermeneutical endeavours are the new tools of the Enlightenment at work – reason, human freedom and competence. No authorities, Church or otherwise, should be permitted to dictate the way in which the Bible is to be interpreted. This approach placed enormous importance on reason and the ability of humans to use it reliably. It was a hermeneutic of commonsense. It represented a kind of logic which had misgivings about contradictions and paradoxes in a text and assumed that truth, including that of the Word of God, could be stated unambiguously. It was the Enlightenment ethos of individual freedom which encouraged Colenso and people like him to assert their freedom from the Church and its control. His rationalistic presupposition was a response to what he perceived as a deficient sense of history. Although Colenso claimed that his entire enterprise of biblical inquiry was prompted by questions raised by his Zulu converts, it was not always guided by them nor did he always use his Zulu experience in unravelling the

---

[84] W. Neil, 'The Criticism and Theological Use of the Bible, 1700–1950: Criticism of the Traditional Use by Rationalists', in *The Cambridge History of the Bible: The West from the Reformation to the Present Day*, ed. S. L. Greenslade (Cambridge, Cambridge University Press, 1963), p. 257.

[85] Alan Richardson, *The Bible in the Age of Science* (London, SCM Press, 1961), pp. 41–2.

[86] Neil, 'Criticism and Theological Use of the Bible', p. 283.

Bible. Often, for example, it was his mathematical prowess which enabled him to check the probability of biblical figures and dimensions.

In spite of his modernistic streak, Colenso remained a conservative. Although he claimed to use reason as a way of understanding faith, nowhere did he contest the inspiration of the Old Testament, nor did he discard the notion that miracles *per se* were false. What concerned him was not 'the miraculous or supernatural revelations of Almighty God' but 'the absolute, palpable, self-contradictions of the narrative'.[87] Thus, he regarded the release of the Israelites as 'the miraculous interposition of God', which worked 'through the agency of Moses'.[88]

For Colenso, what was important was the truth of the Bible, that is, how it witnesses to the truth. At a time when the choice seemed to be between the inerrancy of the Bible on the one hand and its rejection on the other, his solution was to treat the Bible as any other book and allow it to give its own account of itself, its contents, its age and its origin. Although he said that the Bible had to be read like any other book, he had his own view as to how it should be read. It had to be read like any other book but with a discerning mind and an understanding heart. In the end, 'the Bible is not itself, "God's Word", but assuredly "God's Word" will be heard by all who will humbly and devoutly listen for it'.[89] The Bible remained for him 'a book of religious education of mankind'.[90] Implicit in his method was the conviction that the Bible alone was the authority in spite of its fallibility.

Colenso did not see any conflict between divine revelation and human reason, and the Bible had to be approached scientifically and logically. Scientific reasoning is privileged, not in opposition to God's revelation but as itself a gift of God. The reader of the Bible is encouraged to employ whatever resources are available – mathematical skills, history, philosophy and comparative religious texts, in the firm belief that truth is one and belongs to God. Colenso wrote,

---

[87] Colenso, *The Pentateuch*, I, p. 10.   [88] Ibid., pp. 51–2.
[89] Ibid., II, p. 383.   [90] Colenso, *Natal Sermons*, I, p. 13.

the new discoveries of Science, whether in Natural Philosophy or Biblical criticism, *must* be received, indeed, and be received with joy and thankfulness as God's gifts, the gifts of a dear Father to his children ... If the Christian Religion is of God, it must in its fundamental principles be at one with all Truth, with the teaching of the Sciences as well as with that of the Bible.[91]

He went on to assert that 'Religious and Scientific Truth are one, and that, what God hath joined, no man, and no body of men, has a right to put asunder.'[92]

Colenso punctured what was sacrosanct to Victorian Christians, – the Bible – by simultaneously damaging it and redefining it. He never failed to admire the moral grandeur and spiritual beauty of the Bible, but at the same time he had no qualms about attacking its status as an incontestable authority. He pressed home the simplicity and the supremacy of Christian Scripture, while conceding the usefulness of other warrants and authorities. Embedded in his interpretative scheme was the certitude that scripture alone was the authority but, at the same time, that scripture is never alone.

On looking back, the Bible in the hands of Colenso remained largely unharmed, and the source criticism which he applied unremittingly did not in the end destabilize it. On the contrary it did much to reinforce the Bible's authority. He was not the first to engage in such an exercise. There were many before him on the Continent and in England who were wrestling with similar issues. What he and others like him did was to metamorphose the Bible into a different book. Interestingly, the greatest threat to the Bible did not come from the much publicized conflict between the Bible and the then emerging new scientific disciplines such as biology or anthropology, but from 'the less ostentatious advances in the field of history'.[93] In Glover's view, the nineteenth century was 'characterized by a strong historical sense'.[94] The Bible, like any other literary work, was required to measure up to the weighty demands of historical criteria. It was

---

[91] Ibid., p. 37.
[92] Colenso, *The Pentateuch*, IV, p. xxxviii.
[93] William B. Glover, *Evangelical Nonconformists and Higher Criticism in the Nineteenth Century* (London, Independent Press Ltd, 1954), p. 53.
[94] Ibid., p. 13.

these demands, in the end, that caused the Bible to lose its authority as a verbatim oracle of God and turned it into a collection of historically verifiable documents with ethical prescription for the reinvigoration of humankind. In the process its typological and allegorical meanings were cancelled out. Colenso played a considerable part in ensuring their temporary demise. What was gained as a rationally reputable text, as the future narrative critics would say, lost its potential as a good story.

SITUATING COLENSO IN THE COLONIAL DISCOURSE

Colenso's place in colonial discourse is ambivalent. He was favourably disposed towards Africans, especially towards Zulus, and expected that Christianity would be enriched by them. Just as Christianity in the past had benefited from its contact with the philosophies of Persia, Alexandria and Rome, and more recently from German thinking, he hoped for a day when the Zulu culture too would have a great impact on it. He acknowledged the contributions of the African bishops in the earlier councils of Christendom. For him the future survival of Christianity depended on its interaction with African culture:

> Perhaps we may yet have to find that we 'without them cannot be made perfect' – that our nature will only exhibit all its high qualities when it has been thoroughly tried in the case of cultivated black races, as well as white. And surely, with our own experience before us, we cannot presume to assert that the human family will never be benefited by light reflected even from the thinkers of Zululand.[95]

Colenso attempted to understand the Zulu way of life from within, gave a fair description of it and was often generous with his praises. Moved by the exemplary behaviour of Zulus, Colenso saw them as members of the human family, who had, however, 'sunk down gradually' in their moral standards.[96] Although in the dominant discourse of the time Zulus and others were portrayed as stupid and incompetent, Colenso saw them in a positive light. As we saw earlier, they were instru-

---

[95] Colenso, *Bringing Forth Light*, p. 224.
[96] Colenso, *St Paul's Epistle to the Romans*, p. 58.

mental in shaking up his thinking. But his efforts were most deeply motivated by a desire to highlight the likenesses between Zulu and Christian beliefs and practices, to show not only how suggestive and stimulating but also how incomplete Zulu thought patterns were until they were refined by the impact of Christian ethos and Western values. While he generously acknowledged their character and way of life, he remained unable to respect their cultural integrity and tended to define and evaluate it in Christian terms.

With all his egalitarian and progressive tendencies, he believed in the superiority of European and particularly British civilization, though he later came to realize its flaws and became more critical of its ruthless manifestation. He fought for the Zulu cause but operated within Christian religious values rather than opting for secular ideologies. In showing solidarity with the Zulus, he found a richer meaning for Western Christianity and a new endorsement of his own version of traditional Christian values. In the end, the aim was to convert, civilize and christianize all aspects of heathen life. What Colenso desired was that eventually every one should come under the influence of Christianity:

This, as now observed, is purely a heathen ceremony, but has undoubtedly a right meaning at the bottom; and, instead of setting our face against all these practices, our wisdom will surely be, in accordance with the sage advice of Gregory the Great, to adopt such as are really grounded on truth, and restore them to their right use, or rather raise them in the end still higher, by making them Christian celebrations.[97]

On another occasion he said that the aim of the missionary activity was to raise 'a savage nation like the Zulus to the dignity of civilized and Christian men'.[98] This, he reckoned, would be the lasting contribution of missionary work in spite of its other failures.

Colenso's openness to heathens and their culture also has to be placed in the colonial context. This was a time when Christianity was trying to portray itself as the religion of the

---

[97] Colenso, *Ten Weeks in Natal*, p. 93.
[98] Colenso, *Bringing Forth Light*, p. 222.

Empire, as a religion with universal credibility. Its claim to universal ascendancy depended on establishing its superiority in relation to other religions in the colonies. Moreover, there was the feeling that one needed to know these religions before exposing their defects. There was a hive of hermeneutical activity at that time. F. D. Maurice had a great impact on Colenso's theology, though he later fell out with him. In his 1846 Boyle lectures, *The Religions of the World and Their Relations to Christianity*, Maurice was forthright about the vocation of the English 'to subdue the earth, to trade, colonize, and conquer'.[99] He gave a comprehensive account of these religions of the Empire, stating that in spite of the goodness in them there was 'something wrong within, which needed to be purged way',[100] and the only person who could do this was Jesus Christ.

Colenso has to be seen in his historical context. For example, when he spoke of the fatherhood of God and the brotherhood of man as a fundamental principle of his religious faith, we must remember what a father and brother were to him as a member of the bourgeois in the mid nineteenth century. Jeff Guy, who, among Colenso's biographers, has written positively about him without placing him on a high pedestal, puts it in the right perspective:

For him the family was a stabilising and conservative influence in a world disrupted by revolutionary change: it was a hierarchical structure, the father demanding of his sons not only love, but obedience and the unquestioned recognition of his authority. Colenso's univers-
alism and the belief that God's love was present within all human beings implied the need for respect between individuals, but not equality. Communities, and the individuals within them, were ranked and it was the duty of some to lead and of others to follow. When Colenso spoke of the Brotherhood of Man this was an expression of selfless commitment to others, but it was not an egalitarian ideal.[101]

In the last chapter we saw how the colonized in their discursive dealings with the colonizer used the paradigm of resistance. We also need a paradigm for colonizers who engage in oppositional

---

[99] Frederick Denison Maurice, *The Religions of the World and Their Relations to Christianity* (London, Macmillan and Co., 1886), pp. 235–6.
[100] Ibid., p. 233.
[101] Guy, *The Heretic*, pp. 357–8.

discursive practice against their own system. I should like to place such hermeneutical practices within the category of dissidence. Although coopted, the discourse of dissidence successfully subverts it from within. This is precisely what Colenso did. He redefined the nature of the Christian faith in modern and non-biblical terms without jettisoning that faith, and at the same time he rattled both the ecclesiastical and political systems of which he was part.

CHAPTER 5

Textual pedlars: distributing salvation – colporteurs and their portable Bibles

When you come, bring . . . the books, and above all the parchments. 2 Timothy 4.13

White Lady, has God's Book arrived in our country?
Tell the World, 63

There is yet one thing left to do with the Bible: simply to read. Richard Moulton

Biblical scholarship has been relentless in paying attention to the historical investigation of texts, the theological exposition of various narratives and the lexical purity of numerous versions of the Bible, but rarely has it made any serious attempt to study the circulation of the Bible and its effect on ordinary people, especially those who sold them. The aim of this chapter is to begin to rectify this omission, to narrate the intriguing story of its dissemination and its impact on some of those who read it. In order to illustrate this, I will look at the significant role played by colporteurs, a group of men and women employed by the British and Foreign Bible Society, whose specific task was to sell the Bibles door to door. Their activities constitute a significant element in the singular aim of the Bible Society to promote the Bible as *the* Book. They were dedicated hawkers whose specialization lay in carrying the Bibles, Testaments and biblical portions in a sack, and selling them through persuasion or through personal testimonies, thus effecting changes in the lives of the purchasers that eventually led to their conversion. The colporteurs acted not only as hawkers of the Bible, but also as brokers between the Bible Society and the people who bought the Bible. They were ordinary men and women, often from the lower sections of society. Under the colonial practice of writing history in which imperial buccaneers and European missionary heroes were monumentalized, the feats of colporteurs were rarely acknowledged and recorded. One person, however, raised the profile of the work of colporteurs to a mythical status. This was George Borrow. Though not a colporteur himself, Borrow was the Society's agent. An unsuccessful writer, he travelled in Spain between 1835 and 1840 and composed letters to Andrew Brandram, secretary of the Society, describing his extraordinary adventures in distributing the Bible. On his return, he used this material to bring out a volume, *The Bible in Spain* (1843),[1] which became a bestseller at that time. Borrow's book brought to the notice of urban readers in Victorian England the perils and possibilities of peddling God's Book.

The beginning of the twentieth century marked the halcyon days of colportage, and since then the scale of recruitment has not surpassed those momentous figures. At that point the Bible Society had 1,200 colporteurs, more than half of them in India and China. In addition to this, it had on its roll 687 Biblewomen who were appointed to work in countries where women were secluded for cultural and religious reasons. This meant especially India and China where, as the Bible Society's Report put it, women were, 'condemned to live in rigid seclusion',[2] and it was assumed that these women would prefer to hear the gospel from a 'sister's lips'.[3] Generally, colporteurs were local people who were directed and controlled by the Society's own agents or its missionary friends. These colporteurs were not volunteers, but were employed by the Society, though they were more than mere workers.[4] Although they were drawn from

---

[1] See his *The Bible in Spain or The Journeys, Adventures, and Imprisonments of an Englishman, in an attempt to Circulate the Scriptures in the Peninsula* (London, Oxford University Press, 1906 [1842]). Borrow's book spawned a genre of books on bible-selling ventures. See Frederick C. Glass, *Adventures with the Bible in Brazil* (London, Pickering and Inglis, n.d.); Dugald Campbell, *With the Bible in North Africa* (Kilmarnock, John Ritchie, 1944).
[2] *The Leaves of the Tree: A Popular Illustrated Report of the British and Foreign Bible Society for the Year 1906–1907* (London, The Bible House, 1907), p. 55.
[3] *More Golden Than Gold: A Popular Illustrated Report of the British and Foreign Bible Society 1911–1912* (London, The Bible House, 1912), p. 89.
[4] For the history of colportage, the selection process, and the character and qualities

different nationalities and races, spoke many languages and belonged to various Christian denominations, they were re-cruited to perform a singular task: to tell all people that in the pages of the Book they had personally found for themselves the good news of God's redeeming love, and that it was good for all humankind. More importantly, they had to be seen as people who had not only grasped the contents of the Book, but had also grown to love it. They had not only been infected by the Book but were dedicated to spreading that infection to others. Their motto was summed up thus:

Go and teach all nations. Fear neither the difficulties of foreign tongues, nor differences of manners, nor the power of secular governments; consult not the course of the rivers or the direction of mountain ranges; go straight on; go as the thunder goes of Him Who sends you – as the creative Word went which carried life into chaos – as the eagles go, and the angels.[5]

Colporteurs were not particularly known for, nor were they recruited for, their narrative abilities. But the stories and anecdotes of their experiences, which they reported on as part of their job requirement, became very popular, and a stirring testimony to their Christian persistence and determination in awkward situations. These stories were reproduced in the Society's Annual Report, and also in its popular version. These Reports were eagerly read publications of their day.

In this chapter I would like to look at the stories recounted in these Reports and to fathom how the Bible was promoted by the British and Foreign Bible Society, what sort of Bible it projected and how it was perceived by both those who received it gratefully and others who rejected it; the role of the colpor-teurs will also be examined, and how they aided and colluded with the Society's own theological and ideological and expan-sionist ideals. The chapter concludes with some reflections on the idea of promoting a book.

expected of a colporteur, see William Fison, *Colportage: Its History, and Relation to Home and Foreign Evangelization* (London, Wertheim, Macintosh, and Hunt, 1859), pp. 36–50. Fison was a woman, her Christian name Margaret, and like that of most women at the time her gender identity was suppressed.

[5] *After a Hundred Years: A Popular Illustrated Report of the British and Foreign Bible Society for the Centenary Year 1903–1904* (London, The Bible House, 1904), p. 73.

Although the British and the Foreign Bible Society took great pains in translating the Bible into various languages and were involved in the actual publication of these versions, their success was largely dependent upon making them available to the people for whom they were principally produced. This task was undertaken by ordinary men and women who took upon themselves the mission of actually distributing them. A colportage was regarded as 'the noblest jewel in the crown'[6] of the Bible Society's activity. Interestingly, the idea of colportage came from France, and it was borrowed by the British and Foreign Bible Society. It was Jean Daniel Kieffer, the then Professor of Oriental Languages in the Royal College of Paris, who in 1831 developed the concept of door-to-door distribution of Testaments and scripture portions. Colporteurs in France were engaged to sell Bibles, Testaments and Gospel portions at a cheap price, so that those who were disaffected with the Church could read them privately and for personal reasons. They were dedicated to the cause of Protestantism and their efforts go back to the Reformation period, when 'they were among the most active agents in the propagation of the new and illicit ideas'.[7] Like the Bible Society's colporteurs, they observed as a cardinal rule the putting of the Bible, without note or comment, into the hands of those who were thirsting for God's Word, which included fellow-Christians who were denied access to the Bible by the papacy. Their task was to bring to the common people the 'pearl of great price' in a language they could understand, and at a price which they could afford.

The Bible Society's colporteurs carried the scriptures to the remotest corners of the world that were otherwise inaccessible and untravelled – the dense forests of the Orinoco, the upper waters of the Nile, the barracks of Russian soldiers, the banana plantations of Guatemala and the diamond mines at Kimberly. They entered cottages, chalets, camps, bungalows, huts, and tents of nomads. They took advantage of crowds who gathered

[6] George Browne, *The History of the British and Foreign Bible Society: From Its Institution in 1804, to the Close of Its Jubilee in 1854*, vol. 1 (London, Bagster and Sons, 1859), p. 418.

[7] See Lucien Febvre and Henri-Jean Martin, *The Coming of the Book* (London, Verso, 1998), p. 237.

for wakes, festivals and fairs. The Society saw the colporteur in the mould of the Shakespearian character, the pedlar Autolycus who haunted 'fairs, wakes, and bear-baitings'.[8] They used every conceivable method of transport: animals – horse, mule, donkey, camel or elephant – and vehicles and vessels – ancient camel-cart, bullock-cart, carraton drawn by buffaloes in Queensland, wheelbarrow in China, sleigh to reach isolated Russian hamlets and, in time, modern railways, river-steamer, sampan, canoe or bicycle.

Their tenacity and resilience almost raised them to folk-hero status. They braved all kinds of hardship and perils – blizzards in Siberian winters, the heat of Brazil, anarchy in Persia, revolution in South America and freebooters in Mongolia. They were beaten by Roman priests, kicked by Jews, locked up in Austrian prisons, arrested during the Balkan crisis as spies, and called up to serve the colours. A Bulgarian colporteur was captured, chained and imprisoned by Greek soldiers and deported to Crete. In Western China, a colporteur was blown away in a gale, never to be seen again.

BARTERING THE WORD OF GOD

The purpose of the Bible Society was to make God's Book available to people at a purchasable price. It saw its task as producing and selling Bible selections at prices within the means of Eastern peasants and ploughmen. Though the aim was to put the Bible in the hands of every poor person, it was never given free. The Society took the moralistic view that if someone paid for a Bible, however nominal the price, it would have effective and enduring results. However, for those who could not afford them, the Society had alternative plans. It was willing to exchange or barter for a variety of items. A chief in Abyssinia offered his sword in return for the Book. In Mongolia silk scarves were exchanged for the Gospels. A colporteur in Uganda took payment in the form of cowry-shells. In Mongolia the Gospels were exchanged for dried dung. A Korean paid for

---

[8] *In the Vulgar Tongue: A Popular Illustrated Report of the British and Foreign Bible Society 1913–1914* (London, The Bible House, 1914), p. 88.

a copy of the Chinese New Testament with his pipe. 'I've no money', he said; 'wilt thou barter? I'll give thee my pipe, if thou givest me a book. I want a copy of that book very much; please exchange. My pipe cost more than the price thou art asking for the book.'[9]

Food items were sometimes exchanged for the Bibles, Testaments and biblical portions. In South West China, Miao and Lisu tribal people paid with fruits, eggs and pine chips for their new Gospels. In Galicia, Colporteur Christoffel reported that a young man swapped a can of buttermilk for a copy of the New Testament. Three kilos of lentils were offered for a Bulgarian New Testament. In Syria a peasant offered a small sack of nuts. Fish was offered in the Solomon Islands and cheese in Mongolia. In Central America, Colporteur Castills accepted payment in the form of eggs, starch, cocoa-beans, fowls, logwood and firewood – which in real monetary value was considerably less than the cost incurred in producing the books. In North Morocco, a sub-agent accepted barley, eggs, chickens, butter, straw, melons, milk and bread. An old woman in Korea obtained a Testament in exchange for a much-worn-out Buddhist rosary which had long assisted her prayers. When a group of shepherds who had listened with wonder to the Parable of the Shepherds desired to buy a book from the colporteur but did not have any money, they offered him a rabbit which they had caught only an hour before and exchanged it for a copy of the New Testament.[10]

Exchanging the Bibles for food items and for a variety of exotic goods may present the image of the Bible Society as a body with a conscience. The mention of poultry, victuals and bizarre objects might have recalled for English readers of the Reports memories of a cashless, pre-industrial society that they had left behind. What the Reports failed to register was that, with the simultaneous arrival of colonialism and the Bible, the anti-materialistic nature of these societies was about to be changed radically. The introduction of a complex economy based on capitalism and wealth creation meant that economies

[9] *After a Hundred Years*, pp. 71–2.   [10] *More Golden than Gold*, p. 115.

based on barter and an egalitarian way of life were about to be altered beyond recognition.

The reports of colporteurs depict a world being transformed by the Book. They cite, as evidence of this transformation, the changed lives of people and their rejuvenated cultures. They tell stories of people being overpowered by the Book, and its ability to attract and renew men and women and their cultural mores. Their testimonies suggest that readers and cultures have been invigorated by the impact of a text.

Colporteurs file stories of how reading instantaneously changes the internal and external lives of people. The Popular Reports teem with instances of how former gamblers, wife-beaters, cheats, robbers, corrupt merchants, prostitutes, potential killers, all changed their lives after reading the Book. Here are a few: a Japanese barber, who had been a drunkard, found copies of three Gospels on the sea-shore, washed up by the tide. He identified them as 'Jesus books', and took them to his shop thinking that they might be useful to his customers. When business was a bit dull, he began to read them himself. These Gospels, he reckoned, were sent specially for him. As a result, he gave up his drunken habits, believed and was baptized.[11] A San Salvadorian confessed:

I am an engineer by trade, and earn a very good salary. Seven years ago I fell prey to gambling, and have lost money at the rate of $25 per week, sometimes losing that amount at a single stroke. I played until I had scarcely clothes or boots to stand in, and yet all the time vowing that every game should be my last. I tried hard to give it up, but I could not, and all my resolutions were broken as soon as they were made. But a short time ago I bought a Bible from a Colporteur, and as soon as I read it, I felt a new power come into my life. Since then God, through this Book, has broken the awful power of gambling.[12]

[11] *Have Ye Never Read?: A Popular Report of the British and Foreign Bible Society 1912–1913* (London, The Bible House, 1913), pp. 95–6.
[12] *After a Hundred Years*, p. 68.

A rich merchant was so impressed by the story of Zacchaeus that he not only reduced the price of his merchandise but also organized a banquet for the poor in the neighbourhood.[13] In Java a rich opium farmer who used to adulterate the opium he sold gave it up altogether after reading the gospel.[14] In another incident, a man bought a knife to kill his enemy. The colporteur's attempt to dissuade him failed. In desperation, the colporteur took out his New Testament and read from it the sterner passages which threatened the wicked with destruction. On hearing this, the would-be killer abandoned his intention and returned home a changed man.[15]

In the Korean port of Fusan, a proprietress of a wine-shop, who feared neither God nor people, was so notorious that she was known as Jezebel. One day she came across a Gospel portion sold by a gracious little Biblewoman who ventured into her tavern. As the Biblewoman read the Johannine account of the women taken in sin, the Korean realized for the first time that the wages of her life would be death. At once she poured the remaining stock of wine into the drain, closed her shop and returned to her native village transformed.[16]

These stories demonstrate what the text does to readers. It induces them to focus on the need to cultivate moral purity both in their inner personal lives and through their public behaviour. Seized by the text, the reader seems to be emerging from a muddied moral wilderness and despicable delinquent practices with a clear and firm grasp of the distinction between good and evil. Apparently, the text not only disorients but also reorients the reader to embark upon a new way of life.

Cleansing of civilizations

The Bible was seen not only as transforming the lives of ordinary people but also as a catalyst in national and civilizational renewal. The reading of the Bible and conversion to

---

[13] *Like Unto Leaven: A Popular Illustrated Report of the British and Foreign Bible Society for the Year 1923–1924* (London, The Bible House, 1924), p. 82.
[14] *Have Ye Never Read?*, p. 96.   [15] *Like Unto Leaven*, p. 83.
[16] *Have Ye Never Read?*, p. 98.

Christianity were seen as positive steps in neutralizing the mental darkness of Africans and the oriental haughtiness of Asians. The Bible was perceived as providing agency for purifying customs, habits and social institutions. The case of England was projected as a prime example of how the Bible changed a culture. The Reports did not miss an opportunity to hammer home the point that it was the Bible which had made England a great nation. In the words of William Canton, who wrote a multi-volume history of the Society:

For those national traits which have given Britain its place in the world – hatred of falsehood, respect for law and order, love of fair play, reasonableness and a singular freedom from the passionate outbreaks that have marked so much of the history of other nations – we owe an incalculable debt to the Bible.[17]

The Reports repeat the admiring words of natives acknowledging this 'fact'. A South Indian brahmin claimed to have said: 'Where did the English people get all their intelligence and energy, and cleverness and power? It is their Bible that gives it to them. And now they bring it to us and say, "That is what raised us; take it, and raise yourselves."'[18] These attesting voices thus served to function on behalf of British interests and aspirations.

The Reports also mediated the supportive voices of natives who seemed to believe that the Bible was a perfect cure for all the ills of their cultures. Prince Bassey, Duke Ephraim IX of Calabar, is reported to have said: 'Without the Bible a nation is no nation. Every civilized country must have a Bible as its key.'[19] A Christian kaffir who addressed the summer meeting of LMS (London Missionary Society) in London told his audience:

When the Bible came to us we were naked; we lived in caves and on tops of the mountains; we painted our bodies with red paint. The Bible charmed us out of the caves, and from the top of the mountains. Now we know there is a God . . . I have travelled with the missionaries in taking the Bible to the Bushmen and other nations. When the Word of God was preached, the Bushman threw away his bow and

---

[17] *The Immortal Story* (London, The British and Foreign Bible Society, 1927), p. 76.
[18] *For the Healing of the Nations: A Popular Report of the British and Foreign Bible Society for the Year 1915–1916* (London, The Bible House, 1916), p. 70.
[19] *In the Vulgar Tongue*, p. 55.

arrows, the Kaffir threw away his shield. I went to Lattakoo, and they threw away their evil works, they threw away their assegais, and became children of God.[20]

A Bulgarian wrote to the Bible Society's superintendent that under the rule of the Sultan of Turkey his country had no language, no freedom and no literature. But the Bulgarian Bible had done a double service by 'giving language a fixed and standard form, the nation welcomed light and new life'. He went on to say that the 1879 Bulgarian Constitution, which was as liberal and democratic as an Anglo-Saxon Constitution, was influenced by the Bible.[21] The Bible thus offered not only personal salvation but also national redemption in the form of Western standards of manners, social behaviour, governance and sanitation. These corroborative utterances were used as a way of justifying a European presence, social dominance and social engineering.

THE COLPORTEUR'S BOOK

Colporteurs brought to the fore the power of the printed Word. The Bible may lie neglected, dust-covered on a shelf for months, its pages providing wrapping for a cigar or an item of food, but at an opportune moment it will speak a message that will transform a whole life. Colporteurs filed stories of how people came to faith by reading a mere fragment of a Bible or a scrap of a printed portion, discovered accidentally or under unusual circumstances. A Muslim sub-inspector of police, ill and confined to his bed, sent his servant to get him some food. The servant returned with food wrapped in a piece of printed paper on which were words that attracted the attention of the police inspector. The words were so wonderful that he kept the printed page with him in the hope that one day he would trace the book from which it had been torn. The local missionary relieved his curiosity by telling him from where it had come. The inspector immediately bought the book, read it, and that

[20] William Canton, *A History of the British and Foreign Bible Society*, vol. II (London, John Murray, 1904), p. 301.

[21] *The Common Bond* (London, The British and Foreign Bible Society, 1935), p. 91.

led to his conversion.[22] Another story was about a dog in China: a dog was rummaging through a pile of rubbish and came upon part of a book, which it carried it in its mouth and dropped at a camp near by. The soldiers who were at the camp were curious to know what it was and began to read the printed pages. The book was the Old Testament in Chinese, but it was torn, and the torn book was very incomplete. The soldiers guessed that it must have come from the missionary compound and asked for further pages. Dr Mary Stone, who was residing there, supplied them with the full version at least three times since the appetite among the Chinese soldiers was so unquenchable. The result was that a number of soldiers attended the mission service and became deeply interested in the gospel.[23]

The Bible which colporteurs sold was seen as a book which spoke decisively to people from diverse racial, theological and ideological backgrounds. It was a book for all, and anybody could find meaning in it and feel comfortable with it. At a time when denominational rivalries were very fierce, the Society Report set out to show that the Bible was the common bond which united and held together many branches of the Churches and diverse theological opinions: 'Catholic and Protestant, Anglican and Free Churchman, Ritualist and Quaker – all come together around the Bible.'[24] It was hawked as a book which supported differing ideologies like democracy and socialism. It was marketed as a book which gave birth to modern science. In Port Said, when a prospective buyer refused the Bible because it was against science, the colporteur replied: 'That's strange, because it was through studying science that I came to have faith in God and in the book.'[25] Free-thinkers and Freemasons, too, purchased the Book, the latter because the Book of Proverbs went back to King Solomon, the legendary founder of their craft.[26] By making it available and opening it to

---

[22] Ibid., p. 90.

[23] *The Bridge Builders: A Popular Report of the British and Foreign Bible Society for the Year 1922–1923* (London, The Bible House, 1923), p. 74.

[24] *The Common Bond*, p. 37.

[25] *In the Vulgar Tongue*, p. 95.

[26] *The Book Above Every Book* (London, The Bible House, 1910), pp. 95–6.

all, the Bible was seen as a book over which no group had proprietary rights.

In the Bible Society's propaganda, it was emphasized that for personal and national rejuvenation nothing was more critical, more fundamental and more determinative than reading the Bible. Everything else hinged upon it and emanated from it. The Bible was presented as the ultimate standard and measure for moral conduct. As a man in Rio told the colporteur, 'This book has been a moral doctor to me.'[27] It was seen as providing a set of rules for personal and national regeneration. The Bible became the site where the transforming event in a person's or nation's life was initiated and eventually carried through. The colporteur's Bible, at its most positive, functioned at the level of character formation and cultural revitalization.

The Reports were strewn with texts from throughout the Testaments and biblical writings. The Bible was presented as a single, self-contained, coherent text rather than as a compilation of sixty-six writings. The inter-testamental differences collapsed. The Bible was seen as conveying one message which reverberated through the entire corpus. Conceived as a single text, the Bible's internal contradictions were overlooked. The Bible was flattened. The divine authorship and divine purpose united the text of the entire canon. Since it was assumed that there was a single, divine author, any single text was deemed capable of representing the whole of the Bible. The Bible Society's intention was to move away from the practice of earlier generations whose hermeneutical imaginations centred around a few selected passages from the Bible. The Reformers focused on Pauline theology at the expense of other New Testament writings; the Puritans relied on the sacred history of Israel; some of the nineteenth-century Protestants went for the prophetic literature, while others opted for the Epistles to the Hebrews. But the Reports were unequivocal in their position: the business of the whole church was to 'teach the whole Bible'.[28] The intention

---

[27] *The Book and the Sword: A Popular Illustrated Report of the British and Foreign Bible Society for the Year 1914–1915* (London, The Bible House, 1915), p. 86.
[28] *For Such a Time as This: A Popular Report of the British and Foreign Bible Society for the Year 1917–1918* (London, The Bible House, 1918), p. 2.

was to give equal importance and authority to all passages in the Bible. Any text was deemed to be an integral part of the whole canon. Each text was seen as contributing to the essence of the whole. As a consequence, almost anything could be justified with one passage or another.

CHANGED BY THE TEXT

The exciting stories that colporteurs filed tell of the effect the biblical texts had on people who bought and read them. Texts created an emotionally ambivalent impact: on the one hand, they provided encouragement, confidence, hope and a change of perspective to those who found them meaningful; on the other, they produced a negative effect and created fear and rejection in those who resisted them.

Those who despised the Bible were branded as 'careless, profligate and proud', whereas those who benefited from it were hailed as having 'the inquiring mind and the anxious spirit'.[29] The Reports took cases of rejection as illustrations of the hardness of the people's hearts and duly recorded them. A Hindu who read the Book of Ruth complained: 'Sir, why do you have such a book as this in your Bible? The story seems to describe a widow remarrying. If our Indian women read this all the widows will want to marry. Then what a hopeless condition will result!'[30] In Cairo, a Muslim who started reading the scriptures confessed: 'This book condemns many things that I do. It goes against my will and my actions.' A Singhalese goldsmith who bought a copy of the Book of Proverbs was uneasy when he read the eleventh chapter: 'A false balance is an abomination to the Lord: but a just weight is His delight.' At once he flung the book away, declaring that as it was quite against the trade he would never read it.[31] A Persian bought the Book but when he heard that it was the Word of God, he put it down with the words: 'I will not take it, for if I do, I shall no longer be able to commit robbery.'[32] The texts make clear the

---

[29] Browne, *History of the British and Foreign Bible Society*, II, pp. 204–5.
[30] *The Immortal Story*, p. 62.   [31] *The Book Above Every Book*, p. 71.
[32] *For the Healing of the Nations*, p. 55.

need for repentance, and make their readers explore their personal lives.

Colporteurs' stories make it clear that the reading of the Bible effects instant behavioural change in people and show that the authority of the text is so strong that there is no choice but to submit to it. One need not read the whole Bible; even a phrase will be enough to provoke one to change one's life. There is a magic and irresistibility about the texts. A young Chinese named Liu was led to the Lord because he simply remembered the phrase 'a crown of life' from a text: 'I have fought a good fight, I have finished my course; I have kept the faith; henceforth there is laid up for me a crown of righteousness, which the Lord, the righteous judge, shall give me at that day: and not to me only, but unto all them also that love His appearing.'[33]

The text is held in high esteem because of what it exists to do, namely, to be put into practice and gradually to be interwoven into the fabric of personal lives. The underlying hermeneutical assumption is that if one does what the text enjoins, one will conform to biblical Christianity. The ethical interpretation is prominent: texts elicit a vigilantly moralistic stance; they effect behavioural changes leading to spiritual elevation. What is important is the practical obligation, which leads the reader to evangelical integrity and Christian authenticity. The colporteurs made sure that the text was read, that it was put into practice and that the benefits of the changed lives were conveyed to others. Hermeneutics is not the unfolding of the meaning of the texts but the enacting in practice of what they demand. The text is important because it plays a significant part in effecting transformation in the personal lives of people. It unleashes power when it grips a morally sensitive reader.

It is evident from the colporteurs' stories that those who accepted the Bible appropriated it at the level of the literal, plain and obvious meaning of the text. It is the literal sense that conveys the true meaning. It is simply a matter of reading it, finding its true meaning and understanding what it conveys.

---

[33] *The Common Bond*, p. 91.

There is no acknowledgement that biblical texts might be unclear or contradictory. The colporteurs' Bible was error-free; it took no account of complexity and of the mixture of theologies and histories. The Society's insistence on the literal meaning of the text reifies the view of the Bible promoted by the Reformation. It was the Reformers who had rejected the precritical fourfold meaning of the text for a literal meaning. The stories do not show any sign that the Bible could have had more than one meaning and that it could be appropriated at different levels – spiritual, allegorical, historical and typological. The text can mean only one thing, and alternative renderings are implausible and even impossible. The surplus or excess meaning that current hermeneutical theorists espouse is ruled out. The text is essentially seen as authorially controlled, historically determined and theologically defined. The text as fluid, mutable and subject to endless rereading by readers is inconceivable.

In another respect also, the Society's relation to the Bible stands within the Reformation tradition. Scripture is so perspicuous that an unbiased, simple human being who pays attention to its words should be able to grasp its meaning. The Reformers had always argued that the magisterium of the church was unnecessary for an understanding of the basic message of the Bible. They created the myth that simple people freed from any ecclesiastical intervention were safe guides to its meaning. The colporteurs reinforced this by ceaselessly providing stories of people who learned the message of God's redeeming love by simply reading about it for themselves. An Abyssinian Bible reader remarked: 'First we heard about the Bible; then we saw it, but we did not like it; by and by we came to realize that such a Book could be understood even without a teacher.'[34] In a Karen village, when a missionary, after reading the Sermon on the Mount, set about explaining the meaning of the words he had just read, he was interrupted by the chief who said: 'Please, sir, we do not want *your* words; we want the words of the

---

[34] *Have Ye Never Read?*, pp. 98–9.

book.'[35] The following dialogue between a Javanese colporteur
and a local person captures in essence the approach of the Bible
Society:

'Have you been taught the Christian Gospel?'
'Yes, Sir.'
'Who taught you?'
'Nobody.'
'How is that? I suppose you had a Javanese teacher.'
'No, sir, our only teacher was Luke.'
'Who is Luke?'
'The writer of the Gospel we bought some years ago.'[36]

These stories reinforced the Protestant notion that comprehen-
sion of the scriptures depended essentially on the inward
attitude of the reader.

Biblical verses are regularly detached from their immediate
or narrativel context. There is no effort to place the texts in
their historical, literary or social contexts. Nor is there any
acknowledgement that these texts have their own interpretative
history, where over the years various redactors have added or
deleted words. Put at its simplest, the text is read at the redacted
level. Glib connections are made with the text as a ruse for
selling the books. Seeing two carpenters making a ladder, a
colporteur approaches them and reads them the story of Jacob's
vision at Bethel and of the ladder which reached up to the
heavens. The carpenters were so charmed with the narrative
that they immediately purchased the book.[37] There is a reluctance to converse with and interrogate the text. The underlying
implication is that excessive questioning may inevitably lead
one away from the simple task of putting the text into practice.
There is a hesitation to delve too deeply into theoretical meanings. When a Chinese inquirer was puzzled about the great
vision in the Book of Daniel depicting heads of gold, shoulders
of silver and feet of iron and clay, and wanted clarification, the
colporteur sidetracked him by quizzing the inquirer on his

---

[35] *A Fountain Unsealed: A Popular Report of the British and Foreign Bible Society 1910–1911*
(London, The Bible House, 1911), pp. 95–6.
[36] *Our Heritage* (London, The British and Foreign Bible Society, 1934), p. 66.
[37] *In the Vulgar Tongue*, p. 93.

gospel knowledge. What is advocated is to pay attention to a text's practical demands, which sometimes have serious and painful consequences. For instance, a Japanese gambler, when he read the passage, 'if thy right hand offend thee, cut it off', realized that the last joint of the third finger of his right hand had been the offending part, and cut it off.[38] If one wants to unravel the mysteries of the text, there is no better way than by performing it and realizing it in one's own life, even if a single verse is going to bring pain.

The selection of texts reported by the colporteurs is interesting. They rarely mention those which deal with historical or doctrinal matters. The important ones for them are directly related to morality and ethics. Thus the sayings of Jesus and the ethical passages from the Hebrew Scriptures are given equal weight. Psalm 23, the Book of Proverbs and the Parable of the Prodigal Son are projected as having the same hermeneutical purchase. It is interesting to note what texts impressed particular people and attracted them to Christianity. Asked by a colporteur through which missionary agency he had become a Christian, a Chinese convert replied that it was through simply reading a passage in the Bible given him by a woman. The Chinese went on to say that he had felt despair at the uncertainties and disorders in the world, but reading the passage in Revelation 21 which pictured the holy city, new Jerusalem, coming down out of heaven from God, gave him hope and led to his conversion.[39] A Jew in Tangier, who was proficient in Arabic, found that the Arabic version did not come up to the mark and offered himself to do some translating. Taking him at his word, the Society asked him to translate a passage of the Hebrew Scripture. His translating of the Isaian verse, 'He was bruised for our iniquities' (Is. 53), resulted in his becoming a Christian.[40]

An important characteristic of the Society's Reports was that interpretation was seen as a lone task, an enterprise undertaken

---

[38] *A Fountain Unsealed*, p. 68.
[39] *Building the City: A Popular Report of the British and Foreign Bible Society 1921–1922* (London, The Bible House, 1922), p. 69.
[40] Ibid., p. 63.

by a solitary reader engaging with an isolated text. Thus, interpretation becomes a privately concocted and self-serving act, and the meaning of a text becomes the vested property of separate individuals. The Evangelical tradition stressed personal encounter and the importance of individual response. Here, the encounter was not with the risen Lord but with the written Word. In one sense, the reader does not read the text, but is read by it. It is the text which interprets life. The reader is not led by logical steps to a belief in God, but is assailed by the text which, by way of shock, disorientation and disjuncture, prepares him or her for a new awareness. A person is not so much liberated as tamed by the text. The saving knowledge is not seen as a groaning or a travailing leading to awareness of the immanence or transcendence of the divine, as envisaged by Paul in his writings, but almost as a possession and invasion by textual truth. The role of the scriptures is to assist in this illumination and enlightenment. Biblical verses assume authority not because of their theological import or historical authenticity, but because of their power to mould, challenge, control and illuminate the lives of peoples and cultures.

The Bible is portrayed as providing guidance and a safeguard against irresponsible living. One's former life is equated with irresponsibility and a wayward existence which have given way to upright and obedient living. Deliverance is seen as a divesting of former bad habits. These conversion stories are distinctive in that people are attracted to biblical faith because of its ability to change their immoral behaviour.

What we see here is a minimalist hermeneutic at work. It implies that, at best, interpretation is no interpretation at all but an enactment of the Word in people's lives. What is advocated is not even a minimal degree of interpretation, but an active re-enactment of the scriptural words in their day-to-day activities. Each text is clear and changes the lives of people. Simple answers are to be found in the texts for life's complex problems. Interpretation is not a process of drawing out meaning from the text, but a situation one is thrust into. Texts are seen as enforcing moral change and holiness of life. Interpretation is to remain faithful to the Bible's injunctions and moral precepts.

The idea that reading the Bible helps one's theological formation is thoroughly antithetical to the Bible Society's way of
thinking. The reading of scripture does not lead one to systematize Christian doctrines. What is crucial is the saving knowledge embedded in the text and how it is translated into
everyday life.

There is also a sort of hermeneutical circle at work here but
not like the one envisaged by the Latin American liberation
theologian, Segundo.[41] Biblical texts serve as inspiration for
good Christian living and are adapted to accomplish this.
However, certain practices and attitudes are highly valued as
necessary for Christian living and these are confirmed through
reference to the biblical passages. Colporteurs were very clear
as to when the circle began. In the colporteurs' version of the
hermeneutical circle, the Bible is seen as the source of praxis,
and then praxis is clarified and accomplished to meet the
demands of the texts.

OMENS OUT OF THE BOOK: NON-READERLY USE AND
NON-TEXTUAL ATTITUDES

Though the colporteurs' Reports attempt to incorporate into
the narrative the triumph of biblical Christianity, the 'heathen'
often refused to play along with the role assigned to them. The
Bible is frequently sought after by people for purposes other
than reading only, the sole purpose for which the Bible Society
was marketing it. Colporteurs' stories contain instances of
peoples' attachment to a Bible or a Gospel portion as an object
rather than for the meaning of its content. A Brazilian woman
confessed that she did not 'buy the Book to read it, but because
of its beautiful binding'.[42] Likewise it was purchased by large
numbers of people who saw it more as a numinous artefact to
be revered, its benefits perceived as beyond the advantages of
reading. It was bought not so much for the theological truth it
contained, namely the detailed account of God's redeeming

---

[41] For Segundo's proposal see chapter 7.   [42] *A Fountain Unsealed*, p. 93.

activity, but because of its magical, mystical and transcendental properties.

In spite of heavy authorial selection and redaction, the Reports do provide a number of examples of the 'heathen' reversing the purposes for which the Bible was intended. There are a number of ways in which the Bible was put to uses unforeseen by the Bible Society. The Bible was revered as a sacred object which protected people. At Timuen a father and son had been called out to serve in the reserves. The father, receiving the gospel from a colporteur, said to his son: 'Kiss this Book.' Then calling his wife, who was waiting near, he handed her the copy, saying: 'See, this Book will take our place; it will bring comfort. Do thou draw consolation and hope from it. Remember also [to] be grateful to the English society which is so good as to give it to thee.'[43] Similarly, during the Chinese revolution, Colporteur Li was shot at by soldiers but took out a Gospel and waved it; the soldiers recognized the book and the firing ceased.[44] It had a powerful talismatic effect on the imagination of the buyer because it had considerable meaning beyond the benefits of practical reading.

The Book thus served as a fetishized commodity which brought good luck or warded off evil. In Sri Lankan Tamil homes, scripture portions were carefully suspended from the roof near a sick person.[45] It was often used as a talisman or an amulet. In Bohemia a woman was prepared to buy a copy of the Bible if the colporteur could guarantee that her goat would give more milk. In Belgium a woman told the colporteur, Teutsch, that, since reading portions from St Matthew's Gospel, her children had had no whooping-cough, and she went on to tell him: 'Now I possess the complete book, I shall be able to read in St John's Gospel during thunderstorms; no evil can befall me then.'[46] Another wanted Bibles to be put under the tiles of his house, 'so that they may keep off sun strokes, suffering and

---

[43] *Seed Corn for the World: A Popular Report of the British and Foreign Bible Society for the Year 1904–1905* (London, The Bible House, 1905), p. 79.

[44] *Have Ye Never Read?*, p. 61.

[45] Canton, *History of the British and Foreign Bible Society*, II, p. 384.

[46] *In the Mother Tongue* (London, The British and Foreign Bible Society, 1930), p. 71.

sickness'.[47] A Greek wrote: 'Respectfully I have the honour to inform you that I want you to make New Testaments in the Abyssinian language in a very small size, to be used as charms against the devil, for the Abyssinians.'[48] In Chile, as a cure for her lung disease, a woman was recommended to burn the Bible and smoke its ashes.[49] The Bible often played the role that the relics of the monks had during the medieval period – a fetishized commodity now purchasable at a cheaper rate with incalculable spiritual benefits.

The Bible was often purchased for curious, unexpected reasons and with mixed motives. Justice Ranade, one of the most eminent personalities in the then Bombay Presidency, used it as a tool, reading the New Testament with his wife to teach her English.[50] In Serbia, grammar books quoted illustrations from the Bible as examples of good grammatical construction.[51] In North Africa a Frenchman who read Renan's *Life of Jesus* wanted to read the New Testament to check the veracity of the apostolic account.[52] In Algiers a wealthy Jew purchased a copy of the Bible to find out how to divide property in a case of divorce. A veterinary surgeon bought it to find out what it had to say about diseases in horses and mules.[53] Some women who were temple worshippers in Shantung bought portions of the Bible to be used as a safe place to keep their shoe-patterns.[54] A Japanese student who was studying Ruskin's *Sesame and Lilies* started to read the Bible as a way of understanding Ruskin, whose work contained many references to the Bible.[55] These dissenting and often anarchic hermeneutical acts escape their true context but remain embedded in the Society's Reports, which in other respects rhapsodize about the benefits of a simple reading of the Bible. What these hermeneutical 'misuses'

---

[47] *Rebuilding on the Rock: A Popular Report of the British and Foreign Bible Society for the Year 1918–1919* (London, The Bible House, 1919), p. 74.

[48] Ibid., p. 75.   [49] *A Fountain Unsealed*, p. 92.

[50] *The Book of God's Kingdom: A Popular Illustrated Report of the British and Foreign Bible Society 1901–1902* (London, The Bible House, 1902), p. 65.

[51] *Rebuilding on the Rock*, p. 18.   [52] *Have Ye Never Read?*, p. 95.

[53] *Rebuilding on the Rock*, p. 74.

[54] *The Highway in the Wilderness: A Popular Illustrated Report of the British and Foreign Bible Society for the Year 1907–1908* (London, The Bible House, 1908), p. 84.

[55] *A Fountain Unsealed*, p. 93.

indicate is that the promoters of the Bible did not encounter a docile set of natives who could be manipulated at will to reflect the agenda of the Bible Society.

The Christian Bible had a far more significant place in the life of a practising Christian, at least in the Protestant tradition, than did scriptures in the home-life of other faith traditions. While reading and possessing the Bible was central to Protestant Christianity, in other religious traditions, such as Hinduism, access to a sacred text was limited 'not only to specific persons but also to persons in specific conditions – to the twice-born male who had entered a ritually pure state'.[56] These scripture portions were received by the natives both as a rare artefact and a numinous book to be venerated and were accorded the status of a household deity. Like the Hindu's *ishta devata*, scripture represented the nearness of God, and God's protecting care. The role of the simple, universal Word of God was being complicated by being given a place among many household gods. The colonial Book has been resisted as such, reconstituted and placed on an altogether different plane. In the process the univocal Book becomes ambiguous. By making the Christian Scripture a physical object which commands and deserves veneration just like any of their household deities, the colonial Book does not lose its power and presence but comes to be misread and mishandled. In Homi Bhabha's words: 'The book retains its presence. But it is no longer a representation of an essence; it is now a partial presence, a strategic device in a specific colonial engagement, an appurtenance of authority.'[57] What we see here is the strength of the colonial subjects to question and interrogate the English Book in ways other than primarily intended and to put it to use in ways not anticipated by the Bible Society. By appropriating the Bible in their own way, they pose 'questions of authority that the authorities – the Bible included, cannot answer'.[58] Homi Bhabha sees these as

---

[56] Philip Lutgendorf, *The Life of a Text: Performing the Rāmcaritmānas of Tulsidas* (Berkeley, University of California Press, 1991), p. 56.

[57] Homi K. Bhabha, *The Location of Culture* (London, Routledge, 1994), pp. 114–15.

[58] Ibid., p. 115.

'strategies of subversion that turn the gaze of the discriminated back upon the eye of the power'.[59]

COLPORTEURS AND THEIR COLLUSION

The picture we get of colporteurs is that of affectionate, harmless persons, always displaying kindness, dignity and trust. They are portrayed as displaying heroic qualities – resilience, physical hardihood and intrepidity. Their reputation for piety, patience, zeal and self-denying labour was part of their success story. Though these colporteurs were drawn from many nationalities and cultures, the Reports sanitize their national specificities and present them in the image of a rugged Britisher. They come to represent the rational and progressive values of the West. The image we get is that of English virtues of pluckiness and decency, attachment to duty, responsibility and, most importantly, the British sense of humour. The last takes a rather ponderous form: A drunkard told the colporteur: 'I don't want your God, for my God is drink.' The colporteur told him: 'It is a pity that you do not imitate your god, for wine gets better as it gets older, while you get steadily worse.'[60]

The Reports were scrupulous in maintaining the image of a colporteur as one above politics and controversy. The Bible Society's claim was that 'like the Gospel it circulates, it takes no account of political or national divisions'.[61] It was proud of its colporteurs and their non-engagement in politics. They were commended for their neutral, peaceable and exemplary conduct. When asked to address controversial questions such as independence for India, or their views on Gandhi, or why the British were rich and powerful, or why the British held dominion over India and Burma, the colporteurs, ever loyal to their instructions, while eloquent in extolling the virtues of the Bible, often maintained an uncharacteristic silence. When pressed hard for an answer, they resorted to the easy way out, perhaps the only answer they knew, by quoting the saying of

[59] Ibid., p. 112.   [60] *The Book of God's Kingdom*, p. 34.
[61] *Goodwill Toward Men: A Popular Report of the British and Foreign Bible Society for the Year 1920–1921* (London, The Bible House, 1921), p. 18.

Jesus from the Book: 'My kingdom is not of this world, else would My servants fight.'[62] Though the Bible Society claimed neutrality, it was, however, severe against socialist teaching. It warned its readers:

On the continent of Europe, the weight of social hardships and miseries and the iron pressure of militarism have driven multitudes to enter the ranks of Socialism. Englishmen often forget that, outside England, these, 'collectivist' dogmas involve far more than an economic theory or a political programme – as to which the Bible Society stands entirely neutral. The propaganda of Continental Socialism is based on a definitely materialist creed, with secular standards and ideals of life. A foreign Socialist is generally un-Christian, and often fiercely anti-Christian, confronting the Bible with scorn and blasphemy.[63]

Socialists were seen as bitter opponents of the Bible. At Budapest, when a social democrat denounced the Bible as 'poison', the answer the colporteur gave was: 'if the Bible be poison, it is only an anti-toxin against ungodliness and sin'.[64]

Judging by these Reports, it appears that, consciously or unconsciously, these colporteurs had been coopted and had become the mouthpiece of the Society. Whenever they enter the narratives, they reflect the ideals and common concerns of their employers. At the time when the Bible Society was massively disseminating its Bibles, historical criticism was at its height in Europe. The Society dismissed this: 'Most of the problems over which scholars dispute have little practical bearing upon the spiritual content and authority of the New Testament. Plain men still meet God in these pages as they meet Him nowhere else.'[65] Colporteurs' stories of how ordinary people encountered their salvation by mere reading of the Bible, undisturbed by modern biblical theories, helped the Society to withstand the erosion of the authority of the Bible which it attributed to the advent of critical scholarship.

The colporteurs were also successful in implementing the Society's aim of placing immense weight on the text itself as the

---

[62] *In the Mother Tongue*, p. 69.
[63] *Behold a Sower: A Popular Illustrated Report of the British and Foreign Bible Society for the Year 1900–1901* (London, The Bible House, 1901), p. 60.
[64] *Have Ye Never Read?*, p. 40.   [65] *More Golden than Gold*, p. 12.

means to instruct the readers. True to the Society's Protestant tradition they accorded the right of interpretation to the individual. To the Society, it was not the correct ecclesiastical interpretation that mattered, but the place of the texts in the hearts and lives of men and women. In line with the Society's approach, the colporteurs privileged individual over institutional reading.

They also went along with the Society's idea that there was a mass of people out there who had a great desire to read the Bible. The Reports regale their readers with peoples' unquenchable thirst for the word of God. A colporteur wrote from Sri Lanka, then Ceylon, 'The people are ready – able to read and willing to buy.'[66] A Persian colporteur tells of a person who walked ten miles in order to buy a copy for himself, and another tells of an African who waited for thirty years to get hold of a Testament. A wife complained that the expenditure on paraffin oil had gone up ever since her husband had started to read the Bible in the night. An account from Sri Lanka captures the essence of what the Bible Society and its subscribers wanted to hear:

I held service for them in the house, and when I came to the reading of the lesson I took up the big Tamil Bible from the table. It almost fell to pieces in my hands. I turned its pages: they were worn and marked and scored until parts were almost illegible . . . Scattered about Ceylon there must be many solitary Christians like these, who, with but rare opportunities for Church worship and fellowship, find in the vernacular Scriptures a means of grace sufficient to keep them steadfast and separate and faithful to their Lord.[67]

The colporteurs connived with the colonial enterprise of affirming a fraternal bond between the colonizer and colonized. They seem generally to have shared the priorities of the Bible Society: to make the Bible available in all the languages of the world and easily accessible to all; to instil a sense of pride in the Empire; to portray the Bible Society as God's agent; to inform its audience that, through the agency of the Bible, various benighted subjects of the British Empire had acquired Protestant values and attributes; to secure the commitment and

[66] *The Bridge Builders*, p. 52.   [67] *More Golden than Gold*, p. 101.

support of the subscribers; and to make the recipients grateful
to the Bible Society and the English people for disseminating
the gospel to those who greatly needed it.

The work of colporteurs and their spectacular stories inspired
the readers and the subscribers back in England to support the
Society's work; they were manifestly successful in promoting
the colonies as fertile fields for sowing the seeds of the gospel.

CONSTRUCTION OF RACIAL IMAGES

The Society's Reports made much of the fact that the British
Empire embraced a great variety of peoples and places, and
these dominated peoples could be summoned to support the
ethos and values of the Society. This did not prevent them from
offering images tailored to meet the Society's biblicizing priorities. Their depictions of people are often one-dimensional and
self-serving. In these they played on and conformed to current
images. The Reports indicate a variety of imperial perceptions.
India was seen as immobilized by poverty and ignorance and
indifferent to its own people's suffering. Such a representation
of India helped to validate the structures of government and
administration which developed under the Raj. The imperial
presence was seen as putting an end to the inter-tribal wars of
old and laying a foundation of Empire 'amid the chaotic ruins
of Aurangazeb'.[68] China was presented as inflexible, non-
progressive, closed and paralysed by rigid customs, aloof from
other peoples and nations. Because of her haughty imperial
past, China was seen as a place which needed taming. The
Reports identified a number of colonial 'bogeymen' who
needed to be domesticated. In Africa, it was the witch doctor
who was seen as the enemy of progress. In China and India, it
was the priest, in the case of the latter especially the Brahmin
priest, who was seen as obstructive to progress. There is little
sympathy in these Reports for prevailing social and economic
conditions.

Each nationality enters the text to fulfil the imperial ambitions

[68] *The Book of God's Kingdom*, p. 56.

of the Bible Society. The inhabitants of the Empire are presented as pliable in accommodating the purposes of the Society. They do not lead normal lives and are morally suspect, spiritually retarded and materially weak. In these controlled textual spaces, the names of these people are rarely mentioned, though often their social position is described. These potential converts are seen as living and working within corrupt and often complex social and religious contexts from which they need to be isolated, rescued and rehabilitated. In these stories, the readers encounter colonial subjects who are presented essentially as needing European support and protection.

Their attitude to racial stereotyping is ambivalent. On the one hand, they replicate the negative images to justify intervening in the name of civilization, but on the other they make use of these images as a convenient vehicle for promoting the gospel. While Kilgour, a translator for the Society, found it tedious and arduous to translate the ritual regulations of Leviticus, his Nepali assistant found them the most interesting and important part of the Pentateuch because of the Nepalese liking for rites and ceremonies. The Chinese, who revere their ancestors, found the genealogy of St Matthew impressive. Racial and cultural traits were seen as potential propagators for the gospel.

Though readers enjoy the stories set in exotic contexts and the dramatic ways in which the Bible is changing the lives of people, these will not make any sense to the reading public back at home unless they are made to feel that they are participating in momentous historic changes. This was achieved in two ways: first, by endlessly repeating the stories of ever-grateful natives; and secondly, by reminding readers of the high moral role played by the British in the emancipation of the slaves.

The Reports are full of testimonies of ever-grateful natives praising the Society's work: 'I want to thank the Bible Society for the great work that it is doing towards the furtherance of the Gospel.'[69] The British campaign to save Africa from the horrors of slavery is worked into the narrative to encourage

---

[69] *The Highway in the Wilderness*, p. 84.

readers to continue their commitment to the uplifting and improving of vulnerable people. Africa is repeatedly shown as being receptive to and grateful for the humanistic efforts of the anti-slavery movement.

Though continuing to provide damaging stereotypical images of Africans, the underlying message that these Reports offered to the reading public was that, given the chance, the African soul was open to the gospel and redeemable. Africans, however degraded they are, are capable of salvation. Such a perception, viewed against the colonial portrayals of the time, which stressed the animal properties of Africans, was a decidedly positive one. Unlike the European slave merchants, who portrayed them as apes, these Reports viewed Africans as children who needed Christian moral values to realize their real human potential. It gave the readers a sense of understanding, if not respect for Africans. It was their faith in the destinies of 'half-savage tribes' that made them render the scriptures into what the Reports called the 'uncouth and unwritten dialect'[70] of these people. Excited at receiving the Bible in his own language, an African testified: 'I thought He (i.e God) knew the white man's speech only, but He has spoken in our language.'[71] The Bible Society believed that Africans could be rescued by making 'the Book in the speech in which they were born'.[72]

Though these Reports clearly enunciate moral and cultural differences between christianized Europe and the superstitious and polytheistic inhabitants of the far-flung territories, the purpose was not to marginalize or alienate the latter. Their beliefs and practices were denigrated, but the Reports painted a favourable picture for its readers of how, given the chance, people of other faiths would readily and happily shift religious allegiances. The ultimate aim was to convert and eventually incorporate these people, rather than to establish a distinction based on theological, cultural and racial lines. On the one hand, the hermeneutical strategy of these Reports was to project a sense that the Bible was being sympathetically welcomed,

---

[70] *For the Healing of the Nations*, p. 10.
[71] *Tell the World* (London, The British and Foreign Bible Society, 1933), p. 64.
[72] *The Book Above Every Book*, p. 36.

and on the other, their telelogical motive was to bring diverse
and disparate peoples under the influence of Christ in the name
of a common humanity.

The stories of the colporteurs make it clear that, for the
spreading and consolidation of Christian faith, the written Word
and a textualized faith are essential. There were two paramount
reasons for this: first, the supply of the printed word was
indispensable to build up converts and train native preachers
and teachers. In the words of the1908/9 Report: 'Unless a
Christianized people possess the Bible and live by the Bible,
neither the individual believers nor the Church as whole can
ever arrive at maturity and strength.'[73] More significantly, the
printed word was celebrated for its eternal efficacy. Sermons,
missionary addresses, teachings, all may perish but the printed
word remains. As one Report put it, a book 'may be taken up
and read and re-read many a time'.[74] The word of God has now
become practical and portable. Secondly, the Bible had self-
instructive potential. The vernacular Bible is seen as sustaining
people when they are faced with persecution and under trial.
To illustrate this, the Reports provide examples from mission
history. They keep on repeating the case of Madagascar and
Basutoland, where the Church survived persecution because
the local converts possessed Bibles in their mother-tongue.
Bereft of missionaries, ministers and all else, they possessed only
the Bible and drew from its pages peace and comfort when they
endured hardship and persecutions. As a telling proof, the
Report provides the example of some Kalagari Hottentots who
survived war and managed to keep up their Christian faith.
When a chief was asked whether they had a minister to help, he
replied: 'No, but one of us can read, and as we managed to save
one New Testament we built a church, and there for the sixteen
years we have met every Sunday to listen to him reading the

[73] *The Word Among the Nations: A Popular Illustrated Report of the British and Foreign Bible
Society for the Year 1908–1909* (London, The Bible House, 1909), p. 32.
[74] *The Bridge Builders*, p. 52.

Word of God to us.'[75] The Reports make it abundantly clear that people may be deprived of ecclesiastical dispensations such as sacraments and preaching but 'it is the study of the Scripture which maintains and intensifies the spiritual life'.[76] Reading was invested with special self-transformative powers. Reading had now become the new state of grace.

Colporteurs made lofty claims for the Bible. Western civilization, modern science and medicine, democracy, socialism and the abolition of slavery were all claimed to be the result of biblical teaching.

There is an effort to fashion an awareness of a particular type of biblical Christianity in which other sacred texts, oral stories and religious systems are discredited, and biblical vision is upheld. The Reports supported the view that 'most ancient books are dead, or dormant'.[77] The Arabic Koran was seen as archaic, obscure in style and a sealed book even to Arabic-speaking people. A Hindu women confessed: 'In our religion there is nothing to give peace to the mind when we are in trouble, but in your religion there are words to comfort the heart. Your words are good; since hearing them peace has entered my heart.'[78] The Bible is seen as passing judgement on other sacred textual traditions. The Report cites the words of Samuel Marinus Zwemer, Professor of the History of Religions and Christian Mission at Princeton, as authoritative:

The Bible is at once our strongest weapon of conquest, and our most inoffensive method for constructive work. The Bible strikes at the very root of Islam by placing the sublime story of the life of our Saviour over against the artificial halo that surrounds the popular lives of Mahomet. No Moslem can read the Sermon on the Mount without seeing in it an indictment of popular Islam.[79]

Like the stories of Africa, Asia and the Pacific, the stories of the dissemination of the Bible in Europe involve their own kinds of theological and cultural confrontation. European stories offer supporters of the Bible Society a different set of enemies to be confronted – socialism, libertarianism, secularism and, of

---

[75] *The Immortal Story*, p. 75.   [76] Ibid., p. 74.   [77] *Building the City*, p. 57.
[78] *A Fountain Unsealed*, p. 83.   [79] *For the Healing of the Nations*, p. 30.

course, the Romish intolerance. These Reports urged Protestant forces to unite against these common external enemies.

While these Reports treated their home readers to stories of the benighted heathen acquiring valuable Protestant characteristics through the agency of the Bible, in a way they distracted their readers from the Bible Society's more mundane concern to sustain its funds. Firstly, these tales of exotic places and adventurous activities drew the readers' attention away from the fact that the Society had to function as a business, using business methods in order to sustain its work. As we saw in chapter two, its secretary, John Owen, modelled it on Lloyds of London. Sue Zemka, in her study of the Society's strategies, comments: 'In discourse as well as in practice, the Bible Society merged Protestant ideology with the economic rubric and the developing market mechanisms of capitalism.'[80] The Society was in essence a thoroughly Victorian colonial undertaking, successfully combining moral conviction with mercantile methods.

Secondly, the Reports gloss over the Bible Society's advocacy of entrepreneurship and its benefits. They provided a steady diet of information about commercial success contemporaneous with the introduction of the gospel. The 1921 Report notes: 'The natives of its islands (the Pacific), some of whom are still savages and cannibals, are being brought into closer touch with civilization and *commerce*. A vast responsibility rests upon the Christian Church; for unless Christian teaching advances side by side with the *trader*, the consequences will be disastrous for the natives.'[81] The Report also claims that this polyglot region was being effectively civilized through the supply of the Bible in seventy different languages. The reason for the injection of the gospel message was to promote a morality to accompany expanding commercial interests.

Thirdly, the Reports as a whole leave out British dependency on the colonies and the wealth they generated. They underplay

---

[80] Sue Zemka, *Victorian Testaments: The Bible, Christology, and Literary Authority in Early-Nineteenth-Century British Culture* (Stanford, CA, Stanford University Press, 1997), p. 206.

[81] *Goodwill Toward Men*, p. 35; italics mine.

the mercantile role of the British Empire, and its expansionist intentions. The temptations and the corruption which came with it are overlooked, but they emphasize the law and order the Empire claimed to have established. The Reports leave no doubt in the minds of their English readers that Africans, Indians, Chinese and countless other colonized peoples were fortunate to enjoy the security and opportunities offered by English rule. They were beneficiaries of the imperial system. In a way, these Reports helped to avoid possible negative impressions of the Empire, and projected an image of a happy family drawn together under English rule – a corporate undertaking mutually benefiting all. These Reports never discuss the colonial strands in the biblical narrative or its alignment to and reinforcement of colonial intentions and purposes.

A penultimate point: the explosive distribution of Bibles and Gospel portions had fateful consequences. The attempt to put the Bible in every household and make it visible in every market place reduced this extraordinary book to an ordinary one. As we have seen, the Bibles were bought for mixed reasons – merchants using them as cheap wrapping paper, and ordinary people for their ornamental or talismatic value. Thus, what the Bible Society promoted as an uncommon book became common and unremarkable. The easy availability of the printed sacred Word eventually started a trend among other religions to produce their own scriptures in a cheap printed format. In preparing a critical edition of the Hindu epic the *Mahabharata*, Sukthankar claimed: 'Great Britain is a small nation, a young nation, compared to India. And our love of knowledge, love of literature, love of scriptures, is greater. We are the inheritors of the great book, this "book of books" composed at a time when Great Britain was not yet entered on the map of civilised nations.'[82] The Arya Samaj published in 1909 *The Fountainhead of Religion* to demonstrate the superiority of the Vedas, presenting it to graduates 'as an intentional counterpart to the

---

[82] Cited in Peter van der Veer, 'Monumental Texts: The Critical Edition of India's National Heritage', in *Invoking the Past: The Uses of History in South Asia*, ed. Daud Ali (New Delhi, Oxford University Press), p. 140.

presentation of Bibles'.[83] The Christian Bible, far from being a unique, pure and sacred text, not only was now open to all kinds of unholy usages but also faced fierce competition from other sacred texts.

The Bible Society's Reports acted as brokers of cultural representation. They brought to English homes distant peoples who were culturally, historically, geographically and theologically different. Like the travel writings of the period, these Reports transported their readers to various parts of the world, from Australia to Brazil and from Siberia to South Africa. The mapping of peoples and places was a Victorian activity. It was based on the social Darwinist notions of race prevalent at that time. The Reports embedded familiar stereotypes – Maoris as cannibals, Africans as savages, Indians as benighted heathen and Chinese as haughty and proud. They reinforced the Western fascination and preoccupation with the Other. These exotic peoples were brought into the English parlour. The Reports contained information on forms of transport, vignettes, personal stories, anecdotes about lands, people and places. These reassured people back at home that it was England's right to rule, and that the peoples of the Empire were the beneficiaries of such a rule. They discredited the values and customs of other people; they endorsed the necessity for the imperial presence and Christian influence; and they endorsed the power of the gospel to change the lives of wayward peoples. Their textual worthiness is conveyed within a vehicle of popular, entertaining literature whose chief aim was to gain a mass audience, providing readers with materials to thrill, move their hearts and loosen their purses in order to advance the cause.

---

[83] Ganga Prasad, *Meri Atmakatha* (Madras, Arya Samaj, 1932), pp. 31–2.

PART III

Postcolonial reclamations

CHAPTER 6

Desperately seeking the indigene: nativism and vernacular hermeneutics

The Village is our library   Nozipo Maraire

I do not want my house to be walled in on all sides and my
windows to be stuffed. I want the cultures of all lands to be
blown about my house as freely as possible. But I refuse to
be blown off my feet by any.   M. K. Gandhi

I would like to begin by telling you an urban parable. It is about
a peasant and a painter. Actually it is based on an incident that
U. R. Anantha Murthy, the Indian writer and critic witnessed at
an academic conference. In fact the painter in the parable was
also at the same conference. This painter was narrating his
experience of going around villages in North India studying folk
art. Near one of the villages he was attracted by a lonely cottage
at the foot of a hill. Approaching the cottage, he saw through
the window a piece of stone which caught his attention. The
stone was decorated with *kumkum* – the red powder that Indian
women wear on their foreheads as an auspicious mark. The
painter wanted to photograph the stone that the peasant
worshipped and asked if he could take it outside where the light
was better. After taking its photograph, the painter felt uneasy
for having removed the stone that the peasant had revered and
worshipped and expressed his regret. However, he had not been
prepared for the peasant's reply, which astonished him: 'It
doesn't matter,' the peasant told him, 'I will get another stone
and anoint it with *kumkum*.' The painter was staggered by the
hermeneutical implication of his reply: any piece of stone on
which the peasant smeared *kumkum* became God for him. What
mattered was his faith, not the stone. Overwhelmed by the

175

reply, the painter went on to challenge his fellow conference attendees: did they understand the manner in which the peasant's mind worked? Could they apprehend the essentially mythical and metaphorical imagination which informed his inner life? Was it possible for them to appreciate the complex pattern of ancient Indian thought, since they were all caught up in the narrow confines of Western scientific rationality? Should they not have preferred the so-called superstition of the peasant which helped him see organic connections between the human world and the natural world surrounding him, to the scientific rationality of Western science, which has driven the world into a mess of pollution and ecological imbalance?

The painter persisted. He went on to tell his audience that Western education had alienated all of them utterly from this peasant and the seventy-per-cent-illiterate Indian mass who populate the Indian villages. In his simplicity, the peasant still kept alive the mode of thinking and perception which had been revealed to the sages from the dawn of time. If they did not understand the structure and mode of this peasant's thinking, they could not become true Indian writers. Therefore they should free themselves from the enslaving rationalist modes of Western scientific thinking. Only then would they be able to understand the vital connection between this peasant and his world and between him and his ancestors who had ploughed the same plot of land for generations. Western modes of perception – whether liberal, scientific positivist or even Marxist – would not enable them to understand what sustained this peasant. These European-born theories, the painter concluded, would only serve to make them feel inferior, and thus turn their country into an imitation of the West.[1]

Anantha Murthy reports that the instantaneous response of the conference participants was one of embarrassment and shock. They were all profoundly moved by the painter's argument. The painter's peasant stood there before them as an authentic Indian, untouched by the ideas of the grand masters

[1] U. R. Ananda Murthy, 'The Search for an Identity: A Kannada Writer's Viewpoint', in *Asian and Western Writers in Dialogue: New Cultural Identities*, ed. Guy Amirthanayagam (London, Macmillan, 1982), pp. 70–3.

of literary theories, who used the peasant as a mere point of reference to define their positions. The immediate response among the conference attendees was that they had all been alienated from their cultural artistic roots. I will come back to the painter later.

Recently, Third World biblical scholars have turned their attention to the indigenization of biblical interpretation. Central to the task is recovery, reoccupation and reinscription of one's culture which has been degraded and effaced from the colonial narratives and from mainstream biblical scholarship. Vernacular hermeneutics tries to erase the painful memory of this degradation and effacement, and to make a fresh start by returning to one's roots. Impelled by a variety of cultural and political forces, it is an attempt to go 'home'. It is a call to self-awareness, aimed at creating an awakening among people to their indigenous literary, cultural and religious heritage. Etymologically, 'vernacular' connotes the language of the household slaves, hence of ordinary people rather than of the masters or the elites. Vernacular is integral to what the anthropologists call nativism. It favours the indigenous over the exotic. It focuses on cultural nationalism and self-affirmation, in which the colonized and others who have been marginalized seek to vindicate the primacy of the local over the national and international through the language, idiom and culture of the common people. It implies a fierce self-esteem, an assertion of self-hood and self-respect instead of slavish conformity to received ideas, or abject helplessness over one's colonized state. It is undertaken by those who believe in the values of indigenous resources and those who have a deep distrust of the centralizing tendencies of Euro-American critical theories which have failed them. It is a struggle for the historical and political presence of groups suppressed or marginalized by colonization and modernization. It is, by definition, an oppositional category which has come to challenge the very idea of Eurocentricity, modernism and internationalism. Vernacular hermeneutics is not a discrete movement, but part of the ongoing intellectual and critical movement of our time. It is postmodern in its renunciation of the Enlightenment meta-narratives and in its elevation of the local as a site of creativity, and it is postcolonial in its battle against the invasion of foreign and universalist modes of interpretation:

Nativism, in this sense, is an offshoot of the crisis in modernism, a reaction to modernism's alienating aesthetic and its universal claims to knowledge. Nativism, thus, is subaltern – the celebration of the local, the immediate, the marginalised. Hence it is very much a part of the post-modern cultural scenario. There is yet another way of locating nativism. It can be placed in the long and rich tradition of the literature of nationalism and decolonization.[2]

Like any other critical concept, the definition of what is vernacular largely depends on the context. Its meaning is movable and it derives its strength and effectiveness from that to which it is opposed. For instance, during the medieval period in Western Europe, when Latin was the language of learning, English was the vernacular. William Shakespeare's works were practically unknown on the Continent because they were composed in a language which came third after Latin and French. The Indian situation further illustrates the ambivalence of the term. During British colonial rule, with the imposition of first Persian and then English for administration and the elevation and glorification of Sanskrit by the Orientalists, the recovery of languages like Tamil, Marathi, Bengali and other regional tongues, with their attendant linguistic and belief systems, was regarded as providing an ideal vernacular weapon in the hands of the ordinary people in their clash against the domineering presence of Sanskrit, Persian and English. Now, however, the situation has changed dramatically and the old dialectical division which used to be invoked in Indian literary circles between the *margi* (Sanskrit) and *deshi* (regional language) does not lend itself to such clear-cut division. The interrelation between the hegemonic Sanskrit and the humble regional

---

[2] Makarand Paranjape, 'Beyond Nativism: Towards a Contemporary Indian Tradition in Criticism', in *Nativism: Essays in Criticism*, ed. Makarand Paranjape (Delhi, Sahitya Akademi, 1997), p. 173.

languages, or 'vulgar tongues' as the European Orientalists used to call them, is complex and intimate. Indian languages are not self-contained categories; there is much fluidity among them and they continue to interact with one another. For instance, the message of *bhakti*, devotion to God, which was often portrayed as a unique contribution of the vernacular languages of India, was in fact one of the cardinal features of the *Bhagavadgita*, the Sanskritic Scripture which preceded the regional linguistic revival by several centuries. What is more, early converts like Krishna Pillai and Vaman Tilak, although they articulated their new-found faith in Tamil and Marathi, continued to use Sanskrit terms creatively in their writings. Krishna Pillai, for example, utilized phrases such as *sat* (reality), *cit* (consciousness, intelligence) and *ananda* (joy) to convey the idea of God. Today, Sanskrit does not wield the power it used to, nor does it dominate the Indian linguistic landscape. It is no longer a potential threat as a language. It has assumed, in consequence, the same role as a vernacular language, and Sankritic hermeneutical practices such as *dhvani* (poetic experience), *rasa* (aesthetic relish) and *aucitya* (prosperity) are employed by Indians to unsettle the invading foreign critical theories.[3] In such circumstances, Sanskrit is seen as a vernacular corrective to the exegetical protocols set by the metropolitan centres.

Similarly, the imperial role of English has also changed over the years. English in India, in spite of its elitist tone, is seen increasingly as one of the Indian *bhasas* (languages).[4] It played a vital role during the colonial struggle and continued to co-exist with other Indian languages; it also contributed to the task of nation-building in the aftermath of independence. The introduction of English did not result in the de-rooting of the Indian. Except for a lunatic minority who blindly imitated and absorbed

---

[3] For examples of how the Western literary canon has been subjected to these Indian indigenous theories, see *EastWest Poetics At Work*, ed. C. D. Narasimhaiah (Delhi: Sahitya Akademi, 1994). For the application of these theories in Indian Christian hermeneutics, see *BibleBhashyam: An Indian Biblical Quarterly* 5:4 (1979) for the *dhavani* method, and *The Holy Water: Indian Psalm-Meditations*, text by Martin Kampchen and woodcuts by Jyoti Sahi (Bangalore: Asian Trading Corporation, 1995) for the *rasa* method of interpretation.

[4] English accounts for nearly 40 per cent of all Indian publishing.

anything foreign, the English-speaking intelligentsia used the language for broader inter-communal and social contacts. English acts as a medium for transacting trans-regional cultural contracts. The use of English has led to the discovery of India's varied linguistic past and her rich roots, which were hitherto confined to various regions. It was Surendranath Dasgupta's five volumes on Indian philosophy which opened up the richness and intricacies of India's philosophical tradition to those Indians who knew little or no Sanskrit at all. Similarly it was A. K. Ramanujan's *The Interior Landscape: Love Poems from a Classical Tamil Anthology* (Bloomington, Indiana University Press, 1967) which introduced a wealth of poetic tradition from other Indic languages. Though these indigenous literatures and philosophies derive their voice from English, in their explication they remain faithful to the indigenous lexical rule and canon. There is no hint of colonialism in their appropriation of English. English acts as an integrative medium within India's various linguistic groups which otherwise would live in their own communal and linguistic gulags.

English has been successfully nativized by the infusion of an indigenous vocabulary which resonates with the ethos of the sub-continent. The distinctive flavour of Indian English comes through vividly in the writings of Salman Rushdie, Arundhati Roy and others. What is more, in a country like India where language is seen as a vehicle to whip up communalism, English remains a link, and in some ways a unifying force, and is devoid of any communal blemish; so much so that Geeta Dharmarajan claims:

I would like to argue a case for an English that can stand right royally along with the other modern Indian languages – those that are called *bhashas* . . . Such an English *bhasha* would be its own and yet capture all the immediateness that other languages are capable of; it would refrain from being 'bad' yet be able to let us be ourselves, without having to hide our deepest sentiments and emotions behind the restrained facade of 'proper' English.[5]

---

[5] Geeta Dharmarajan, 'Treading Euclid's Line', in *Katha Prize Stories*, vol. IV, ed. Geeta Dharmarajan (New Delhi, Katha, 1994), p. 12.

What is vernacular depends on who is using what and against whom. Hence regional *bhashas*, Sanskrit and English can all be used creatively to revise and envision an alternative to invading, disabling and alienating forces and tendencies.

The vernacular has had until now only a limited valency in theological circles. Its role has been chiefly to translate books produced in Western languages. What Koyama, the Japanese theologian who began his career as a theological educator in Thailand, says of that country is also generally true of other Third World countries:

In Thai theological education, the function of the vernacular has been largely to explain Western theological words and ideas. The religious images shaped in the Thai spirituality for centuries are either ignored or subordinated to the images imported from the West. The vernacular has lost its own dignity. This goes against the Pentecostal affirmation of every language.[6]

The loss of the vernacular was due to the growing distance of the second and third generations of Indian Christians from their traditional cultures. Though eventually they drifted away from their own cultures, the early converts were organically steeped in them and maintained an organic link with them. The effortless ease with which they delved, with great profit, into their linguistic, regional, cultural and religious idioms and reworked them into Christian themes is hardly evident in the current theological literature. Present-day Indian interpreters who show competence and acquaintance with Western learning and literature have to make a special effort to employ indigenous themes. The other misfortune is that, because of the civilizing motive of Christian missionaries, Christians have been forced to study indigenous texts in the context of Christian texts. As a result, the greater part of Hindu, Buddhist and Confucian textual traditions has become irrelevant, and the few parts that have become meaningful are due to the forced imposition of Christian/Western categories.

---

[6] Kosuke Koyama, 'Theological Education: Its Unities and Diversities', *Theological Education Supplement* 1:30 (1993), 101.

VERNACULARIZATION AND BIBLICAL INTERPRETATION

Vernacular interpretation seeks to overcome the remoteness and strangeness of these biblical texts by trying to make links across the cultural divides, by employing the reader's own cultural resources and social experiences to illuminate the biblical narratives. It is about making hermeneutical sense of texts and concepts imported across time and space by means of one's own indigenous texts and concepts. In opening up the biblical narratives, vernacular reading draws on three dimensional aspects of a culture – ideational (world views, values and rules), performantial (rituals and roles) and material (language, symbols, food, clothing, etc.). In other words, using indigenous beliefs and experiences, cross-cultural hermeneutics attempts to provide important analogies with ancient texts of which readers from other cultures may not be aware. What, in effect, such readings have done is to make culture an important site for hermeneutics.

Conceptual correspondences

Surveying the field, one can identify at least three modes of vernacular reading – conceptual correspondences, narratival enrichments and performantial parallels. The first mode – conceptual correspondences – seeks textual or conceptual parallels between biblical texts and the textual or conceptual traditions of one's own culture. Such an attempt, unlike historical criticism, looks beyond the Judaic or Graeco-Roman contexts of the biblical narratives and seeks corresponding conceptual analogies in the readers' own textual traditions. Indian Christian interpreters of an earlier generation were pioneers in this mode. K. M. Banerjea (1813–85) demonstrated the remarkable similarities between biblical and Vedic texts. He selected overlapping narrative segments touching upon the Creation, the Fall and the Flood from the great wealth of *Vedic* writings, and juxtaposed these with passages from the Bible, emphasizing, however, that the expectations of the Indian texts were fulfilled in Christianity: 'The *Vedas* confirm and illustrate

Scripture traditions and Scripture facts, and how Christianity fills up the vacuum – a most important vacuum – in the *Vedic* account of the sacrifices, by exhibiting the true *Prajapati – the Lamb slain from the foundations of the World*.'[7]

There are a number of examples of creative borrowing from indigenous concepts. G. S. Vethanayagam (1774–1864) employed the theistic mystical tradition of the *Saiva bhakti* to explicate the death of Christ. Dayanandan Francis, who has done an extensive study of the creative utilization by Tamil Christians of their own tradition, describes Vethanayagam's ingenious use of *Saiva bhakti* thus:

His attention is focussed on the feet of Jesus. He visualizes his master nailed to the cross. He approaches the feet of Jesus as would a Hindu *bhakta* approach the feet of his Lord. The highest point of mystical union in theistic *Saiva Sidhanta* is the close and intimate contact between the feet of the Lord and the head of the *bhakta*. The feet *(tāl)* and the head *(talai)* almost become one while they maintain their distinctive identity. The two words *tāl* and *talai* when joined together become *tādalai* according to grammatical rules of combination. The phrase *tādalai* sounds as one word while it obviously contains two words which have not lost their identity. The union between the *bhakta* and the Lord is similar to this. Vedanayagam longs to experience similar union with the Lord Jesus Christ under whose feet he wishes his head should settle. His longing is that the settlement should be firm and enlivening. So he beseeches that the nails piercing through the feet of Jesus should also pierce through his head. He believes that when this kind of oneness is attained his image will vanish like the iron in the furnace and the image of Christ will be enshrined in it. He sings: In order that this wicked one might vanish in your image like a piece of iron burnt in fire / And that I settle under Thy feet upon the cross so that the nail on Thy feet might pierce through my head.[8]

Dayanandan Francis himself has relocated the Gospels of Mark and John within the Tamil poetic context and has opened up the magic casements of theTamil world for Christian

---

[7] K. M. Banerjea, *Two Essays as Supplements to the Arian Witness* (Calcutta, Thacker, Spink & Co., 1880), p. 79.

[8] Dayanandan Francis, 'Brief Remarks on the Relevance of the Indian Context for Christian Reflection: A Tamil Perspective', in *Christian Contribution to Indian Philosophy*, ed. Anand Amaladass (Madras, The Christian Literature Society, 1995), pp. 118–19.

readers. His *Vazhvalikkum Vallal* (The One who gives life)[9] and
Iraivanin Tirmainder (God's Holy Son)[10] weave Tamil aesthetics
with the Gospel narratives. Another Tamil convert, H. A
Krishna Pillai (1827–1900), made use of the practice resorted to
by Tamil lovers in the *Sankam* literature,[11] where the lover, as
evidence of his love for his beloved, rides, screaming and
bloody, on a thorny cart made out of a palmyra trunk, in order
to compare to the death of Christ, with his head crowned with
thorns, hanging on the cross enduring untold agony.[12] Similarly,
A. J. Appasamy (1891–1971) borrowed key ideas from *bhakti*, the
Hindu devotional tradition, to make sense of Johannine spirituality. He conscripted concepts like *moksa*/liberation, *antar-
yamin*/indweller, *avatar*/incarnation, as a way of getting into the
thought world of John. In doing so, he invested these Hindu
concepts with Christian meanings and at the same time accen-
tuated the role of Jesus.[13]

In China, Wu Lei-ch'uan (1870–1944) was engaged in a
similar exercise. In his case he was trying to integrate Confucian
and biblical concepts. He utilized the Confucian fundamental
concept of highest virtue, *jen* (love), and also *Tien-tzu* (Son of
Heaven) and *Sheng Tien-tzu* (Holy Son of God), to elucidate the
Holy Spirit and the role of Jesus.[14] Similarly, K. K. Yeo utilizes
the Chinese philosophical concept of yin/yang and the Confucian understanding of *T'ein Ming* (Mandate of Heaven) and *li*
(law/propriety), as well as *jen*, to communicate biblical notions
of God, humanity, rest, and will of God.[15] Also falling within

---

[9] See his *Vazhvalikkum Vallal* (The One who gives life) (Madras, The Christian
Literature Society, 1981).

[10] See his *Iraivanin Tirumainder* (God's Holy Son) (Madras, The Christian Literature
Society, 1984).

[11] Tamil bardic and classical literature produced between 300 BCE and 200 CE, regarded
as the most creative period of Tamil writing. Sankam means academy, a normative
body of poets who adjudicated the worthiness of literary creations.

[12] See his *Ratchanya Yathrikam* (Madras,The Christian Literature Society, 1972; Tamil).

[13] See his *Christianity as Bhakti Marga* (Madras, The Christian Literature Society, 1928)
and *What is Moksa?* (Madras, The Christian Literature Society, 1931).

[14] John Y. H. Yieh, 'Cultural Reading of the Bible: Some Chinese Cases', in *Text &
Experience: Towards A Cultural Exegesis of the Bible*, ed. Daniel Smith-Christopher
(Sheffield, Sheffield Academic Press, 1995), pp. 122–53.

[15] Khiok-Khng Yeo, *What Has Jerusalem to Do with Beijing?: Biblical Interpretation from a
Chinese Perspective* (Harrisburg, PA, Trinity Press International, 1998), pp. 51–161.

this mode are the Japanese theologian Kitamori's employment of *tsura* to explain the pain of God;[16] the South African artist Mbatha's use of *ubunto* to appropriate the story of Joseph as that not of an individual but of a community; and Gerald West's recovery of African notions of *indlovukazi* (first wife), *inthandokazi* (favourite wife) and *isancinza* (helper to the wife) as an interpretative key to explain the matrilineal presence and power and to determine the role of Leah, Rachel, Bilhah and Zilpah.[17] A fellow South African, Madipoane Masenya, draws on the North Sotho *bosadi* (womanhood) to read the Naomi–Ruth story. Acknowledging the patriarchal orientation of both biblical and South African world-views, Masenya mines the narrative for the exemplar value of the story. The relationship between Naomi and Ruth, according to Masenya, depicts 'an example of female love, mutual respect, and bonding, and models how women, particularly mothers-in-law and daughters-in-law, should behave, especially in an African-South African context'.[18]

In this same mode, insights from popular culture are also summoned to illuminate biblical texts critically. Hendricks, the African American, calls for the use of cultural expressions such as blues, soul and jazz to formulate a guerrilla exegesis.[19] Australian Aboriginals attempt to translate Aboriginal Dreaming stories in Christian terms, citing passages from both Testaments to convey the essential moral message.[20] The reclamation of two pivotal Indian tribal values – anti-pride and anti-greed, which resonate with the Markan narrative (10.17–27 and 10.35–45) – as an alternative model for a world driven by greed

---

[16] Kazoh Kitamori, *Theology of the Pain of God* (Richmond, VA, John Knox Press, 1965), pp. 135–36.

[17] Gerald O. West, *Contextual Bible Study* (Pietermaritzburg, Cluster Publications, 1993), p. 58.

[18] Madipoane J. Masenya, '*Ngwetsi* (Bride): The Naomi–Ruth Story from an African-South African Perspective', *Journal of Feminist Studies in Religion* 14:2 (1998), 90.

[19] Osayande Obery Hendricks, 'Guerrilla Exegesis: A Post Modern Proposal for Insurgent African American Biblical Interpretation', *The Journal for the Interdenominational Theological Center* 22:1 (1994), 92–109.

[20] Anne Pattel-Gray, 'Dreaming: An Aboriginal Interpretation of the Bible', in *Text & Experience: Towards A Cultural Exegesis of the Bible*, ed. Daniel Smith-Christopher (Sheffield, Sheffield Academic Press, 1995), pp. 247–59.

and consumerism is a further example of the utilization of elements from popular culture.[21]

Narratival enrichments

The second mode is to re-employ some of the popular folk tales, legends, riddles, plays, proverbs and poems that are part of the common heritage of the people and place them vividly alongside biblical materials, in order to draw out their hermeneutical implications. C. S. Song, the Taiwanese theologian who pioneered the method of creatively juxtaposing myths, stories and legends with biblical narratives, often went beyond the written word to the symbolic meaning. In *The Tears of Lady Meng*, Song uses a well-known Chinese folk tale and blends it with the biblical theme of Jesus' death and resurrection.[22] Peter Lee juxtaposes the Book of Ruth and a Chinese drama of the Yuan period, 'The Injustice done to Ton Ngo'. Both stories are about a daughter-in-law and her devotion to her mother-in-law. Both emerge out of a patriarchal society, though they differ in their plots.[23] The ethical and metaphysical perspectives shine through the stories. Samuel Rayan, in his essay, 'Wrestling in the Night', juxtaposes in an imaginative way three texts, two ancient – The *Bhagavadgita* and the Book of Job – and one modern – the posthumous writings of a young girl, eponymously entitled the *Poems of Gitanjali*. These three represent three religious traditions – Hindu, Jewish and Islamic. In spite of the time span and different religious orientations, Arjuna, Job and Gitanjali testify that sorrow and pain are universal.[24] All three in different ways wrestle with death, pain, love and God, and through sorrow and pain grow in faith and love. Africans, too, are engaged in retrieving their folk tales. The

---

[21] George M. Soares-Prabhu, 'Two Mission Commands: An Interpretation of Matthew 28: 16–20 in the light of a Buddhist Text', *Biblical Interpretation: A Journal of Contemporary Approaches* 2:3 (1995)), 264–82.

[22] C. S. Song, *The Tears of Lady Meng: A Parable of People's Political Theology* (Geneva, The World Council of Churches, 1981).

[23] Peter K. H. Lee, 'Two Stories of Loyalty', *Ching Feng* 32:1 (1989), 24–40.

[24] Samuel Rayan, 'Wrestling in the Night', in *The Future of Liberation Theology: Essays in Honor of Gustavo Gutiérrez*, ed. Marc H. Ellis and Otto Maduro (Maryknoll, NY, Orbis Books, 1989), pp. 450–69.

Parable of the Two Brothers, a popular story among the Sukuma people of Tanzania, has interesting parallels with the Lukan Prodigal Son. Both these stories have a father and two sons and in both the younger son is received back into the family and rewarded. Although in their plots and in their thematic emphasis they may differ, the additional insights that the Sukuma parable provides, such as values of community and unity, serve to enrich the biblical story.[25] Jyoti Sahi finds another dimension in the same parable, but this time from an environmental perspective. He reads concurrently the legend of the Uranos, the indigenous people of Central India who tell a similar story to that of the Prodigal Son. Compared to the biblical and the African parables, both of which deal with the interpersonal, this legend is essentially about alienation from one's own environment. It is about a son finding fortune in an alien land. In this parable of the Uranos, the Karam tree, which symbolizes the ancient tradition and is the metonymy for the father in the Gospel parable, is rejected and uprooted. The son goes through a long process of rediscovering his roots, and eventually finds peace and harmony with his environment.[26]

Archie Lee engages in a postcolonial intertextual rereading of two poetic traditions, Hebraic and Chinese. He investigates Psalm 78 and the Book of Poetry (Odes) or *Shih Ching* and demonstrates how, in their retelling, these texts privileged a particular royal ideology. One legitimizes the rule of David and Judah as compared with that of the marginalized Ephraim, and the other elevates the Chou dynasty at the expense of the colonized Shang people: 'These imperial powers have made use of religious power of the chosenness of God and the threatening concept of the Mandate of Heaven.'[27] In Lee's view it is crucial to listen again to the missing voices like those of Jeremiah and the suppressed Shang, who 'represent the other side of the missing part of the story which at least expresses disagree-

---

[25] Joseph Healy and Donald Sybertz, *Towards an African Narrative Theology* (Maryknoll, NY, Orbis Books, 1996), pp. 104–6.
[26] Jyoti Sahi, 'Reflections on the Image of the Prodigal Son', *Indian Theological Studies* 34:1, 2, 3 (1997), 181–3.
[27] Archie C. C. Lee, 'The Recitation of the Past: A Cross-Textual Reading of Ps. 78 and Other Odes', *Ching Feng* 39:4 (1996), 192.

ment'.[28] Lee's contention is that to arrive at a full reality one needs to engage in such a hermeneutics.

Recently Yuko Yuasa has utilized the Japanese Noh-drama to illuminate biblical texts. Noh drama tradition traces its roots to Ameno Uzume, the eighth-century Japanese singer, dancer and goddess from whom most of the performing arts in Japan draw their inspiration. Noh-drama method aims to bring liberation through performance. According to the ancient myth, Ameno Uzume dances to free people from despair, thus ushering new vigour, purpose and harmony into their lives. Yuasa links the theme of Ameno Uzume to biblical Miriam. Miriam like Ameno Uzume, led people in tambourine playing and dancing. Miriam, along with the other women during the Exodus, celebrated the end of slavery in Egypt through dance. 'Experiencing the liberation from the past by dancing', writes Yuasa, 'with such powerful leaders as Miriam and Ameno Uzume, people are led to recognize that life is not determined by the old self. This realization of one's being born anew gives us a hope, preparing us for faith in the resurrection.'[29] Yuasa notes another positive aspect, too. 'Performing arts often reveal God as actively moving in us to help us identify ourselves with the dynamic god through our movements. This is the direct fruit of performing sacred texts.'[30]

Performantial parallels

The third mode is to utilize ritual and behavioural practices which are commonly available in a culture. The Johannine saying of Jesus, 'Very truly, I tell you, unless you eat the flesh of the Son of Man and drink his blood, you have no life in you. Those who eat my flesh and drink my blood have eternal life, I will raise them up on the last day, for my flesh is true food and my blood is true drink' (6.53–5), may sound awkward and cannibalistic to those who are reared in Western Enlightenment values. But if one reads it analogically to Malawian witchcraft

---

[28] Ibid., p. 193.
[29] Yuko Yuasa, 'Performing Sacred Text', *Concilium* 3 (1998), 85.
[30] Ibid., p. 88.

talk, as Musopole has done, the saying takes on a different meaning – 'anyone who feeds on Jesus takes into themselves the very life-force of Jesus to re-inforce their own lives'.[31] Such a reading could be understood metaphorically as a eucharistic saying, or literally as witchcraft talk.

The African concept of trickster, though it differs from context to context, is also a helpful medium through which to appraise the behaviour of some biblical characters who, viewed from a Western moral perspective, may seem dubious and deceitful. From an African trickster point of view, such actions are recognized as performed by people who lack power and live in hopeless situations. The trickery in question is something men and women often turn to in situations where they have no other recourse. The reason given by Hebrew midwives for their unwillingness to discharge Pharaoh's order to kill all male children born to Israelites (Exod. 1.15–19), Abraham's deceptive statements to Pharaoh and Abimelech (Gen. 12.10–13; 20.1–18), Delilah's attempts to woo and overcome Samson (Jud. 16) and Rachel's answer 'the way of woman is upon me' (Gen. 31.35), as a way of foiling her father-in-law Laban's attempt to verify the truth of whether she has stolen the family gods or not, are examples of the trickster role played in the Bible by individuals who are otherwise powerless.[32]

The importance of olfaction as a rite of passage and transition in some African cultures could also open up some of the difficult biblical passages which exegetes, raised in the Enlightenment mode of thinking, try to expurgate or explain away. One such verse is Isaiah 11.3. Modern translations read: 'And his delight shall be in the fear of the Lord.' If translated literally, it would read, 'He shall smell in the Lord.' Such a translation causes uneasiness among cultures which fail to see a potent link between odour and discriminatory powers. God discerns through the senses of smell and taste just as much as through the oral and visual. In African traditional religions this is a

---

[31] A. C. Musopole, 'Witchcraft Terminology, The Bible, and African Christian Theology: An Exercise in Hermeneutics', *Journal of Religion in Africa* 23:4 (1993), 352.

[32] Naomi Steinberg, 'Israelite Tricksters: Their Analogues and Cross-Cultural Study', *Semeia: An Experimental Journal for Biblical Criticism* 42 (1988), 1–13.

common practice. In these religions there is a Chief Sniffer, whose role is to sniff every entrant at the worship with a view to checking whether the intentions of the worshipper are good or evil. Some African independent Churches have instituted the role of a Chief Sniffer. Ian Ritchie, who has studied this phenomenon and has been arguing for the democratization of the means of knowing, points out that olfaction in many African religions is 'considered a means of discernment in many respects superior to any other sense, for it can reveal important things not accessible through any other sense'.[33] Because of the disuse of olfactory language among contemporary commentators, there is a reluctance among them to accept the idea of a God or Messiah who would discern by a sense of smell. The Hebrew Bible is full of olfactory images, olfactory language and olfactory metaphors of knowledge. The current Western hermeneutical paradigm is heavily biased towards a visual mode of knowledge and equates seeing, especially with seeing of the text, with knowing. African culture, like the Hebrew, is free of this exclusively textualist and visualist paradigm and is in an advantageous position to appreciate the Isaian and similar passages in the Bible.

THE VERNACULAR IN METROPOLITAN CONTEXT

The emergence of indigenous ways of reading the Bible by the people of the Third World has given the impression that vernacular hermeneutics is something recent, exotic and confined to the cultures 'out there', and that Western readings are devoid of such practices. Biblical interpretation, however, has always been culturally specific and has always been informed and coloured by reigning cultural values; Western scholars themselves have not always been entirely free from such tendencies. Even a casual glance at the history of hermeneutics will

---

[33] I rely here on the manuscript form of Ian Ritchie's two articles – 'Bodily Ways of knowing in the Hebrew Bible: Implications for Biblical Studies' and 'The Nose Knows: Bodily Knowing in Isaiah 11.3'. Though these articles have been accepted for publication, I have been unsuccessful in getting the bibliographical details; my apologies to Ritchie.

reveal that there has never been an interpretation that has had no reference to, or dependence on, the particular cultural codes, thought-patterns or social location of the interpreter. A classic example of an earlier cultural appropriation was the *Heliand* (Saviour), the ninth-century Saxon epic poem of the life of Christ, in which the four Gospels were re-expressed in Germanic terms, with Christ re-imagined as a Germanic chieftain, and the disciples as clan warriors assembled by him for his private army for the battle:

In its pages Christianity and northern European warrior culture came far closer to a synthesis . . . This synthesis provided an evangelical basis for the imaging of Christian discipleship in soldierly terms and opened the imagination and the conscience to create the ideal of the northern Christian soldier – the knight. This evangelical synthesis, it might be further argued, even though originally intended as poetic metaphor, facilitated, and was the embodiment of a founding element of the culture of Europe.[34]

What the unknown author does with the familiar gospel narratives, such as the infancy narratives, the Sermon on the Mount, the Beatitudes, the Lord's Prayer, the Passion and Resurrection, is to accommodate them to suit the prevailing warrior-aristocratic values:

Its anonymous author envisioned dynamic poetic equivalents so that the impact of the original text, in its Mediterranean cultural context, might be transferred by poetry analogously to a new North-Sea context. Such a task of inculturation had not been undertaken since the evangelists themselves.[35]

Another notable example where prevailing cultural codes were summoned to illuminate a difficult biblical concept is the often baffling notion of the death of Christ. Anselm's answer to the problem was to use the 'analogy of the situation of a medieval peasant insulting a king. Reconciliation would not be achieved until satisfaction had been made for the affront to the king's honour.'[36] Luther's reinterpretation of justification by

---

[34] G. Roland Murphy, *The Saxon Savior: The Germanic Transformation of the Gospel in the Ninth-Century Heliand* (New York, Oxford University Press, 1989), p. viii.

[35] Ibid., p. 28.

[36] Michael Winter, *Problems in Theology: The Atonement* (London, Geoffrey Chapman, 1994), p. 63.

faith, which dispensed with a mediator, utilized the then emerging modernism's core value, individualism. Such mobilization of contemporary cultural codes supports Bultmann's claim: 'Every theological exposition of the saving event and the Christian's existence is constructed with contemporary conceptions.'[37] Bultmann himself utilized Heidegger's existential philosophy to interpret the New Testament. A recent example of culture-specific reading in the West was the work of the Bible and Culture Collective. Uneasy with the interpretative practices which emerged in the wake of modernity, this group attempted to recover the Bible by subjecting it to postmodern concerns. The introduction to the *Postmodern Bible* reads:

In reaction, we are arguing for a *transformed* biblical criticism, one that would recognize that our cultural context is marked by aesthetics, epistemologies, and politics quite different from those reigning in eighteenth- and nineteenth-century Europe where traditional biblical scholarship is so thoroughly rooted. We are also arguing for a *transforming* biblical criticism, one that undertakes to understand the ongoing impact of the Bible on culture, and one that, therefore, benefits from the rich resources of contemporary thought on language, epistemology, method, rhetoric, power, reading, as well as the pressing and often contentious political questions of 'difference' – gender, race, class, sexuality and, indeed religion – which have come to occupy center stage in discourses both public and academic. In short, we hope in this volume to contribute to the process of bringing biblical scholarship into meaningful and ongoing engagement with political, cultural, and epistemological critiques that have emerged 'in modernity's wake' . . . and that have proved so fruitful in other literary studies and cultural criticism.[38]

SOME AFFIRMING AND CONSTRUCTIVE THOUGHTS

With such a breadth of possible readings, one has to admit that the efficiency and utility of vernacular hermeneutics as a

---

[37] Rudolf Bultmann, *Faith and Understanding* (London, SCM Press, 1969), p. 279.
[38] The Bible and Culture Collective, *The Postmodern Bible* (New Haven, Yale University Press, 1995), p. 2.

critical tool is somewhat limited at present. One should not idealize the indigenous, endow it with redemptive properties and see it as a vehicle of deliverance for our entire hermeneutical malaise. Positively, vernacular hermeneutics has enabled Christian interpreters to gain credibility and cultivate deeper contact with their own people, who otherwise would have regarded Christians as foreigners in their own country. It has also helped to reverse the missionary condemnation of indigenous cultures. The mobilization of cultural insights has served as an acknowledgement that religious truths were present in indigenous cultures prior to the arrival and introduction of Christianity. Even before Vatican II and the current theology of religions popularized the notion of positive elements embedded in other faith traditions, earlier interpreters like Banerjea were able to establish this.

Drawing creatively on the indigenous archive, vernacular hermeneutics has played a significant part in rectifying an often one-sided picture of biblical concepts. For instance, God is often portrayed in male categories. Re-accentuating *Saiva* and *Vaisnavite* concepts of God as male and female, Krishna Pillai and Tilak were able to re-channel and weave these into Christian discourse. Marshalling what is explicit in their tradition, they were able to draw attention to the gaps, omissions and implicit elements in the biblical narratives The lyrics these men wrote after their conversion demonstrate how the concepts of two traditions intermingle. Tilak's hymn, still widely used in Indian Christian worship, is a case in point:

> Refrain:Tenderest Mother-Guru mine,
> Saviour, where is love like Thine?
> A cool and never-fading shade
> To souls by sin's fierce heat dismayed: (Refrain)
> Right swiftly at my earliest cry
> He came to save me from the sky: (Refrain)
> He chose disciples – those who came
> Consumed by true repentance' flame (Refrain)
> For me, a sinner, yea, for me
> He hastened to the bitter Tree (Refrain)
> And still within me living, too,
> He fills my being through and through (Refrain)

My heart is all one melody –
'Hail to Thee, Christ! All hail to Thee! (Refrain)[39]

Creatively intermixing and synthesizing biblical faith with indigenous religion, vernacular hermeneutics has not only transformed the biblical faith; it has also enabled indigenous cultures, for instance, Mayan identity in Guatemala, to survive.[40]

At a time when hermeneutical practices emphasize textual and visual modes as a means to knowledge, vernacular hermeneutics provides a corrective with its emphasis on the non-visual senses; it reverses the bias towards rationalistic understanding and opens up the richness of non-rationalist modes of interpretation.

Significantly, vernacular hermeneutics did not try to speak to an imaginary or real metropolitan centre. It is evident from the writings of Krishna Pillai, Tilak and others, that the West or the academy did not occupy a central position in their hermeneutical articulations. Certainly they learned and borrowed ideas and techniques from external resources, but they reshaped them, often adding their indigenous texture to meet local needs, and in a few cases they turned their articulations against the European invaders. More importantly, they did not convey their message exclusively through the mode of the dominant thinking. They did not see their task as representing or measuring up to the protocols set by outsiders, but went about their business of redefining imported Christian values to fit the local idiom and ethos. What is remarkable about their literary production is the fact that their audience was an immediate one, and one whose immediate interests they served.

Negatively, in pressing for corresponding cultural elements, vernacular hermeneutics tends to overuse the positive aspects of ancient cultures, and, in doing so, it inclines to overlook their dehumanizing aspects. Vernacular hermeneutics does not

---

[39] See *The Experimental Response of N. V. Tilak*, ed. P. S. Jacob, Confessing the Faith in India Series, no. 17 (Madras, The Christian Literature Society, 1979), p. 102.

[40] Susan Hawley, 'Does God Speak Miskitu? The Bible and Ethnic Identity Among Miskitu of Nicaragua', in *Ethnicity and the Bible*, ed. Mark G. Brett (Leiden, E. J. Brill, 1996), pp. 315–42.

become automatically virtuous because it draws on native traditions. It can become hegemonic and intolerant of other modes of local communication such as oral or other minority language traditions. The uneasy relationship between Indian dalits and the tribals is a case in point. Indigenous cultures carry along with their enlivening aspects a baggage of feudal, patriarchal and even anti-egalitarian traditions. Vernacular hermeneutics does not gain value because it is expressed in the songs of an *adivasi* (indigenous people) or an illiterate peasant, or is found in a few folk-forms and in the writings of modern rural and dalit writers. It is valuable when it celebrates the plurality of the native traditions; but when it creates an exclusive and a protective past, in the process silencing other voices and hindering the growth of communal harmony, and views contemporary perceptions and attitudes as poisonous, then it has to be challenged. Manipulated by the unscrupulous, vernacularism can degenerate into another form of crude resurgence and an undiscerning glorification of rural and feudal values. Nothing is axiomatically admirable because it is indigenous and local.

It is too simplistic to think that everyone who writes in one of our regional languages and utilizes autochthonous idioms, symbols and ceremonies is always free, emancipated and represents the true India, and that those who write in English and use contemporary Western modes of interpretation are by contrast always conniving with Anglo-American or Sanskritic imperialism. It is tempting to believe that indigenous people have access to privileged knowledge in unravelling the mysteries of ancient texts. To believe so would be to re-inscribe a hierarchy of hermeneutics in which some have an unequal access and relation to texts. A vernacular writer may actually engage in anti-native cultural practices and turn against his or her own cultural traditions, while a non-native writer in English may actually aid and energize indigenous traditions. The exciting way in which European missionaries have utilized Sanskritic, Tamil, Bengali and numerous other languages is a case in point. Vernacularism can easily degenerate into chauvinism, jingoism or narrow-minded communalism.

Christian vernacular hermeneutics tends to be apologetic and triumphalistic in tone. Since most of the *bhasa*-tradition writers were recent converts, they were well qualified to expose the defects of the religion they left behind. Krishna Pillai's *Ratchanya Camaya Nirnayam* (1898) (*The Determination of the Religion of Salvation*)[41] is an illustration of this. Utilizing his knowledge of the Hindu Scriptures, he constructed his vision of the true image of God, demonstrated how it fitted in with the biblical notion of God and went on to expose the failure of his former Hindu deities to measure up to the standard set by their own texts. Nehemiah Goreh (1825–95) is another who was very severe on his own tradition. Using his profound knowledge of Hindu Scriptures, Goreh was able to refute many of the Hindu claims. In 1860 he published *Shaddarashna Darpa* (literally, *Mirror of Six Systems*, i.e. the traditional six systems of Hindu philosophy – *Samkhya, Yoga, Nyaya, Vaiseshika, Mimamsa* and *Vedanta*). The book, written in Hindi, was primarily aimed at the Hindu reform societies of the time, the Arya Samaj and Brahmo Samaj, who were at that time engaged in a rejuvenation of Hinduism. The book was a devastating attack on Hindu philosophical systems and in the process it demolished the exaggerated claims the European Orientalists had hitherto made for the ancient wisdom of India; it also demonstrated that when exposed to reason and logic these systems were full of inconsistencies and defects. His message to his erstwhile Hindus was that 'their education in their own *Sastras* does not enlighten them'.[42]

The other negative feature of vernacular hermeneutics is that it often makes excessive claims for Christianity and it is prone to triumphalistic tendencies. Thus, the unusual form of altruism, *aram*, the highest form of virtue, which the Tamils claim as their own inventive property, and which is textualized extensively in their literature, especially in the *Sankam* writings, is denied its South Indian origin and is attributed to Christian influence. Satiasatchy's contention is that such a supreme form of love, which surpasses all human standards and defies all religious

---

[41] See H. A. Krishna Pillai, *Ratchanya Camaya Nirnayam* (Sivakasi: Chandra Printers, 1898).

[42] C. E. Gardner, *Life of Father Goreh* (London, Longmans, Green, and Co., 1900), p. 231.

laws and regulations, belies its Tamil origin and is more akin to the New Testament understanding of *agape*; and that it must have come to India with St Thomas and been subsequently absorbed by the Tamils into their lives and literature:

Hence we may concede that to Christ's life-style of *agape*, as possibly introduced by Thomas and as communicated by traders and travellers, the Tamil mind has possibly reacted. Consequently, we have instances, legendary and historical, recorded in Tamil literature from which we have reasons to concede that *agape* in course of time, in some form or other and in varying degrees, began operating in the minds and lives of the Tamils.[43]

In making such an assertion, Sathiasatchy not only perpetuates the claim that anything religiously good can only come out of the Judaeo-Christian tradition, but also denies the possibility that Tamils could have arrived at this independently. Such claims and denials alienate the Indian Christian community further from their neighbours.

The protagonists of vernacular hermeneutics have often used the argument that interpreters should stick with what they know best, write about things with which they are familiar, explore their own cultural heritage and drink from their own wells. This way, they argue, one acquires credentials and credibility, and demonstrates one's authentic roots. Such an argument, in effect, tries to tell the dalits, burakumin, aboriginals, women and the other subalterns that they should deal with and focus on their own territory and not venture beyond their limited space and imagination. The words of the Pulitzer prize-winning author, Annie Proulx, are quite apposite here: '[This] strikes me as the worst possible advice you can give someone, because you are recommending that they not explore life, they do not look beyond their horizons, they not travel or move about, but concentrate on a small scope that is their own internal thoughts and relationships.'[44] Edward Said, too, has expressed his uneasiness about the formation of hermeneutical

[43] P. A. Sathiasatchy, 'Theological Exploration Into Ancient Tamil Poems', in *Doing Theology with the Poetic Traditions of India: Focus on Dalit and Tribal Poems*, ed. Joseph Patmury (Bangalore, PTCA/SATHRI, 1996), p. 36.
[44] See her interview in the *Guardian* 6 June 1997.

enclaves: '[I] have no patience with the position that "we" should only or mainly be concerned with what is "ours" any more than I can condone reactions to such a view that require Arabs to read Arab books, use Arab methods, and the like.'[45] A contemporary critical practice must retain the right to adapt, adulterate, amalgamate and parody any theories in its struggle to achieve a coherent understanding in a pluralistic world. To cling only to an exclusive single position is to deny other possibilities and options.

Vernacular hermeneutics became a celebratory event when people led a settled life and thought in terms of cultural wholes. But now, at a time when there is an intermixing of cultures at both popular and elitist levels, when local/global and vernacular/metropolitan divides are shrinking and peoples' lives are being rearranged by globalization, finding cultural-specific analogues may be an increasingly difficult task; alternatively, of course, the new multi-vision may throw up its own hitherto undiscovered parallels. It is important to see the global/vernacular, rural/metropolitan as relational and relative concepts. To treat vernacular and metropolitan hermeneutics as contrastive pairs – one as narrow, stable, intuitive and closed, and the other as open, progressive, rational and fluid – is to miss the point. The interconnection between the vernacular and the global is now so deep that it is very difficult to determine what is native and what is non-native. If vernacular means isolation, exclusion and purging of foreign elements, narrow-minded communalism and whipping up of anti-feelings, then it is doomed to fail. A hermeneutics which is capable of distinguishing between local and non-local, and yet achieves continuity and unity between vernacular and metropolitan, is one that is worth upholding and promoting: 'The boundaries of the local need to be kept open (or porous) if the local is to serve as a critical concept.'[46] If vernacularization is held to mean the hermeneutical cleansing of imported elements extraneous to one's culture, then surely it

---

[45] Edward W. Said, *Culture and Imperialism* (London, Chatto & Windus, 1993), p. xxviii.
[46] Arif Dirlik, 'Global in the Local', in *Global/Local: Cultural Production and the Transnational Imaginary*, ed. Rob Wilson and Wimal Dissanayake (Durham, NC, Duke University Press, 1996), p. 42.

is bound to be a disaster. But on the other hand, if it means critical freedom to resist cultural imperialism and to challenge dominant ideologies, then it will continue to be an important hermeneutical category.

The threat to the vernacular way of thinking comes not necessarily from the importation of literary theories from outside, but from within. It comes from the rapid social and cultural changes that are taking place within traditional societies. Among other things, it is caused by rapid movement, displacement and resettlement of people due to local wars, environmental disruption, and so forth. When the preservers and guardians of traditional wisdom and values are uprooted, lose touch with their native knowledge, diminish in numbers and begin to disappear, being gradually replaced by a generation exposed to and seduced by global values, then the traditional belief-system is in real trouble.

Let me digress here and narrate a modern parable. It is about the outward progression of an Indian Christian. There was an old villager simply called Muthu. His son was Gnanamuthu, a trained teacher and a potential candidate for the order of catechist. Gnanamuthu had a son, who went to the local mission college, blossomed into Mr John Gnanamuthu, BA, BL, and ended up as an advocate at the Madras High Court. He acquired a motor car. His son went to Cambridge and gained a blue in tennis, he called himself John Hoskyns Gnanamuthu, Esq. – J. H. G. Muthu for short. Rajaiah Paul, from whom I borrowed this parable, comments that the short Muthu was culturally 'a weakling compared with his grandfather, the plain Muthu'. The older Muthu's spirituality was plainly visible because it was drawn from and sustained by his own immediate past and cultural forms. Whereas, according to Rajaiah Paul, 'the Cambridge blue's faith is smothered by his blazer with the college crest, and the flickering flame of his spirituality has long ago been extinguished by the cold of an English university education and by a deluge of intellectual irrelevancies'.[47] What this imaginary story indicates is a rapid

[47] Rajaiah D. Paul, *The Cross Over India* (London, SCM Press, 1952), p. 111.

lapse of cultural memory and an uneasy relationship with one's heritage, as one moves through different processes of intellectual and cultural mutations.

The other threat to the vernacular way of thinking comes from an excessive preoccupation with identity and authenticity. Recently, Robert Allen Warrior has urged native scholars to move away from detached and essentializing tendencies and not to abandon themselves to intellectual strategies and categories of Western thought patterns in their output, but to recover the intellectual sovereignty of the native poetic practice. What he was advocating was that hermeneutical deliberations should be grounded in and continuous with native narrative practices and be circumscribed by them. In evaluating and recommending some of the works of the Native American writings, Warrior writes: 'What we need to learn [from their work] is that we do not have to wait to discover some essentially Indian form of writing before we can begin to try to make critical sense of our past, present, and future.'[48]

Vernacular hermeneutics, like any other textual practice, cannot be a surrogate for real engagement with the everyday business of living. Invoking the native culture and insisting on its purity is less important than real involvement with the ongoingness of life. In an ever-increasingly multi-cultural society like ours, where traditions, histories and texts commingle, interlace and overlap, a quest for unalloyed pure native roots could prove to be dangerous. It could cause complications for the everyday business of simply living with neighbours of diverse cultures, religions and languages. The prime concern for the interpreter must be to facilitate communal harmony rather than to resuscitate a projected, invented or imagined hypothetical identity or a past entombed in a bygone age.

At a time when the world is ever shrinking and being linked by transnational capital and multinational corporations, when the globe is celebrated as a village where everyone is interconnected and when the idea of a stable home is an elusive concept, to look for a native or a vernacular heritage may be a

---

[48] Robert Allen Warrior, *Tribal Secrets: Recovering American Indian Intellectual Traditions* (Minneapolis, University of Minnesota Press, 1996), p. 117.

futile or even a utopian endeavour. In such circumstances, it is
not always easy to identify an authentic native person. One of
the tests prescribed in the Hebrew Scriptures – using vernacular
as a way of ascertaining identity – may not be appropriate
today. The Book of Judges describes how the men of Gilead,
under the leadership of Jephthah, unmasked the Ephraimite
infiltrators crossing the river Jordan by asking them to pro-
nounce the word for 'running stream', *shibboleth*. If the infiltrators said '*sibboleth*', their dialect exposed them as fugitives from
Ephraim, and the text reports that forty-two thousand Ephrai-
mites were slain (Jud. 12). At a time when vernacular cultures
and languages are intermingled with those of the metropolis, it
is not always feasible to use dialect as a test of identity. In our
enthusiasm to recover the native, we may put ourselves in the
double predicament of finding redeeming values both in the
indigene and in the text. Both have to be approached cautiously.
By eulogizing the ascendency of the native and revalorizing the
text, we may end up fixing, absolutizing and immobilizing both.
We may eventually find ourselves advocating and reaffirming
the 'cosy indigene', and endowing the text with unwarranted
numinous and magical properties. In our desire to resurrect the
real native, it is worth while heeding Rey Chow's warning – not
to sanctify the image of the native nor to regard native as the
site of genuine knowledge. She goes on to say that 'our
fascination with the native, the oppressed, the savage, and all
such figures is therefore a desire to hold on to an unchanging
certainty somewhere outside our own 'fake' experience.'[49] In
projecting an idealized native, we may be culpable of fabri-
cating our own version of 'orientalism' and of partaking in myth
making.

As a way of ending, let us go back to the painter and the
peasant. Though Anantha Murthy was moved by the painter's
remarks, on reflection he says that he had a nagging doubt:

Isn't the authentic Indian peasant, whose imagination is mythical and
who relates to nature organically, also an imported cult figure of the
Western radicals, who are reacting against their materialist civiliza-

---

[49] Rey Chow, *Writing Diaspora: Tactics of Intervention in Contemporary Cultural Studies*
(Bloomington, Indiana University Press, 1993), p. 53.

tion? What if these spiritual reactions in the West are their way of keeping fit, and the 'decline of the West' theory is glibly-repeated humbug? . . . As a result we keep reacting rather than creating; we advocate the absurd, or in reaction to it admire the authentic Indian peasant – all of them masks to hide our own uncertainties. In the morass of poverty, disease and ugliness of India, isn't the Westernized Indian unauthentic and inconsequential, and the traditional peasant an incongruous and helpless victim of centuries of stagnation?[50]

Third World theologies, desperately looking for a new mode of perception in the face of new forms of colonialism and the threatening features of globalization, are certainly attracted by the simple peasant/aborigine/tribal who has remained through the centuries impervious to the cultures of the conquerors. It is also tempting to freeze a part of the indigene's life as if it represented the whole, and confine him or her to the local. Such an indigene may be no more than a creature of the hermeneutical imagination. Even if that imaginary indigene exists, he or she, like the peasant at the foot of the hill, may not be the least bit interested in the issues discussed here. But as Anantha Murthy says, 'it is important to know that he [or she] exists; our hypersensitive, highly-personal nightmares will at least be tempered with the irony of such knowledge'.[51]

[50] Ananda Murthy, 'The Search for an Identity', p. 72.
[51] Ibid., p. 76.

CHAPTER 7

Engaging liberation: texts as a vehicle of emancipation

I don't particularly think liberation should need theology.

Gayatri Chakravorty Spivak

In the 1980s, after nearly twenty years of liberation theology, Juan Luis Segundo, one of its pioneers, delivered a lecture in Toronto, and in it he delineated the shifts within Latin American liberation theology. In the course of the lecture Segundo identified two types of Latin American theology: one initiated by middle-class professional theologians, and the other by ordinary people. The features of the first line of theology were the conversion of the professional class of theologians to the cause of the poor; their detection of the ideological manipulation of the gospel by the institutions and the powerful, to maintain their hold; and their commitment to provide long-term pastoral care with a new de-ideologized and humanizing gospel recoverable from the ancient texts. Segundo told his audience: 'Thus it was not the oppressed people, but the middle classes, beginning with students, who received the first features of this liberation theology as a joyful conversion and a new commitment.'[1] The context for the first model was the university, and its proponents were a theologically trained cadre. The middle class acquired a new theological vision and made liberation their new commitment at the cost of risking their physical comforts and material privileges.

The second model of Latin American theologizing, Segundo observed, arose as a result of the irruption of the populist

[1] Juan Luis Segundo, *Signs of the Times: Theological Reflections*, tr. Robert R. Barr (Maryknoll, NY, Orbis Books, 1993), p. 71.

movements with their indigenous religiosity. This happened
both within and outside the Church. The emergence of the
common people had indicated that they 'had neither understood nor welcomed anything from the first theology of liberation, and had actually reacted against its criticism of the
supposed oppressive elements of popular religion'.[2] The middle
class, Segundo observed, had enthusiasm, raised hope and
showed concern for the poor, but they were so integrated into
European culture that they did not appreciate the religiosity
and the spirituality of the indigenous. No doubt the professional
theologians shared the same goal of humanizing and liberating
those who suffer under oppression on the Continent, but
Segundo opined that one could not conceal the fact that 'we are
faced here with two different theologies under the same name:
different in scope, different in method, different in presuppositions, and different in pastoral consequences'.[3]

It is nearly twenty years since Segundo made these observations. Since that time Latin American theology has gone
through other paradigm shifts,[4] but more significantly, as a
theology which started as a local enterprise catering to local
needs, it has now broadened to become part of 'a truly global
flow',[5] and has attained a sense of universal status. However, its
assumed homogeneity, its domineering posture and its tendency
to speak for all the Third World were dented by forces both
within and from outside. Building on, and in some cases taking
issue with, Latin American liberation theologies, Africans,
Asians, women, and various indigenous and disadvantaged
people have worked out their own version of liberation theology.
The purpose of this chapter is to sketch how the Bible has been
appropriated in the welter of liberation theologies.

Based on Segundo's analysis, one can see three phases within

---

[2] Ibid., pp. 73–4.   [3] Ibid., p. 75.

[4] For paradigm shifts within liberation theologies, see essays in *Liberation Theologies on
Shifting Grounds: A Clash of Socio-Economic and Cultural Paradigms*, ed. G. de Schrijver
(Leuven, Leuven University Press, 1998).

[5] Robert Schreiter postulates that as part of globalization, along with the circulation of
culture and information, theologies too travel. Examples of such travelling theologies
are Latin American liberation theology, and the Western feminist theologies. See his
Robert J. Schreiter, *The New Catholicity: Theology Between the Global and the Local*
(Maryknoll, NY, Orbis Books, 1997), pp. 1–27.

liberation hermeneutics. One, Latin American liberation theology undertaken at a grand macro-level, engages in a universal
discourse of liberation. It provides overarching categories which
make sense only from a cosmopolitan perspective. In the
interpretation of the texts, its aim is to read the text 'in the light
of our Latin American reality', or through 'Latin American
Eyes' and, by extension, including all those who are oppressed
in distant continents. It is stripped of all Latin American
particularities, and aims to speak for all the oppressed. For
instance, in Gutiérrez's seminal work, *Theology of Liberation*, his
own country, Peru, is hardly mentioned. In his introduction to
Job, he writes:

In this reading of the Book of Job I shall keep my attention on what it
means to talk of God in the context of Latin America, and more
concretely in the context of the suffering of the poor – which is to say,
the vast majority of the population.[6]

In the process of working out its hermeneutic, it by-passed all
specificities and assumed some kind of universal proportion and
intention. In her preface to the North American edition of *The
Amnesty of Grace*, Elsa Tamez reminds her readers of the universal implication of her work: 'Even though this study has
arisen in a context of exclusion, oppression, and poverty, its
message is for everyone.'[7] I would like to call this mode of
interpretation classic liberation hermeneutics.

The second phase is the reading of the Bible undertaken at
the grass-roots in the base Christian communities by non-
trained readers. They see the Bible as the product of a community and see their task as recovering it from an individualistic,
'spiritual'-apolitical reading, for the empowerment of the community. This reading practice was initiated in Latin American
base ecclesiastical communities and indigenous communities.
The appropriation of the Bible during the Samoza regime by
the peasants from Solentiname became an important hermeneutical occasion. This mode of interpretation later flowed into

---

[6] Gustavo Gutiérrez, *On Job: God-Talk and the Suffering of the Innocent* (Maryknoll, NY,
Orbis Books, 1987), p. xviii.
[7] Elsa Tamez, *The Amnesty of Grace: Justification by Faith from a Latin American Perspective*, tr.
Sharon H. Ringe (Nashville, Abingdon Press, 1993), p. 8.

other parts of the world, particularly to South Africa and the Philippines. I would like to call this approach the Peoples' Reading.

The third phase is the emergence of specific-reference liberation reading engaged in by a wide variety of minority voices – dalits, women, burakumin, indigenous people and people who were victimized by both internal and external forces. In the 1980s the victim culture began to emerge and historical suffering became a kind of certificate of legitimacy. It was the 'product of damage'. People stopped hiding their ethnicities and gender differences and saw their goal as awaking and nourishing their wounded identities. Victimhood became not only a rallying point but a central focus of identity. I would like to call this identity-specific reading.

CLASSICAL LIBERATION HERMENEUTICS

There is no need to rehearse here the origins and development of Latin American liberation theologies. There is enough literature dealing with it. However, let me highlight some of the interpretative features which have become the hallmarks of liberation hermeneutics.

Commitment to eradicate poverty comes first, and the reading of the text follows as a critical reflection upon it, tangibly accomplishing the intentions behind the sacred writings;

affirmation that reality is one and liberation is seen as an all-encompassing phenomenon. Traditional dualisms such as sacred/secular, individual/communitarian are coalesced into one unified history. History is seen as the medium of God's self-disclosure, and the site of the historical activity of God;

privileging the poor as a significant hermeneutical category. Every new situation rescues a new interpretative concern which earlier interpreters had either neglected or overlooked. Liberation hermeneutics made the poor a favoured exegetical concern;

it also made a compelling case for biblical scholarship to

come to grips with the problems of people and serve
them rather than be taking refuge in theories and
philological debates;

abhorrence of the idea of a neutral reading of the text. An
interpreter has to take an option; liberation theologians
unapologetically, openly and consciously side with the
poor, and it is from this perspective that a reading is
undertaken;

the credibility of the Bible rests on a proper pre-understanding.
The Bible has meaning only when it is read with a
particular viewpoint. The reading of the Bible from a
specific perspective does not threaten the catholicity of
the gospel, rather it liberates the gospel message from its
neutrality and brings out its multifaceted dimension.

Liberation hermeneutics was responsible for introducing two
hermenutical categories – 'hermeneutical circle' and 'hermeneutics of suspicion'; which have since entered the lexicon of
biblical scholarship. It was Segundo who first mooted the idea
of a hermeneutical circle.[8] According to him, one first analyses
the everyday reality of the context with all its problems and
conflicts, then one goes to biblical texts to listen to their
message, and then one returns to the context bringing in the
newness that the gospel introduces to the situation. The hermeneutics of suspicion, on the other hand, seeks to expose the
ideological bias in biblical interpretation. José Bonino identified
in the early days of liberation theology that what is often
mistaken for an objective reading is ideologically biased. This
was before it became fashionable to see a link between social
location and interpretation. For instance, looking at the way the
sayings of Jesus on the rich and poor have been exegeted by the
dominant hermeneutics of the time, Bonino was able to expose
how it reflected class values:

Even a cursory look to biblical commentaries in the Protestant
tradition shows the almost uniform ideological train of thought: riches
(in themselves) are good – therefore Jesus could not have condemned

---

[8] Juan Luis Segundo, *The Liberation of Theology*, tr. John Drury (Maryknoll, NY, Orbis Books, 1976), pp. 7–38.

them as such, nor rich people as such – consequently the text must mean something else.[9]

Such ideological blindness, Bonino went on to declare, was found even in honest and responsible exegetes. Bonino cites the example of Joachim Jeremias:

He – perhaps correctly – argues in the parable of the rich man and Lazarus, 'Jesus does not want to comment on a social problem.' But when [verse] 25 (Luke 16.19–31) poses the reversal of the condition of the poor, Jeremias argues for the 'ideological supposition' and asks: 'Where had Jesus ever suggested that wealth in itself merits hell and the poverty in itself is rewarded by paradise?'[10]

To this Bonino himself came up with answers which an interpretation free from bourgeois presupposition could not have failed to see:

One: that Jesus never speaks of wealth *in itself* or poverty *in itself* but of rich and poor as they are, historically. The 'in itself abstraction is clearly a piece of liberal ideology. Second: a whole number of texts, or rather practically all texts dealing with the subject (with the exception of Matthew 13.12 and parallels if interpreted in this connection), point in the clear direction of this reversal, whatever explanation we may want to give them. Moreover, its relation to one trend of the prophetic tradition – to which Jesus is evidently related in several other aspects of his teaching – makes it all the more clear. We reach the real ground of Jeremias' interpretation in the strange affirmation that 'Jesus does not intend to take a position on the question of rich and poor.'[11]

Next, as a way of highlighting the classic liberation hermeneutics, I would like to look at Gutiérrez's *On Job* and Elsa Tamez's *The Amnesty of Grace*. I have purposely chosen these writings to set aright the popular misperception that liberation hermeneutics revolves around a single biblical narrative – the Exodus. Gutiérrez himself has often tried to rectify this false impression. In his discussion with the theology faculty of the Catholic Institute of Lyons, he told his audience that, although the Exodus motif is important for Latin America, it has been

---

[9] José Miguez-Bonino, 'Marxist Critical Tools: Are They Helpful in Breaking the Stranglehold of Idealist Hermeneutics?', in *Voices from the Margin: Interpreting the Bible in the Third World*, new edition, ed. R. S. Sugirtharajah (Maryknoll, NY, Orbis Books, 1995), p. 60.

[10] Ibid., p. 60.   [11] Ibid., pp. 60–1.

overstated, and that liberation hermeneutics from the outset had been mining other biblical passages which are a key to the understanding of liberation, for instance, passages that profitably deal with poverty.[12]

Gutiérrez's Job

The starting point for reading Job, for Gutiérrez, is God-talk – how do we talk about God particularly from within the situation of innocent suffering? The theological focus for him is not the one which Western theology has been trying to wrestle with since the holocaust – how do we speak about God after Auschwitz? Rather, how does one engage in theological discourse while Ayacucho[13] lasts? It is talking about God while ordinary people daily experience violation, deprivation and death in Latin America. It is not about a theological reflection based on a past event like Auschwitz, important though it is; the Latin American question is about the present innocent suffering of the poor when everything in their daily life seems to be a denial of the presence of the love of God. With these questions, Gutiérrez turns to the Book of Job because he finds in it that the 'innocence that Job vigorously claims for himself helps us to understand the innocence of an oppressed and believing people amid the situation of suffering and death that has been forced upon it'.[14] While conceding that the Book of Job addresses other pertinent theological issues such as the transcendence of God, the problem of evil, personal suffering and grief, Gutiérrez's conviction is that central to the narrative is the question of innocent suffering.

Gutiérrez acknowledges that the Book of Job does not provide a neat answer for the question of innocent suffering; Job's faith has prompted him to inquire into finding an appro-

---

[12] See Gustavo Gutiérrez, *The Truth Shall Make You Free: Confrontations*, tr. Matthew O'Connell (Maryknoll, NY, Orbis Books, 1990), p. 29. For appropriation of various texts of the Bible by Latin American interpreters, see *Subversive Scriptures: Revolutionary Readings of the Christian Bible in Latin America*, ed. and tr. Leif E. Vaage (Valley Forge, PA, Trinity Press International, 1997).

[13] Ayacucho is a rampantly poor and violent city in the Peruvian mountains.

[14] Gutiérrez, *On Job*, p. xviii.

priate language about God that makes sense to the suffering people. Job conveys that there are two ways of speaking about God – prophetic and mystical – both are interlaced, and reinforce and inspire each other. Prophetic language allows one to draw nearer to God because of God's predilection for the poor. An aspect of this language is justice. In the early stages, Job was too concerned about his own suffering, and this becomes the site for his protest. Gradually Job realizes that he is not alone, that suffering is not something peculiar to him and that there are many like him. From then on his protests become stronger because he is open to other sufferings, and they include the plight of others as well. Now he protests in the name of all innocent victims. It is this kind of prophetic language, Gutiérrez urges, that Christians should recapture in their discourse and praxis.

Mystical language, on the other hand, speaks about the gratuitous love of God – the unmerited love God has for the poor. The poor are privileged not because they are morally superior or materially deprived, but because of the gratuitousness and universality of God's utter freedom to love. God is committed to the poor not because they are inherently good, but because God is good and God prefers the least in the world. Gutiérrez writes: 'The ultimate basis for the privileged position of the poor is not in the poor themselves but in God, in the gratuitousness and universality of God's *agapeic* love.'[15]

For Gutiérrez, both languages – prophetic and mystical – are necessary and therefore inseparable. The language of contemplation acknowledges that everything comes from God's unmerited love and it opens up 'new horizons of hope'; and the language of prophecy attacks the structural causes which deprive the poor and keep them in the unjust situations in which they find themselves. It is the language which looks for ' "the suffering features of the Christ the Lord" in the pain-ravaged faces of an oppressed people'.[16] This twofold language, in Gutiérrez's view, is the language of Jesus presaged by Job. While Job stutters, Jesus speaks out clearly and explicitly. It is on

[15] Ibid., p. 94.   [16] Ibid., p. 97.

the cross that Jesus talks with great expressiveness about God. Gutiérrez's contention is that we 'must humbly allow the cry of Jesus on the cross to echo through history and nourish our theological efforts'.[17]

In reading *On Job*, we see a shift in methodological orientation in Gutiérrez's thinking. The celebrated phrases which he wrote in *Theology of Liberation* and which became a kind of manifesto for liberation theology – commitment as a first act, and theology as a critical reflection upon praxis as a second act[18] – have now given way to contemplation and praxis as the first act, and reflection on it as the second act.[19] In his changed understanding of speaking about God, Gutiérrez writes:

> The point I want to make can be stated thus: God is first contemplated when we do God's will and allow God to reign; only after that do we think about God. To use familiar categories: contemplation and practice together make up a *first act*; theologizing is a *second act*. We must first establish ourselves on the terrain of spirituality and practice; only subsequently is it possible to formulate discourse on God in an authentic and respectful way. Theologizing done without the mediation of contemplation and practice does not meet the requirements of the God of the Bible.[20]

The accent here seems to be placed more on contemplation and emancipatory spirituality than on action and social transformation, for which liberation theology came to be known in its heady days. In a statement which suggests the repudiation of one of the basic tenets of liberation theology, Gutiérrez goes on to say: 'The ultimate basis of God's preference for the poor is to be found in God's own goodness and *not in any analysis of society or in human compassion*, however pertinent these reasons may be.'[21] These changes in thinking could be attributed, among other things, to pressures from the Roman Catholic hierarchy, and

---

[17] Ibid., p. 103.
[18] Gustavo Gutiérrez, *A Theology of Liberation: History, Politics, and Salvation*, tr. Caridad Inda and John Eagleson (Maryknoll, NY, Orbis Books, 1973), p. 9.
[19] For a moving personal account of the shift in his methodology, see his introduction to the revised edition of *A Theology of Liberation*, especially pp. xxviii–xxxvi: Gustavo Gutiérrez, *A Theology of Liberation: History, Politics, and Salvation*, tr. Caridad Inda and John Eagleson (Maryknoll, NY, Orbis Books, 1988).
[20] Gutiérrez, *On Job*, p. xiii.
[21] Ibid., p. xiii; italics mine.

the apparent failure of the socialist experiment in Eastern Europe. In the face of these, liberation theology seems to be distancing itself from an earlier liberative critical theory and practice, and to be moving to a more conservative type of theological discourse.

Tamez's Paul

Tamez engages in a similar theological pursuit, but this time her hermeneutical aim is how to talk about justification in Latin America when there is cultural, social and psychological dehumanization. The doctrine of justification, as it is perceived in Latin America, offers good news to the oppressor rather than to the poor. It is viewed in an abstract, individualistic and generic sense. Going beyond confessional and denominational debates which focus on faith and works, law and grace, Tamez tries to make justification meaningful to the excluded; she redefines sin as being structural and as the cause of the deaths of innocent millions in Latin America.[22] Unlike the denominational theologies which see sin in private and pietistic terms, Tamez places it in a social context, and hence her contention is that justification has to be seen in social terms. In her rereading of Paul's Romans, Tamez detects correspondences between the Pauline and the Latin American contexts. Her claim is that Paul himself addressed questions about the power of the structural sin which has enslaved all humanity, and which Paul recognized as an indestructible power. Tamez reckons that sin is a reality woven into Paul's historical context. To triumph over this, Paul engages in two types of interrelated languages. Echoing Gutiérrez's view of prophetic and mystical languages, Tamez sees in Paul a similar twofold theological vocabulary: one talks about the faithfulness of God; the other talks about the redemption of the poor and about human solidarity among them as a consequence of such an act of God. Tamez explains Paul's position thus:

One type of language speaks about faith in God: the absolute certainty of the solidarity of God with the condemned, which is

---

[22] Tamez, *Amnesty of Grace*, p. 14.

manifested in the love of God in Christ. No one and nothing will be able to separate us from that love (Romans 8:38–39). The other type of language speaks of the faith response in the human being: 'In all these things we are more than conquerors through him who loved us' (Romans 8:37).[23]

To overcome the perceived subjectivism and individualism of justification, Tamez sees justification as God's loving care on the Cross. The Resurrection constitutes an integral component of justification. On the Cross, God not only heard the cry of his son but the cries of all those who were abandoned. In raising Jesus, God offered to the excluded the possibility of resurrection. Without resurrection one would remain in the former life – the life of hopelessness. For Tamez, justification has more to do with the affirmation of life than with forgiveness of sin. Reconciliation with sinners is only an aspect of justification, but the very essence of justification is God's solidarity with those who are on the periphery and are threatened with death. She writes

The revelation of the justice of God and its realization in justification proclaim and bring about the good news of the right to life for all people. The life granted in justification is recognized as an inalienable gift, because it proceeds from the solidarity of God, in Jesus Christ, with those who are excluded. Such a life of dignity makes human beings subjects of their history. God 'justifies' (makes and declares just) the human being in order to transform the unjust world that excludes, kills and dehumanizes that same human being.[24]

Such an act of solidarity, according to Tamez, has vitalized the excluded into regaining their dignity as free people of God. The logic of grace declares an amnesty for all those who are excluded. No more are they the objects of law or manipulated by the structures. Now, as the result of the work of Jesus on the Cross, they emerge as fully humanized subjects, to do 'justice and rescue the truth which has been imprisoned in injustice'. To put it differently, justification is God in solidarity with humanity in Jesus Christ – the prototype of the excluded, as a result of which, human beings discover their dignity and self-affirmation.

[23] Ibid., p. 112.   [24] Ibid., p. 14.

To sum up: there are certain similarities between the hermeneutical enterprises of Gutiérrez and Tamez. Both speak from
within the context of Latin America and try to recontextualize
the biblical message within that context. In this, their interpretative practices resonate with Leonardo Boff's notion of 'the
correspondence of relationships'. Unlike 'the correspondence of
terms' which sees facile parallels between the present context
and past texts, 'the correspondence of relationships' is a much
more finessed mode where the current political, social and
economic struggles of people are seen as the prism through
which to look at a similar political, social and economic engagement depicted in biblical narratives.[25] Both exegete at the
redacted level of the texts, and their commentarial style reflects
the current narrativel way of commenting rather than the
technical line-by-line approach. They both use the Bible as a
check and a corrective to the prevalent teachings of the Church.
For both, the credibility of the Bible is defined by and based on
its essential content – Jesus Christ. 'The life of Jesus Christ, his
death and resurrection of which we read in the Scriptures', in
Tamez's view, must be 'reinterpreted with the purpose of giving
life to every human being.'[26] It is Jesus who replaces the Bible as
the authority. Finally, Gutiérrez and Tamez concur in their
theological proposal, too. Both emphasize the generosity and
compassion of God, social responsibility and the benevolence
that prevails among the disadvantaged, prompted and inspired
by God's graciousness.

While rejecting the universalizing tendencies of Western
theologies, these two interpreters end up reproducing a micro-
cosmic version of the very theology they tried to reject. The
Book of Job and the Pauline writings are reread, without the use
of any specific Latin American theological nuances or indigenous cultural resources, but from the perspective of liberal
and modernist values of solidarity, identification and liberation.
Their hermeneutics retains some features of liberal theology.

---

[25] Clodovis Boff, 'Hermeneutics: Constitution of Theological Pertinency', in *Voices from
the Margin: Interpreting the Bible in the Third World*, ed. R. S. Sugirtharajah (London,
SPCK, 1991), pp. 9–35.
[26] Tamez, *Amnesty of Grace*, p. 122.

The understanding of justification based on the reconstruction of Paul and the message that God shows unmerited love towards the poor are actually closer to liberal thinking. The justification (for Tamez) and the gratuitousness of God's love (for Gutiérrez) are ultimately effected through the death of Jesus, and the difference is that it is the poor who replace sinners as recipients. In their use of the Bible too, Gutiérrez and Tamez replicate the classical liberal view which advocates that the Bible must be related to the context wherein God's presence is already evident. Their hermeneutical proposal sounds as though it is replicating the liberal message, couched in liberation language: Jesus loves me. This I know for the Bible tells me so.

RADICAL READING WITHIN THE MARGINS: PEOPLES' APPROPRIATION OF THE BIBLE

The second line of hermeneutics to emerge within the liberation framework is the peoples' appropriation of the Bible, where it is read with intimacy and authority in the community of the faithful. This mode of interpretation exploded in Latin American Christian base communities, and as a result the professional and trained biblical scholars were forced to take up the cause of the new 'liberating exegesis'. This conversion was seen as the new evangelization whereby theologians were evangelized by the poor. The theologians themselves went on to affirm the valency of the poor: 'We ought to be in the discipleship of the poor' (Dussel); 'The Church is born of the poor' (Boff); 'The history of the kingdom is moved by the hidden power of the poor' (Gutiérrez). In marking this movement, Vitor Westhelle wrote:

Instead of the Exodus motif stressed by theologians who would see themselves leading the people away from the land of slavery, or a John the Baptist calling for repentance and announcing the coming of a new person, now the images were reversed. Instead of Exodus, there was *eisodus*, the entry into the lives of the people, the incarnation, and *kenosis*.[27]

---

[27] Vitor Westhelle, 'Elements for a Typology of Latin American Theologies', in *Prejudice: Issues in Third World Theologies*, ed. Andreas Nehring (Madras, Gurukul Lutheran Theological College and Research Institute, 1996), pp. 91–2.

The appropriation of the Bible by ordinary readers is known variously as 'popular', 'pastoral', and 'communitarian' reading but, for our purpose, I have chosen to define it as the Peoples' Reading. Pablo Richards, who has established himself along with Carlos Mesters as a pioneer and a theoretician in the communal mode of interpretation, describes this reading as

[G]enerally carried out in the Base Ecclesial Communities found among the people of Latin America, which attempts to recover the original historical and spiritual meaning of the Bible, according to the experience of the presence and revelation of God in the world of the poor in order to discern and communicate the word of God.[28]

The key to the interpretation is to view reading as a single act where the text and life coalesce. In this act, according to Mesters, the principal hermeneutical task is not to interpret the Bible but to interpret life with the help of the Bible: 'The main concern is not to find out what the Bible says in itself, but to learn what it has to say about life. For that reason it is seen as a "mirror".'[29]

Although communal reading of the Bible originated in the Latin American context to meet specific hermeneutical and ecclesial needs, this mode of interpretation has now also been profitably transferred to, and appropriated in, other parts of the world. Gerald West in South Africa[30] and Carlos Abesamis in the Philippines[31] have utilized the method by looking at biblical narratives and using an important but often neglected tool – ordinary people's critical consciousness of their own society and the text. Though they emerge from different reading encoun-

---

[28] Cited in Saulo Maurico de Barros, 'Popular Reading of the Bible: A Liberating Method', MA dissertation (University of Birmingham, 1998), p. 5.

[29] Carlos Mesters, *Defenseless Flower: A New Reading of the Bible*, tr. Francis McDonagh (Maryknoll, NY, Orbis Books, 1989), p. 81.

[30] See Gerald O. West, *Contextual Bible Study* (Pietermaritzburg, Cluster Publications, 1993); Gerald O. West, *The Academy of the Poor: Towards a Dialogical Reading of the Bible* (Sheffield, Sheffield Academic Press, 1999); see also *Semeia: An Experimental Journal for Biblical Criticism* 73 (1996), 'Reading with: An Exploration of the Interface between Critical and Ordinary Readings of the Bible – African Overtures'.

[31] See Carlos H. Abesamis, *A Third Look at Jesus: A Guidebook Along the Road Least Travelled* (Quezon City, Claretian Publications, 1999). For other examples of reading the Bible in local congregations see Dhyanchand Carr (ed.), *Towards An Asian Theology of Hope: Reading the Bible with New Eyes*, nos. 1 and 2 (Hong Kong, Christian Conference of Asia. n.d.)

ters, there are certain common elements within these approaches. I shall tease out some of the common features of the
Peoples' Reading and support this reading with exegetical
examples from the interpretation that came out of the community at Solentiname.[32]

Solentiname, in Nicaragua was one of the base Christian
communities which attracted attention in the 1980s. Its popu-
larity was due to two factors: first, its involvement in the
revolutionary struggle against the rule of General Anastasio
Somoza and, second, its production of commentaries. The
peasants at Solentiname became popular for their biblical
commentaries, both textual and visual,[33] which came out of
their weekly meetings. The community was composed of nearly
ninety peasants gathered from thirty-eight isles in the Lake of
Nicaragua. It became the spiritual home for these poor people.
Ernesto Cardenal who, to the annoyance of the Roman Catholic officialdom, joined the Sandinista government after the
overthrow of Somoza, acted as the 'expert' who enabled the
peasants to wade through the complex maze of biblical history,
theology and interpretation.

The Peoples' Reading revolves around the following
elements.

The Bible is their own book, and there is the firm belief that
the Bible is addressed to today's poor in their joys and sorrows,
and in their hopes and fears.

The Bible assures them that the present pitiable state they

---

[32] For other examples see Tereza Cavalcanti, 'Social Location and Biblical Interpret-
ation: Tropical Reading', in *Reading from This Place*, vol. II: *Social Location and Biblical
Interpretation in Global Perspective*, ed. Fernando F. Segovia and Mary Ann Tolbert
(Minneapolis, Fortress Press, 1995), pp. 201–18; Shigeyuki Nakanose, *Josiah's Passover:
Sociology and the Liberating Bible* (Maryknoll, NY, Orbis Books, 1993), especially
pp. 113– 51. In the first part of the book Nakanose subjects Josiah's Passover in 2
Kings to sociological analysis and demonstrates how the reactivated festival strength-
ened the power of small elite groups, and concentrated the power in the institutions;
he then goes on to describe what happens when this is read in relation to the
Brazilian base communities.

[33] For their comments on biblical passages see Ernesto Cardenal, *The Gospel in
Solentiname*, tr. Donald D. Walsh, vols. I–IV (Maryknoll, NY, Orbis Books, 1982); for
their visual representation of biblical narratives see Philip Scharper and Sally
Scharper, *The Gospel in Art by the Peasants in Solentiname* (Maryknoll, NY, Orbis Books,
1980).

find themselves in is changeable. The current poverty is not an accident of history, nor pre-ordained, but human made. As such, the Bible has the evangelical potential to bring out changes in the social order. Oscar, one of the peasants who figures predominantly in the Solentiname commentaries, tells his fellow Nicaraguan peasants that, if they are not interested in the transforming power of the Bible, they might as well read 'any damned thing', or 'any stupid book'.[34]

It is their faith that makes grass-roots Christians read the Bible. They are not unduly worried about the threat posed to the biblical narratives by historical criticism, nor is their faith in the biblical God undermined by theological controversies which tend to rattle the faith of urban and secular Christians. It is not the 'death of God' which makes the poor turn to the Bible, rather it is the death of the poor. The Bible is not read from the perspective of belief versus unbelief but from the perspective of liberation versus oppression.

The study of the Bible is undertaken collectively and it takes place in a community. Therefore everything is seen in a communal fashion. Biblical doctrines such as sin, grace and salvation are defined in collective terms rather than in individualistic or pietistic terms.

The Bible helps people to feel a oneness with the Palestinian peasants and places them in a similar context of redemption and exploitation. The Bible, for instance, helps the Nicaraguan peasants to see easy parallels between Roman-occupied Palestine and Somoza-ruled Nicaragua. In one of the sessions, Cardenal reminds them that: 'The tragedy in Managua tonight, and in the whole country, is very much like the painful scene described in the Gospel.'[35] The peasants show little concern for historical distance and readily associate themselves with the hopes and fears of the first-century Palestine peasants. Thus, Somoza becomes the new Herod; the Nicaraguan children who were killed during the Managuan earthquake are likened to the innocent babes slaughtered during Herod's rule; Somoza's betrayal of Sandino reenacts Judas' betrayal of Jesus. Che

---

[34] Cardenal, *The Gospel in Solentiname*, III, p. 255.
[35] Ibid., I, p. 41.

Guevara, Allende and Camillo Torres become new liberators in the fashion of Jesus. Rigoberta Menchú, the Guatemalan Nobel Prize winner, recalls how she and her activists, in their Bible study sessions, saw parallel relationships between themselves and the biblical figures:

Take 'Exodus' for example, that's one we studied and analysed. It talks a lot about the life of Moses who tried to lead his people from oppression, and did all he could to free his people. We compare the Moses of those days with ourselves, the 'Moses' of today. . . We began looking for texts which represented each one of us. We tried to relate them to our Indian culture. We took the example of Moses for the men, and we have the example of Judith, who was a very famous woman in her time and appears in the Bible . . . She held her victory in her hands, the head of the King. This gave us a vision, a stronger idea of how we Christians must defend ourselves.[36]

The Bible becomes credible for the grass-roots communities because of its ability to stimulate them to action and participation. The appeal of the Bible is that it not only contains liberative memories of an oppressed people but it also provokes participation. In the words of Fernando: 'I don't understand how you can read the Gospels and get spiritual lessons for your life out of it and not get involved in the Revolution. This Book has a very clear political position for anyone who reads it simply, as you read it.'[37] It is a social document with implications for social change.

The ordinary people see in a text two meanings – historical-explicit and implicit-prophetic. For them it is the latter meaning which is crucial because it offers them wider possibilities. It is this distinction that prevents the peasants from falling into a literalistic trap. Thus they are able to distinguish between the literal and symbolic meaning of Jesus' command to share clothes and food with the person who has none. To put it in William's words:

I don't think this should be understood so literally – that if I have two shirts I have to give one away. . . That's all right, but we're not going to stop there, just looking for somebody who doesn't have a shirt.

---

[36] Rigoberta Menchu, *I. Rigoberta Menchu: An Indian Woman in Guatemala*, ed. Elisabeth Burgos-Debray, tr. Ann Wright (London, Verso, 1984), pp. 131–2.
[37] Cardenal, *The Gospel in Solentiname*, I, p. 85.

What this means, it seems to me, is that we have to change the system where some people have lots of extra shirts and others don't have any. This is levelling the roads, I said before.[38]

People as exegetes view the biblical milieu in socio-economic categories. Interpretative history tends to portray the biblical milieu as a theological battleground for varying factions such as the circumcision or anti-circumcision party, Judaizers and anti-Judaizers, or as a site for competing theological claims such as faith and work, and law and grace. Peasants do not see the New Testament period in terms of theological division but in categories of the just and unjust, the oppressor and the oppressed, and the poor and the rich. Nicodemus is not seen as an upholder of a pious and outmoded Jewish religion, but as a defender of a class system under a false religious facade. The religious leaders who came before Jesus were not false prophets and sectarian leaders but leaders who supported the oppressive political system. The unjust person is not one who is irreligious, or a pagan who follows a different religion, but the oppressor or the collaborator of the oppressor.

People do not approach the Bible with the Enlightenment world-view and critical rationality. The miracles, the angels and the virgin birth do not pose any threat to their faith or embarrass them. They accept the supernatural without any qualms. It is not a question of demythologizing the biblical stories but of remythologizing and incorporating them. When reading Acts 12.1–17, the community did not agonize over the scientific verifiability of the angel's intervention in releasing Peter, but secularized it and, through an act of analogical crossover, validated the genuineness of a biblical event. Listen to how Dona Maria explains the narrative:

When Dom Pedro Casaldáliga (the bishop of São Félix do Araguaia, Brazil, a supporter of the communities) was a prisoner in his house, no one knew. There was no means of communication. Seven well-armed police officers kept watch at the house and refused to let anyone enter or leave. Exactly like Peter's prison in the Bible. But a young girl went in. No one took any notice of her. She was an ordinary girl, in cheap flip-flops. She took a note from Dom Pedro out of his prison, went

---

[38] Ibid., p. 107.

straight to the airstrip, got a lift to Goiânia, and told the bishops who were meeting there. They got busy and got Dom Pedro freed. The girl was the angel of God who made the gates of Peter's prison swing open.[39]

Thus, little girls, community workers and freedom fighters become the present-day angels. Jesus' healing of the deaf-mute is seen as a conscientizing process. For them, the gospel becomes irrational and illogical when it does not speak against injustice, hunger, exploitation and hoarding of wealth and private property. For Oscar it was difficult to believe in the miracle of the healing of the deaf-mute; but what concerned him most was why Jesus should separate the deaf-mute from his village to heal him.

People's exegesis could be described as pre-critical, and perceived to be taking as their point of departure the Pauline dictum – 'the letter kills but the spirit makes alive'. People as exegetes unconsciously nurture pre-critical reading practices such as those which are literal, typological and allegorical. They take the text literally when it fits with their experience. They interpret typologically when they link their situations with biblical personalities or events. Thus the three Herods become three Somozas; Castro and Che are identified with Christ; Nicodemus is seen as the follower of Somoza; paying tributes to Caesar is the same as paying taxes to Somoza; giving false witness is likened to the spies collaborating with the state. They interpret allegorically when they search for hidden meanings underlying the primacy and the obvious meaning of the narratives. The purpose of interpretation is not to seek historical information about the biblical record but to deal with the issues that face them. The emphasis is not on the text's meaning in itself but rather on the meaning the text has for the people who read it. Exegesis for them is essentially an 'analogical leap'. It is through this analogical leap that the authenticity of a biblical event is determined. The biblical events become alive and authentic only when they coincide with similar current historical events in Latin America, Asia or Africa.

The Bible then becomes the fundamental criterion for dis-

[39] Mesters, *Defenseless Flower*, pp. 3–4.

cerning life. The narratives exist not as a historic and subversive revelation of ancient past but as a present reality, thus altering the perceived understanding of biblical revelation. The artistic depiction of the nativity scene by the Solentiname peasants is indicative of this radical shift. The thatched roof, verdant scenery and the indigenous attire the figures wear are all from Solentiname.[40] The hermeneutical impact of such a visualization is that the divine child born in ancient Palestine, true to his name – Immanuel, God with us – not only had meaning for the first century, but also continues to have meaning for twentieth-century Solentiname. The present reality helps people to decipher the divine revelation within the world and see it as an ongoing theophany.

Irruption within the irruption: indigenous reading

Within the Peoples' Reading of the Bible, there emerged another voice which took theologians aback. It came from the indigenous population of Latin America. The one moment which dramatically crystallized the indigenous people's attitude to the Bible was when Andean Indians wrote a letter to Pope John Paul II in 1985, signed by leaders of several Indian organizations:

We, the Indians of the Andes and America have decided to give you back your Bible, since for the past five hundred centuries it has brought us neither love, peace or justice. We beg you take your Bible and give it back to our oppressors, whose hearts and minds are in greater need of its moral teachings. As part of the colonial exchange we received the Bible, which is an ideological weapon of attack. The Spanish sword used in the daytime to attack and kill the Indians, turned at night into a cross which attacked the Indian soul.[41]

---

[40] Scharper and Scharper, *The Gospel in Art*, pp. 10–12.
[41] 'Pope Asked to Take Back the Bible,' *The Telegraph* 7 February 1985; also see Pablo Richard, '1492: The Violence of God and Future of Christianity', *Concilium* 6 (1990), 66. This was not the first time that the indigenous people of Latin America returned the Bible to the Church hierarchy. Unlike the polite petition of the present-day Andeans, five hundred years ago the Inca of Peru 'threw on the ground the book where the words of God were found'. For this act, he and his people were killed. See Elsa Tamez, 'Quetzalcoatl Challenges the Christian Bible', unpublished paper, SBL Annual Conference (San Francisco, 1992), p. 7.

For many years, the dominant Churches worked with the idea of a single Latin American culture and defended a faith which came from Europe. Indigenous religious practices were viewed from biblical prophetic tradition and denounced as idolatrous and superstitious. Now the indigenous people demanded that their culture be taken into account in all hermeneutical deliberations. Elsa Tamez confesses that the demand for the recognition of their religion and sacred tradition to be on a par with Christianity found biblical scholars, mestizos, white Catholics and Protestants 'unprepared'. They thought that this kind of hermeneutical agenda belonged to Asian Christians: 'We believed that on this continent there didn't exist any religion except Christianity and we thought that the Judaeo-Christian Bible was the only canon that had to be re-read from the perspective of the oppressed.'[42] Thus they were forced to realize that their interpretative focus had to move from making options for the poor, to options for the poor as the 'Other'. The Other until now were identified as pagan or infidel. The Cuna theologian Wagua comments:

And even today it does not always altogether free itself from this in its relations with our communities. The church has always been very sensitive to human rights, to the poor and needy, the marginalised in the dominant society, but when it has been a question of the 'other', she has regarded him as an enemy, a pagan, infidel, Moor, Indian . . . in other words they are *different*.[43]

To address the new issues, Latin American hermeneutics devised new lexicons such as 'insertion', 'inculturation' and 'to live and be identified with people'. It was no longer criticizing the religious and cultural practices of the people but was willing to learn and to be instructed by people. The people's syncretic way of articulating the faith was no longer dismissed as compromising the gospel, but came to be regarded as a 'form of resistance and inculturation of Christianity'.[44]

[42] Tamez, 'Quetzalcoatal Challenges the Christian Bible', p. 9.
[43] Aiban Wagua, 'Present Consequences of the European Invasion of America', *Concilium* 6 (1990), 53.
[44] Leonardo Boff, 'The New Evangelization: New Life Bursts in', *Concilium* 6 (1990), 134.

The indigenous hermeneutic, or the Indian reading, as Pablo Richards terms it, follows the pattern of the basic ecclesial communities – based on the Augustinian model that life is the first book and the Bible is the second book. Indigenous reading tries to rescue the authentic spirit of both the biblical and the people's own religious tradition. The colonial framework for domination was based on the distinction between soul and body. The Spanish and the West were identified with the soul and thereby identified with the spiritual and the divine, whereas the indigenous people were seen as the body, representing materialism and barbarism. It was this dichotomous thinking which underlay Western exploitation of the indigenous people. The spirituality of the indigenous people, on the other hand, was inclusive, and the spirit was not only identified with the soul but also with the entire human being and with life. Pablo Richard defines the indigenous reading thus: 'The Bible as whole is now interpreted in terms of life/death opposition rather than soul/body opposition. An interpretation of the Bible from the perspective of the Indian, the female and the body is thus a spiritual interpretation carried out under the same Spirit with which the Bible was written.'[45]

To conclude this section: recently, literary theorists have come up with a whole host of readers – from the 'implied' reader to the 'ideal'; from 'model' to 'mistaken'; and from 'subjective' to 'strong'. Unlike the fictive readers conjectured by theorists, what we have here are real flesh and blood readers who have feelings and emotions that they bring to the texts.

---

[45] Pablo Richard, 'The Hermeneutics of Liberation: A Hermeneutic of the Spirit', in *Reading from This Place*, vol. II: *Social Location and Biblical Interpretation in Global Perspective*, ed. Fernando F. Segovia and Mary Ann Tolbert (Minneapolis, Fortress Press, 1995), p. 273; see also his 'Biblical Interpretation from the Perspective of Indigenous Cultures of Latin America (Mayas, Kunas, and Quechuas)', in *Ethnicity & the Bible*, ed. Mark G. Brett (Leiden, E. J. Brill, 1996), pp. 297–314. For how Miskitu Indians constructed and reconstructed their self-identity in the political and social context in which they found themselves, especially during and after the Sandinistas rule, see Susan Hawley, 'Does God Speak Miskitu? The Bible and Ethnic Identity Among Miskitu of Nicaragua', in *Ethnicity and the Bible*, ed. Mark G. Brett (Leiden, E. J. Brill, 1996), pp. 315–42; and especially pp. 337–8, where the Bible once again became a weapon, this time turned against the Sandinistas, and they were identified variously as Antiochus Epiphanes, the Egyptians, the Canaanites, Philistines, Babylon and Rome.

What the Peoples' Reading demonstrates is that the Book which has been used as a tool of civilization has now become a tool for vitalizing their culture and life. People draw on and invoke their past and present history. They read events and episodes from their lives into the biblical narratives, and read out of them political and social praxis.

Linking oneself with biblical motifs, personalities and events raises a few questions. Identifying oneself with biblical events may produce pomposity and a false sense of security and spiritual pride. The tendency will be to see oneself as God's chosen and others as damned and rejected by God. Any hermeneutics based on the quest for easy biblical identity is bound to produce self-righteousness. The trouble with easy identification with biblical motifs, events and biblical characters is that one tends to see oneself and one's enemy in biblical stereotype. Two recent examples are the Zionist movement and Afrikaners in South Africa. Such parallelism does not give much scope for fresh dialogue and understanding. One tends to overlook the enormous political, cultural and historical differences between the present time and the biblical period. But the serious consequence of such an analogous identification is that nobody sees anything as it really is. Such a use of the Bible wrests the present from its reality. What is needed is a hermeneutics of distance. At a time when there is a relentless attempt to bridge the gap between the text and the reader, it may sound strange that I advocate this. There is already a hermeneutics of proximity in operation in many reading communities. The fusion between the ancient text and the reader already exists in the minds of ordinary readers. The ordinary readers easily identify with the Bible, biblical events and biblical characters. Existentially we may not have difficulty in seeing the relevance of the Exodus or the Exile, but we must admit that these events are not about us.

In the dialogue between indigenous cultures and the Bible, it is the Bible which functions as the adjudicator. As in colonial days, the Bible is summoned to judge people's cultures and traditions. Pablo Richard asserts the role of the Bible: 'The Bible is an instrument, a criterion, a canon, for discerning the presence and revelation of God in indigenous culture and religion.'[46]

IDENTITY-SPECIFIC READINGS

The third feature within liberation hermeneutics is the emergence of hermeneutics informed by identity questions. These voices represent the cultural, gender and ethnic identities of people who were gaining new confidence but were excluded from the mainstream theological discourse, and also from liberation theology, by a failure to address the concerns of those who were outside the high culture and patriarchy. They were Indian dalits, women, tribals, Native Americans and Aborigines, whose history has for so long and so often been one of pain and neglect. This time the reading was not against missionaries or colonialists, but against their own interpreters whose hermeneutical output was seen as pollution-based, and hierarchically and patriarchally influenced. Their reading practice was partly a reaction to the continual neglect and the intimidating and universalizing tendencies of theologies, particularly those of their own people.

These hermeneutical practices, like all liberation hermeneutics, arise out of being wounded and hurt. Having been once sidelined, the marginalized emerged to tell their own story on their own terms and, in the process, they discovered a new self-identity, self-worth and self-validation. They were not only pioneers in removing the distortion and mystification perpetuated by the reigning theologies both within the Third World and outside, but also in using those theologies to reinstate their legitimate position and affirm their wish to take their place in reinvigorating theological discourses. These minority groups turned to biblical narratives not so much to find answers to abstract questions but to rediscover who they themselves were and where they were going. They excavated what they regarded as the 'pure', 'radical' origins of the gospel, hoping to be empowered by it.

[46] Richard, '1492: The Violence of God and Future of Christianity', p. 66.

Taking leave of texts: Native Americans

One of the earliest subaltern groups to raise uneasiness about liberation hermeneutics was Native Americans. Robert Warrior, a member of the Osage Nation of American Indians, in his influential essay, 'Canaanites, Cowboys, and Indians', challenged one of the pivotal motifs of liberation hermeneutics, the Exodus narrative, which according to him overlooked an important hermeneutical constituent in this equation – the indigenes in the narrative, the Canaanites, those who were already living on the land, and by extension the Native Americans.[47] Warrior sees parallels between Native Americans and the biblical Canaanites, who were dispossessed of their homeland, and rooted out by a foreign invader.

The obvious characters in the story for Native Americans to identify with are the Canaanites, the people who already lived in the promised land. As a member of the Osage Nation of American Indians who stands in solidarity with other tribal people around the world, I read the Exodus stories with Canaanite eyes. And, it is the Canaanite side of the story that has been overlooked by those seeking to articulate theologies of liberation. Especially ignored are those parts of the story that describe Yahweh's command to mercilessly annihilate the indigenous population.[48]

For Warrior, the narrative is about a conquering and not a liberating God. The uncritical preoccupation of liberation hermeneutics with the Exodus motif, though it has hermeneutical purchase, is inappropriate for the Native Americans. First, for liberation hermeneutics, what the redemption narrative presents is more important than the violation it causes to the indigenous people. Secondly, the indigenes' status is secondary and defined in relation to what Yahweh is going to achieve for the Israelites. The indigenes were assimilated into other

---

[47] For the unsuitability of the first Exodus for the Palestinians, and for Naim Ateek's call for the second Exodus which speaks of greater realism and understanding of land and indigenous people, see Naim S. Ateek, 'Biblical Perspectives on the Land', in *Voices from the Margin: Interpreting the Bible in the Third World*, new edition, ed. R. S. Sugirtharajah (Maryknoll, NY, Ortis Books, 1995), pp. 267–76.

[48] Robert Allen Warrior, 'Canaanites, Cowboys, and Indians', in *Voices from the Margin: Interpreting the Bible in the Third World*, new edition, ed. R. S. Sugirtharajah (Maryknoll, NY, Orbis Books, 1995), p. 279.

people's identity, and their own history came to be regarded as suspect and a danger to the safety of the Israelites. What is perturbing for Warrior is that white America's self-image as the new chosen people enabled the Puritans to draw hermeneutical implications from the conquest narratives and treat Native Americans as Amelkites and Canaanites, who were to be either converted or exterminated. While conceding that the conquest stories may be historically suspect and scholars may dispute the veracity of annihilation, Warrior's contention is that the narrative as such remains and continues to provide political and spiritual sustenance to many: 'As long as people believe in the Yahweh of deliverance, the world will not be safe from Yahweh the conqueror.'[49] The narratives encourage the victims to participate in their victimhood. Victims who read such narratives may not be aware of the history nor of the implied colonial theology located within the narratives. With reference to such readers, Warrior writes: 'The peasants of Solentiname bring a wisdom and experience previously unknown to Christian theology, but I do not see what mechanism guarantees that they – or any other people who seek to be shaped and moulded by reading the text – will differentiate between the liberating god and the god of conquest.'[50] His argument takes on an added significance in the case of indigenous people from all over the world who were subjected to the genocidal 'reverse Exodus' from literally their 'Promised Land'. Warrior goes on to suggest that the native people have to look elsewhere for a cogent and an alternative vision of 'justice peace and political sanity'.[51]

Disentangling the text: dalit hermeneutics

In India, the dalits (once called outcastes) are trying to bring to the fore the glaring social reality of the caste system and

[49] Ibid., p. 284.
[50] Ibid., pp. 282–3.
[51] Ibid., p. 285. For the internal debate elicited by this article among the Native American interpreters see pp. 100–4 in *Native and Christian: Indigenous Voices on Religious Identity in the United States and Canada*, ed. James Treat (New York, Routledge, 1996).

endeavouring to work out a hermeneutics based on the principle of equality. Before we look at their proposal, I include here a brief account of the Bible's entanglement with high culture and the caste Christians. When the Bible was first introduced in India, it found a favourable niche among the caste Christians, and it was they who among Indian Christians enthused over it. Initially, in a country brimming with sacred texts, the entry of the Christian Scripture was problematic. It had to fight its way to gain recognition. J. S. M. Hooper, writing the history of the introduction of the Bible in India, noted:

It is also to be remembered that India has never suffered from a dearth of religious literature, and that at one end of the scale of her vast population there has always been a section whose religious pride has become proverbial; and this arrogance has been based on the exclusive possession of an ancient sacred literature. As the nineteenth century brought its changes in the structure and outlook of Indian society this Brahmin pride became the common stock of India's new self-consciousness and self-respect . . .[52]

Once the Christian Scripture found its place, it was the caste Christians who first appropriated it and made profitable hermeneutical purchase out it. Some of the early converts to Christianity in the colonial days came from a brahminical background; they made productive use of their ancient texts and saw interconnections between their texts and the Bible.[53] They went on to articulate Christian theology and, in the process, they were also to construct a self-identity which underwent tremendous changes as the result of colonialism and its attendant Western values and Christian principles.

The caste Christians conferred on the Bible a similar status to that of their own Vedas. For instance, Nehemiah Goreh, an early brahmin convert, accorded the Bible the same standing as that of the divine *Śruti* (= 'that which is revealed') and

---

[52] J. S. M. Hooper, *The Bible in India with a Chapter on Ceylon* (London, Oxford University Press, 1938), p. 6.

[53] For examples of high-caste Christians' appropriation of the Bible by an earlier generation see R. H. S. Boyd, 'The Use of the Bible in Indian Christian Theology', *Indian Journal of Theology* 22:4 (1974), 141–62. For recent attempts see James Canjanam Gamaliel, *Dharma in the Hindu Scriptures and in the Bible* (Delhi, ISPCK, 1999); Koshy Abraham, *Prajapathi: The Cosmic Christ* (Delhi, ISPCK, 1997).

bestowed on the patristic writings the same status as *smriti* (=
'that which is remembered').[54] Thus, he and others like him
conceded that the Bible was an authority and an aid in spiritual
matters just as Hindu Scriptures were. They also saw the Vedas
and the Bible as part of a textual continuum and claimed that
the unadulterated Vedic religion was closer to biblical faith.
Indian converts like Banerjea, whom we encountered earlier,
asserted that Indian caste Christians were descendants of
brahminical Aryans, and that among the ancient peoples only
the Hebrews and the Aryans had developed a cultured sense of
sacrifice; Banerjea saw in Jesus the supreme example of a
Prajapati (Lord of Creatures). They drew heavily upon the high
culture in their exposition. These caste Christians interpreted
the Bible utilizing brahminical philosophical concepts, such as
Advaita in the case of Upadhyay and *Visistadvaita* in the case of
Appasamy, to explicate the gospel, especially the Johannine
texts. At a time when the missionaries called for a complete
disjuncture from Hinduism, seeing the interconnections
between the two textual traditions enabled upper-caste Christians to advocate continuity between the two religious traditions. The impression they created was that Christians stood to
gain from the use of Hindu Scriptures because these would
enhance the gospel. A. J. Appasamy's production of *Temple
Bells*, an anthology culled from Hindu Scriptures, went a long
way to assert the complementarity of the Hindu Sacred writings.[55] The idea was that the perceptions of God drawn from
the high brahminical culture would enhance the understanding
of the biblical God.

The increasing association of brahminical texts with the
Bible and caste Christians' identification of the Bible with high
culture posed problems for dalits. The ancient Indian Scriptures, the pride of brahminical literacy and religiosity, were out
of bounds for the dalits and they were prevented from reading
them. The very books which were seized upon as the embodiment of brahminical spirituality prescribed punishment for

---

[54] See Boyd, 'The Use of the Bible in Indian Christian Theology', p. 143.
[55] See *Temple Bells: Readings from Hindu Religious Literature*, ed. A. J. Appasamy (Calcutta,
Association Press, 1930)

dalits – the pouring of molten lead into their ears for even inadvertently hearing the recital of the passages. It was these very scriptures that kept them outside the caste system and brought them untold misery which were now being evoked to illuminate and enhance biblical texts.

While caste Christians made great hermeneutical strides, the missionaries' presentation of the Bible sent confusing signals to the dalits. On one level, the missionaries projected the Bible as the new Moses, leading an Exodus from caste-ridden Hinduism. But on another level, the missionaries were reluctant to press home the egalitarian potency of the gospel. With a long-term view of attracting brahmins, the missionaries were concerned about biblical elements which might cause offence to brahminical sensibilities. For instance, the passages related to the ritual slaughter of cows – feasting on a fatted calf as Abraham did with his heavenly guests or the killing of a fatted calf to celebrate the return of the Prodigal – would be seen by brahmins as sacrilegious accounts, for the cow was regarded as a sacred animal. The New Testament portrayal of Jesus as son of a carpenter, of his Galilean peasantry and his fisher-folk disciples would give the impression that the founder and followers of Christianity came from the lowest and vilest in the society. Noting the uneasiness among the caste Christians, Abbé Dubois, a Roman Catholic missionary, wrote:

But, above all, what will a Brahmin or any other well-bred Hindoo think, when he pursues in our holy books the account of the immolating of creatures held most sacred by him? What will be his feelings, when he sees that immolating of oxen and bulls constituted a leading feature in the religious ordinances of the Israelites, and that the blood of those most sacred animals was almost daily shed at the shrine of the god they adored? What will be his feelings when he sees that, after Solomon had at immense expense and labour built a magnificent temple in honour of the true God, he made a *pratisha* or consecration of it by causing 22,000 oxen to be slaughtered, and overflowing his new temple with the blood of these sacred victims?[56]

Dubois went on to say that with such shocking details, the

---

[56] Abbé J. A. Dubois, *Letters on the State of Christianity in India* (New Delhi, Associated Publishing House, n.d.), p. 16.

brahmins would look on the book as an abominable work, and were bound to throw it away and consider themselves polluted by having touched it. His solution was not to introduce what he called 'the naked text of the Bible' to the unprepared minds of prejudiced Hindus, but to produce a translation which would be in keeping with the style of the literary norms of Hindu Sacred Scriptures:

In fact, a translation of the Holy Scriptures, in order to awaken the curiosity, and fix the attention of the learned Hindoo, at least as a literary production, ought to be on a level with the Indian performances of the same kind among them, and be composed in fine poetry, a flowery style, and a high stream of eloquence, this being universally the mode in which all Indian performances of any worth are written. As long as the versions are executed in the low style in which we find these, you may rest assured that they will only excite contempt, and tend to increase the aversion already entertained by the natives against the Christian religion.[57]

The other aspect of missionary hermeneutics was that the missionaries did not see any inconsistency with the gospel in their affirmation of caste differences. Robert De Nobli even went on to claim that 'the caste system as such was not unchristian'. Summoning texts like Matthew 5.17, they were able to endorse the notion that Jesus did not come to abolish social practices but to fulfil them. The Bible was presented as maintaining the status quo, and the missionaries pointed out that neither Jesus nor Paul was against slavery nor actively involved in its eradication. The Society for the Propagation of the Gospel wrote to its members:

The Society does not countenance the adherence of the Christian converts to any former religious restrictions, which are not consistent with their Christian liberty, yet it cannot be in the power or wish of the Society to abolish all distinctions of ranks and degrees in India; nor do they consider themselves entitled to do more than to remind the Christian converts, that with respect to spiritual privileges, there is in Jesus Christ neither bond nor free, neither high nor low; yet that such privileges are in no way incompatible with the various distinctions of rank and degrees in society which are recognized in the

---

[57] Ibid., p. 22.

Gospel itself, where persons of several ranks and conditions receive respectively admonitions and counsel adapted to their state.[58]

Viewed against such a background, the current dalit Christians have an ambiguous attitude towards the Bible. In it they see both egalitarian and enslaving potential. In between these two positions, there are those who challenge the very validity of the canonical scriptures for the dalit cause: Polykayal Yohanan, one of the dalit proponents, writes:

In the New Testament there are certain epistles by St Paul and others. To whom did Paul write these epistles? To the Romans, Corinthians etc. They were not written to the Pulayars of Travencore. Therefore, there is no revelation in those epistles for you, but only for the Romans, Corinthians etc. The revelation to you Pulayas of Travencore is through me.[59]

Those dalits who see liberative potential in the Bible, would like to go beyond its tainted association with the brahminical texts, and would like to replace them with dalit modes of thinking. Arul Raja proposes the following as a basis for dalit biblical hermeneutics.[60]

First, hermeneutics should take into account the oral nature of the dalit culture.The Biblical texts have to be transmitted to the dalits as if they are orally communicated stories. He posits, 'The Bible could be of some service to the Dalits in their

[58] Cited in Duncan B. Forrester, *Caste and Christianity: Attitudes and Politics on Caste of Anglo-Saxon Protestant Missions in India* (London, Curzon Press, 1980), p. 34. The book is an important source, providing changing perspectives on caste by both missionaries and Indian Christians.

[59] Cited in V. Devasahayam, 'Conflicting Roles of Bible and Culture in Shaping Asian Theology: A Tale of Two Indian Theologies', a paper presented at the Programme for Theology and Culture in Asia Consultation, November 1998, Hong Kong (unpublished), pp. 12–13.

[60] For examples of dalit hermeneutics see Maria Arul Raja, 'Assertion of Periphery: Some Biblical Paradigms', *Jeevadhara: A Journal of Christian Interpretation* 27: 157 (1997), 25–35; Maria Arul Raja, 'Towards a Dalit Reading of the Bible: Some Hermeneutical Reflections', *Jeevadhara: A Journal of Christian Interpretation* 26: 151 (1996), 29–34; M. Gnanavaram, '"Dalit Theology" and the Parable of the Good Samaritan', *Journal for the Study of the New Testament* 50 (1993), 59–83; Dhyanchand Carr, 'A Biblical Basis for Dalit Theology', in *Indigenous People: Dalits: Dalit Issues in Today's Theological Debate*, ed. James Massey (Delhi, ISPCK, 1994), pp. 231–49; V. V. Devasahayam, *Doing Theology in Biblical Key* (Madras, Gurukul Lutheran Theological College and Research Institute, 1997); also the thematic issue of *Jeevadhara: A Journal of Christian Interpretation* 22: 128 (1992): 'Biblical Reflections on Dalit Christians'.

attempts to regain their human dignity only if it is presented to the Dalits as the pre-literate oral narrative in this age of post-literate oral (electronic) communication.'[61]

Secondly, if the Bible is to be made an effective instrument for dalits, then religiosity latent in their culture should be activated and brought into dialogue with biblical religiosity. In dalit religiosity, the Divine is available at all times and can be approached without any intermediaries, such as priest or the printed word, without the practice of purity regulations which debar people and without prescriptions about what to eat and what to wear. Arul Raja notes: 'Because the Divine is never distant from the dalits, they do not seem to have the need for incarnation of self-emptying as understood in the biblical tradition.'[62] Against this theological landscape, if the biblical God is portrayed as one upholding the pollution-purity laws as prescribed by deuteronomic and priestly writers, such a God may not be an attractive proposition to the dalits. Arul Raja proposes two ways in which the dalit idea of the Divine could be a connecting link to the biblical notion of God. First, the dalits experience the Divine through the symbol of goddesses. In dalit religiosity, goddesses are free from any personal spouses and are rather seen as superintendents guarding the interests of the people and ensuring their procreation. Goddesses' personal sexuality is not part of their myth making. Their asexual nature and their role in protecting the afflicted through solidarity could be a common ground for dialogue between a dalit goddess and the biblical God who demonstrates similar values. Though there is a gender distinction between the male biblical God and a female dalit goddess, both exhibit a mixture of benevolence and cruelty, gentleness and barbarity. The second way is the shedding of blood for the sake of the afflicted: the dalit gods/godesses are 'mortals-turned deities' who are killed in the very act of protecting the villagers from cultural and ritual oppression. A similar idea is evident in the biblical God who shows concern for the marginalized by shedding the blood of God's son.

---

[61] Maria Arul Raja, 'A Dialogue Between Dalits and Bible', *Journal of Dharma* 24:1 (1999), 43.
[62] Ibid., p. 45.

Given the long history of being at the receiving end of biblical notions such as 'election', 'land', 'people', 'aliens', 'conquest' and 'holy war', dalits treat such lexicons with deep suspicion and aversion. In the light of this detestation, Arul Raja advocates preferential status for those biblical stories 'of wandering people seeking a land', rather than for those of 'the settled people conquering other nations'.[63] It is the former which will appeal to the imagination of the dalits.

The presentation of the Bible as a grand story with propensity to speak for all, and its claim to possess universal solutions, will not make sense to dalits. It is important to emphasize the servanthood of the Bible, and its power to energize the dalit struggle; Arul Raja writes:

[T]he dalit modes of perception feel out of place with the logic of logocentric, idealistic or positivistic outlook, determinacy, belief as system, literary-based communication or text bound interpretation . . . The dalit way of understanding reality innately acknowledges its sense of fluidity, particularity, indeterminacy, partiality and contextuality.[64]

Reflecting a postmodern mood, the dalit mode of thinking does not aim to control or to be controlled by the Bible. Dalits see their task as wresting the Bible from brahminical management and its alleged brahminical alliance. The Bible's valency depends upon its ability to espouse dalit causes and, more pertinently, its potentiality to resonate with the dalit mode of thinking.

There are certain features which are common to Indian dalits and Japanese burakumin. Both are ostracized on the basis of pollution-purity laws, and their stigma is hereditary. Burakumins were seen as filth (*eta*), as) non-people (*hinin*) and as those who live in ghettos (*buraku*). They were treated as the inferior caste and ranked below warriors, farmers, artisans and merchants. The burakumin, the people discriminated against on the basis of ceremonial pollution, have recovered the biblical symbol – a crown of thorns, which is made up of brambles, the most hated and useless of all plants, and a contrast to the

---

[63] Ibid., p. 48.   [64] Ibid., p. 44.

Japanese imperial throne of chrysanthemums – as a symbol which points to their pain of marginalization and also future liberation.[65]

Depatriarchalizing the text: women's readings

Learning from, and at the same time disputing with, Western feminist theologies, women from the Third World have worked out their own biblical hermeneutics.[66] They have mined biblical motifs, personalities and events to reconstruct their identity. They have unearthed various models which provide a framework of reference: from Esther, as an inspiration for women obliged to preserve their lives by remaining in oppressive relationships, to the daughters of Zelophehad who stood up in front of Moses and other leaders and demanded their right to the name and the inheritance of their father, as a way of asserting their identity and nurturing their faith. Among these retrievals of biblical material, one that is most challenging and innovative is the recovery of Mark's Gospel, by the Japanese feminist theologian Hisako Kinukawa.[67]

The major thrust of her work is exposing the ways in which patriarchy, both Jewish and Japanese, prohibits and represses the salvational message of the Gospels. In her introduction she writes:

As a woman, I can feel closer to the women in the Bible, since our experiences as women have so much in common with theirs. Such common experiences of shame/honour with boundaries of power, sexual status, and respect for others, in a group-oriented society of dyadic personalities, provide me with a powerful methodological

---

[65] Teruo Kuribayashi, 'Recovering Jesus for Outcasts in Japan', in *Frontiers in Asian Christian Theology*, ed. R. S. Sugirtharajah (Maryknoll, NY, Orbis Books, 1994), pp. 11–26; also his 'Theology of Crowned with Thorns', in *God, Christ & God's People in Asia*, ed. Dhyanchand Carr (Hong Kong, CCA Theological Concerns, 1995), pp. 90–114. See also Tanimoto Kazuhiro, 'Mission for Buraku', in *Identity and Marginality: Rethinking Christianity in North East Asia*, ed. Werner Ustorf and Toshiko Murayama (Frankfurt am Main, Peter Lang, 2000), pp. 141–52.

[66] For feminist biblical hermeneutics from the perspectives of Asia, Africa and Latin America see *Semeia: An Experimental Journal for Biblical Criticism* 78 (1997).

[67] Hisako Kinukawa, *Women and Jesus in Mark: A Japanese Feminist Perspective* (Maryknoll, NY, Orbis Books, 1994).

device for studying the women and their experiences in Mark's Gospel.[68]

Hisako Kinukawa draws on cultural anthropology to demonstrate that the New Testament communities and some Asian societies are governed by norms of honour and shame. She concedes that in spite of their similarities there is a basic difference between the two. Unlike the patriarchy based on honour/shame of the Palestinian culture, in Japan it is the culture of shame which is predominant. It is further reinforced by Japanese imperial ideology and principal Japanese religions such as Shintoism, Buddhism and Confucianism.

Kinukawa employs a wide variety of critical methods: the traditional historical-critical method to situate the text in its proper context; audience-oriented critical rhetorical studies to address the question of male representation in both the Markan text and the subsequent interpretative history of it; and cultural anthropology to unveil socio-cultural patterns embedded in the text. Her choice of Mark was due to the fact that it was written in the earliest stages before patriarchalization enveloped the whole system. She is of the view that, in spite of the androcentric mind-set of the author, she could recover the women hidden in the texts, who will help her to reclaim the message. The key to Kinukawa's hermeneutics is the mutual interaction between women and Jesus which was instrumental in gradually dismantling the hold of patriarchy. Violating the norms of the time, it was women who took the initiative and prompted Jesus to follow suit in breaking down the barriers of patriarchy. Kinukawa writes: 'The women led Jesus to become a responding "boundary breaker". Having spent his whole life in the culture of honour/shame which was fully male-oriented, and which expected women to bear all the shame, Jesus did not take initiative until women prepared him by stages to break down the boundaries.'[69] The actions of the Haemorrhaging Woman (Mark 5.25–34), the Syrophoenician Woman (Mark 7.24–34) and the Anointing Woman (Mark 14.3–9), are illustrative of redrawing the boundaries. Each woman, in her own way,

---

[68] Ibid., p. 16.   [69] Ibid., p. 139.

was able to redefine purity, ethnic and sexual barriers. The
Haemorrhaging Woman challenged purity laws which prevented women from being integral to society and classified
them as unclean and contagious. It was she who made the first
move and touched Jesus with a view to recovering from her
physical illness and also to being reinstated in the society. The
Syrophoenician Woman rattled the exclusive ethnic zones
erected around communities at the time. In her persistence and
assertive dialogue with Jesus, she not only got her daughter
restored to life but also helped Jesus to broaden his particular-
istic and culture-bound understanding of people who were
outside the Jewish fold. The Anointing Woman tore down the
sexual barrier by breaking into a closed male fellowship and
carried out the prophetic task of preparing Jesus for his death.
These women acted out of their desperation to initiate an
encounter with Jesus, which led to his awareness of being a
suffering servant and eventually caused him to attain his
Christhood. These encounters, according to Kinukawa, 'were
reciprocal and both sides received and learned something'.[70]

By paralleling realities that coexist between the New
Testament women and current burakumins, Korean comfort
women and ordinary Japanese women who suffocate under the
burden of patriarchy, Kinukawa concludes that the Markan
women invite and provide an example of resistance for all these
women so that they 'may experience life-communion with
Jesus'.[71]

To sum up so far: these identity-specific hermeneutics highlight the marginalization of Native Americans, dalits and
women as a slur on the mainstream society in which they live.
They utilize the status of marginalization as a point of entry
into the text. They see reading as both a resisting and a
validating act. For them the Bible continues to be the principal
source of liberation but it now comes to be perceived as a far
more complex writing. Unlike the classical liberation hermeneutics which seeks to speak on behalf of the poor, here we see
that the poor themselves represent their cause and delineate

---

[70] Ibid., p. 139.   [71] Ibid., p. 144.

their agenda. What they have gone on to claim, especially in the case of Kinukawa and Warrior, is that different subaltern groups can forge strategic partnerships with each other so that different identities do not cancel out common concerns.

CONCLUDING REMARKS

In its desire to espouse liberation at a time when there is cynicism and weariness about emancipatory causes, liberation hermeneutics has valiantly and almost single-handedly helped to maintain liberation at the centre of theological discussion. To keep the momentum of liberation alive, liberation hermeneutics has drawn on both modern and postmodern tendencies. It embraces features of both, and at the same time distances itself from them. Liberation hermeneutics' chief focus is liberation which itself comes out of a modernistic agenda. Liberation is one of the grand stories of modernity which is still to play out its potential in many Third World countries, and liberation hermeneutics has rightly aligned itself with this modernistic cause. Liberation hermeneutics becomes redundant when it implicates other grand stories of modernity in its interpretative pursuits. Two such narratives which dominate liberation hermeneutics are 'salvation in history', and 'the Jesus Christ saga'. Liberation hermeneutics operates within the existing biblical approaches, and it accords God's self-disclosure through historical events in the life of Israel a primary status in its hermeneutical endeavours. It was this very model which was appropriated by missionaries and colonialists in order to subjugate and subdue other people's culture and history. The salvation-in-history model raises the question of the experience of God. It emphasizes a fuller account of history and historical consciousness. This approach tends to project an interventionist image of God – a God who lives outside history and who, from time-to-time, intervenes in the affairs of the world. This means having to wait patiently from event to event to see how God operates in the ongoingness of life.

Let me turn to the other grand story that liberation hermeneutics reifies, the Jesus Christ saga. In its approach, liberation hermeneutics is overtly Christocentric. The authoritative Jesus reconstructed by liberation theology is not the Jesus behind the text, but within the text. His actions are seen as acts of God mediated in solidarity with humanity as depicted in the canonical texts of the New Testament. In fulfilling this task, the interpreter assumes an apostolic and canonical status in interpreting the significance of Jesus for the marginalized community of faith. The notion that Jesus is at the heart of the Bible gives rise to an unconscious conviction that the Bible cannot err.

In relation to the Bible, liberation hermeneutics is postmodern and postcritical, especially when it looks for 'images' and 'types' in the Bible. Boff writes:

We need not, then look for formulas to 'copy', or techniques to 'apply' from scripture. What scripture will offer us is rather something like orientations, models, types, directives, principles, inspirations – elements permitting us to acquire on our own initiative, a 'hermeneutic competency', and thus the capacity to judge – on our own initiative, in our own right -'according to the mind of Christ', or 'according to the Spirit', the new unpredictable situations with which we are continually confronted. The Christian writings offer us not a *what*, but a *how* – a manner, style, a spirit.[72]

Such an approach helped to turn liberation hermeneutics away from being literalistic. But at the same time what is so striking about liberation hermeneutics is its textualism. It emphasizes the written word. For liberation hermeneutics, ultimately it is in the Bible that the message of liberation is to be found, and it is recoverable through a variety of critical means. Raul Vidales asserts that liberation theology's 'starting point is the original, pristine witness of Scripture'.[73] The text remains the centre of debate. The hermeneutical suspicion with which ideological interpretation of the text is viewed is not accorded to the Bible. Pablo Richard maintains that 'the problem is not the Bible itself, but the way it has been interpreted . . . The Bible gives us the testimony of the word of God, it is also the canon or criterion of discernment of the Word of God today.'[74] There is

---

[72] Boff, 'Hermeneutics: Constitution of Theological Pertinency', p. 30.

[73] R. Vidales, 'Methodological Issues in Liberation Theology', in *Frontiers of Theology in Latin America*, ed. Rosino Gibellini (London, SCM Press, 1980), p. 38.

[74] Richard, '1492: The Violence of God and Future of Christianity', p. 66.

an inherent biblicism in its approach. The texts which speak of dehumanizing aspects are conveniently passed over.

In its attempts to recover the biblical message, liberation hermeneutics employs the now suspicious historical-critical tools, the very tools worked out at the foundry of modernity. But where it deviates from modern shortcomings of historical criticism is in its usage. These tools are marshalled to serve the modernist project of making the gospel relevant to the educated, secularized middle-class Christians who are unsure of their faith. Liberation hermeneutics makes use of the very same tools to liberate the gospel, and make it serve for the non-persons whose faith remains unshakeable in spite of the emergence of rational thinking. Liberation hermeneutics has made historical tools more ethically responsible. Though historical criticism retains its archaeological and philological pursuits, it is now employed by liberation theologians to discern the interconnection between the social-political world of the text in its past context as well as in the contemporary context.

Liberation hermeneutics is postmodern in its desire to take the Other – the poor, women, indigenous and all the marginalized peoples – seriously. In doing so, it rightly overrides the Enlightenment concern with the non-believer, and focuses on the non-person. But this does not preclude reifying the poor, and it functions within the Enlightenment paradigm of dichotomous thinking – rich/poor, oppressed/oppressor and have/have-nots. Moreover, it is prone to romanticize the poor. What Pablo Richards says about the indigenous people of Latin America is true of other marginalized peoples:

The indigenous peoples, with their millennial history, with their cultural and religious tradition, and recently, with their own native method of evangelization and their native theology, are much better prepared to read and interpret the Bible than the Western European Christian who has a millennial history of violence and conquest, impregnated with the erudite, liberal and modern spirit.[75]

---

[75] Pablo Richard, 'Indigenous Biblical Hermeneutics: God's Revelation in Native Religions and the Bible (After 500 Years of Domination)', in *Text & Experience: Towards a Cultural Exegesis of the Bible*, ed. Daniel Smith-Christopher (Sheffield, Sheffield Academic Press, 1995), p. 271.

Eleazar Lopez goes still further and accords a privileged access to the poor because of their deprived status. In his view, indigenous people are the conservers of the gospel content, and it is much more 'preserved among our peoples, because of the purity of heart possessed by the poor, than in the contaminated vessels of the Church'.[76]

Liberation hermeneutics is modernistic in its attempt to speak for all, and in setting hermeneutical goals. It sees its role as a testimony, a testimony to what it has witnessed of human suffering and degradation. Not all liberation hermeneuts are economically disadvantaged. They believe that interpretation has a witnessing function, as did the sages of old who urged: 'Open your mouth for the dumb, for the rights of all those who are left desolate, open your mouth, judge righteously, maintain the rights of the poor and needy' (Prov. 31.8–9). In its over-zealousness to represent the poor, liberation hermeneutics has ended up as a liberation theology of the poor rather than a theology of liberation by the poor. The goal now is not social change but pastoral concern. Political activism is replaced with the Church's traditional concern for good work and charitable projects.

In conclusion: this is not the time to assess the impact of liberation theology, but I would like to end with a comment which comes from a sense of solidarity and shared concern. When it emerged, liberation theology gave the impression that it was going to be a great force in altering the way we do theology itself, and in ushering in an era of radical changes. Sadly these failed to materialize. In its interpretative proposals, liberation hermeneutics continued to be conservative. In its appropriation of the Bible, in its expositions, in its obsession with Christ-centred hermeneutics, it remained within conventional patterns. A theology which started out as socially progressive remained largely conventional and theologically cautious. It did not engage in an overall reappraisal of, nor did it desire, a reconfiguration of the basic theological concepts. This reluctance could be attributed to several factors: a lack of

---

[76] Cited in Richard, ibid., p. 271.

critical self-reflectivity which is crucial to any emancipatory theory and practice; pressure from conservative forces within the Church hierarchy; over-eagerness to get the methods correct; and the seductive effects of dialoguing with Western theologians. Whatever the reasons, over the years, without much self-criticism and a willingness to re-perceive ancient doctrines, liberation hermeneutics has faded into a pale imitation of itself. Instead of being a new agent in the ongoing work of God, liberation hermeneutics has ended up reflecting upon the theme of biblical liberation rather than being a liberative hermeneutics.

CHAPTER 8

Postcolonializing biblical interpretation

> If post-modernism is at least partially about 'how the world dreams itself to be "American"', then, post-colonialism is about waking from that dream, and learning to dream otherwise.   Diana Brydon

> In life one must for ever choose between being one who tells stories and one about whom stories are told.
> **Shashi Tharoor**

Until now liberation hermeneutics has been seen as the distinctive contribution of Third World biblical interpreters. Recently another critical category, postcolonialism, has emerged as its rival, and has staked a claim to represent minority voices. On the face of it, both liberation hermeneutics and postcolonialism share a common interpretative vocation – for instance, de-ideologizing dominant interpretation, a commitment to the Other and distrust of totalizing tendencies. However, a closer look in the last chapter revealed that liberation hermeneutics is still stuck with some of the vices of the modernistic project – excessive textualism, disparagement of both major and popular religions and homogenization of the poor. Also it seems shy about breaking with them. What I propose to do first in this chapter is to delineate the characteristics of the new entrant to the critical arena – postcolonialism – and outline some of its theoretical and praxiological intentions and assumptions; second, to deal with the applicability of postcolonialism to biblical studies; and third, to map out the affinities and differences between postcolonialism and liberation hermeneutics. In the concluding part I will try to answer some of the questions constantly asked about postcolonialism, and I will end with my own qualified support for the theory.

Briefly, let me try to spell out what postcolonialism as a descriptor stands for. At the outset, I must admit that the task is not an easy one because of the definitional ambiguity that surrounds the notion.[1] To begin with, there is a reluctance and shyness among the theorists to spell out the purpose and parameters of the discourse; they elect to be freelance and thus make vagueness a cardinal virtue. Each scholar, depending on his or her academic speciality, subject status and institutional connection, has devised a different set of definitions, examples and emphases. For instance, in her preference for the term postcolonial rather than neocolonial, Tejeswani Niranjana has rightly pointed out that each discipline, due to its own disciplinary demands, will reach its own definitions, and what political scientists come up with need not necessarily be suitable for cultural theorists. To have two different definitions, she writes, 'is not to posit two separate realms of analysis, but merely to suggest that a term appropriate at one level may not be as accurate at another'.[2] Then there is the vexed issue of using or not using the hapless hyphen. This has caused constant hermeneutical squabbles among practitioners and their critics. Does post-colonialism, in its hyphenated form, mark the end of colonization? Or in its unhyphenated form, postcolonialism, does it indicate the continued messy and complicated history

---

[1] Recently, there have been several introductory texts that wrestle with the aim and ambit of the discourse. See Padmini Mongia (ed.), *Contemporary Postcolonial Theory: A Reader* (London, Arnold, 1996); Peter Childs and Patrick Williams, *An Introduction to Post-Colonial Theory* (London, Prentice Hall, 1997); Ania Loomba, *Colonialism/Postcolonialism* (London, Routledge, 1998); Leela Gandhi, *Postcolonial Theory: A Critical Introduction* (Edinburgh, Edinburgh University Press, 1998); Bart Moore-Gilbert, *Postcolonial Theory: Contexts, Practices, Politics* (London, Verso, 1997); Bart Moore-Gilbert, Gareth Stanton and Willy Maley, *Postcolonial Criticism* (London, Longman, 1997); Bill Ashcroft, Gareth Griffiths and Helen Tiffin, *Key Concepts in Post-Colonial Studies* (London, Routledge, 1998); *A Companion to Postcolonial Studies*, ed. Henry Schwarz and Ray Sangeeta (Oxford, Blackwell Publishers, 2000); John McLeod, *Beginning Postcolonialism* (Manchester, Manchester University Press, 2000); Ato Quayson, *Postcolonialism: Theory, Practice or Process?* (Cambridge, Polity Press, 2000).

[2] Tejaswini Niranjana, *Siting Translation: History, Post-Structuralism, and the Colonial Context* (Berkeley, University of California Press, 1992), pp. 7–8.

colonialism leaves in its awake? At least at present it is the unhyphenated version which is gaining dominance in academic circles. As Ato Quayson noticed, the new consensus emerged as a way of distinguishing it from its 'more chronologically inflected progenitor'.[3] Its significance is not related to a chronology which privileges the Empire days and celebrates freedom in the aftermath of the Empire. It is about both the state of affairs in colonial times and the state of affairs that exists in the fraught aftermath of imperialism. Then the whole discourse is torn between its use of mutually incompatible critical categories such as Marxism and poststructuralism. Added to this is the constant changing of frames of reference within the field.

It is important at the very outset to reiterate that while 'postcolonial' indicates an epoch, postcolonial criticism is not limited to such a time frame. As Stuart Hall put it, it needs to be seen as a 'reconfiguration of a field, rather than as a movement of linear transcendence between two mutually exclusive states'.[4] Postcolonialism is about a set of measures worked out by diasporan Third World intellectuals in order to undo, reconfigure and redraw contingent boundaries of hegemonic knowledges. Or, as the inaugural issue of *Postcolonial Studies: Culture, Politics, Economy* editorialized it, the term postcolonialism is 'undeniably and necessarily vague, a gesture rather than a demarcation, [and] points not towards a new knowledge, but rather towards an examination and critique of knowledges'.[5] And the editorial went on to claim that, in conjunction with other critical currents of the time, postcolonialism sees its task as 'a discursive protestation *against* "major" knowledges, and *on behalf of* "minor"/deterritorialized knowledges, as quintessentially political and oppositional'.[6] For our purposes and at the risk of over-simplifying, I define postcolonial criticism as a

---

[3] Quayson, *Postcolonialism*, p. 1.
[4] Stuart Hall, 'When Was "the Post-Colonial"? Thinking at the Limit', in *The Post-Colonial Question: Common Skies Divided Horizons*, ed. Iain Chambers and Lidia Curti (London, Routledge, 1996), p. 254.
[5] Sanjay Seth, Leela Gandhi and Michael Dutton, 'Postcolonial Studies: A Beginning', *Postcolonial Studies: Culture, Politics, Economy* 1:1 (1998), 8.
[6] Ibid., pp. 8–9.

textual and praxiological practice initially undertaken by people who were once part of the British, European and American Empires, but now have some sort of territorial freedom while continuing to live with burdens from the past and enduring newer forms of economic and cultural neo-colonialism. It was also undertaken by ethnic minorities who live in diaspora, namely British blacks and British Asians in England, and racial minorities in the United States and Canada – African Americans, Native Americans, Hispanic Americans and Asian Americans – who had been victims of old imperialism, who are now current victims of globalization and who have been continually kept away from and represented by the dominant First World elements. Postcolonialism involves investigation into various colonial archives and discussion on a variety of issues ranging from slavery to migration, from gender to ethnic matters. Postcolonial criticism tries to conquer the past by comprehending it, and to overpower the present by exorcizing it.

Historical background

The arrival of postcolonial discourse on the theoretical scene is crucial. Its advent was facilitated by three key events which occurred more or less simultaneously: the failure of the socialist experiment as practised in the Soviet bureaucracy; the rise of global capitalism and the market economy, which resulted in the disruption of both metropolitan and village economies; and the loss of political momentum among the Third World countries who had covenanted to create a non-aligned movement in Bandung. Utilizing the space offered by the Western academy in the 1980s, diasporic intellectuals of Third World origin returned to the problem of interpreting the understanding of colonialism formulated by both colonialists and nationalists. Though the critique emerged from different disciplinary needs, postcolonialism provided an interventionary impulse. It has now come to be widely acknowledged that Edward Said,[7]

---

[7] Edward W. Said, *Orientalism* (Harmondsworth, Penguin, 1985).

Gayatri Chakravorty Spivak[8] and Homi Bhabha[9] are progenitors of the theory and practice of postcolonialism, and that the text that played the most important part in opening up the debate and making the issue visible was Edward Said's *Orientalism*, published in 1978. In it he describes the means by which the West conceptualized the Other, and made the colonial world susceptible to certain kinds of textual management. Since the publication of the book, terms such as orientalism and orientalist have become a handy descriptor for the West's way of managing the Third World.

STREAMS OF POSTCOLONIALITY

Surveying the field, one can see three streams of postcolonialism at work. The first carries the notion of invasion and control; the second places enormous investment in recovering the cultural soul; and the third stresses mutual interdependence and transformation.

The first stream was about textual practices and resistance to colonial supremacy with its superintending of other peoples' lives, territories and cultures. The purpose of the discourse here was to expose colonial control and domination, with a view to gaining eventual independence and liberation. It included essayists, cultural critics and political activists ranging from the Trinidadian C. L. R. James and the Martiniquan Aime Cesaire to the Sri-Lankan Ananda Coomaraswamy.[10] They were agitating for cultural and intellectual emancipation at a time when territorial freedom was little more than a utopian dream. Here the hermeneutical engagement was locked into a battle between two unequal homogeneous entities – the invader and the occupied. Ironically, the debate was shaped by the language

---

[8] Gayatri Chakravorty Spivak, *In Other Worlds: Essays in Cultural Politics* (New York, Routledge, 1988); Gayatri Chakravorty Spivak, *The Post-Colonial Critic: Interviews, Strategies, Dialogues*, ed. Sarah Harasym (New York, Routledge, 1990); Gayatri Chakravorty Spivak, *Outside in the Teaching Machine* (New York, Routledge, 1993); Gayatri Chakravorty Spivak, *A Critique of Postcolonial Reason: Toward a History of the Vanishing Present* (Cambridge, MA, Harvard University Press, 1999).

[9] Homi K. Bhabha, *The Location of Culture* (London, Routledge, 1994).

[10] For an introduction to and a critique of the authors mentioned here, refer to any of the readers mentioned in note 1.

of resistance and the epistemological assumptions of the occupier who supplied and informed anticolonial attitudes to class, culture, gender, subjectivity, and so forth.

The second stream concentrated on recovering the 'cultural soul' from the intellectual and cultural grip of the master. Here we see two ploys at work. One is bent on recouping the pure essence of the native soul and culture which is momentarily debased and disgraced; and the other is engaged in exposing the wiles of the master and the speciousness of his claims to preeminence. The former was espoused by, among others, Ananda Coomaraswamy, who emphasized the immense potentiality and perennial usefulness of indigenous cultural energies. The latter was exemplified by Fanon and Memmi, whose distinguished works exposed the illegitimacies of the master culture. Both camps believed in the spiritual and theological superiority of African and Asian cultures which were undermined by the current Western supremacy. They tended to rely on essentialist notions of a civilized native soul and uncontaminated indigenous cultures, and they thrived on utilizing such polarizing categories.

The third stream is about mutual interdependence and transformation. The emphasis here is on the construction of an identity based on the intertwined histories of the colonizer and the colonized. Its aim is to go beyond totalisms, essentialisms and dichotomies, and transcend the modernist notion of assimilating the marginalized and the minorities into one monolithic cultural whole. The key words here are hybridity and liminality, which denote an in-between-space. It is a space where one is equally committed to and disturbed by the colonized and the colonizing cultures. In Homi Bhabha's words, it is the 'Third Space'[11] which emerges from an analytical scrutiny of diverse cultures rather than from integrating them.

Though chronologically these streams emerge out of different contexts, they are neither linear nor monolithic; they sit side by side and interact constantly. More importantly, the protagonists, too, cannot be boxed into discrete categories.

Anti-colonial reading is not new. It has gone on whenever a

---

[11] Bhabha, *Location of Culture*, pp. 36–9, 218.

native put quill pen to paper to contest the production of knowledge by the invading power. Postcoloniality begins when subjects find themselves thinking and acting in certain ways. What is distinctive about the current enterprise, however, is that far from being locked into the colonial paradigm where colonialists set the ground rules, it concedes more importantly, the complexity of contact between the invader and the invaded. It goes beyond the binary notions of colonized and colonizer and lays weighty emphasis on critical exchanges and mutual transformation between the two. Postcolonialism does not mean that the colonized are innocent, generous and principled, whereas the former colonizers, and now the neocolonizers, are all innately culpable, greedy and responsible for all social evils. Not only is such a notion an inverted form of colonialism but it also absolves the Third World elite from their patriarchal and vassalizing tendencies. The current postcolonialism tries to emphasize that this relationship between the ruler and the ruled is complex, full of cross-trading and mutual appropriation and confrontation.

Postcolonial theory offers a space for the once-colonized. It is an interpretative act of the descendants of those once subjugated. In effect it means a resurrection of the marginal, the indigene and the subaltern. It means engaging with the mass of knowledge which is produced on their behalf and which is in the domain of Euro-American interpretation. It is an act of reclamation, redemption and reaffirmation against the past colonial and current neocolonizing tendencies which continue to exert influence even after territorial and political independence has been accomplished. It is a tactic, a practice and a process. It means finding ways of operating under a set of arduous and difficult conditions which jeopardize and dehumanize people.

POSTCOLONIAL CRITICISM AND BIBLICAL STUDIES

Applied to biblical studies,[12] postcolonial criticism hopes to

---

[12] For recent attempts, see *Semeia* 75 (1996): 'Postcolonialism and Scriptural Reading'; *Jian Dao: A Journal of Bible and Theology* 8 (1997): 'A Postcolonial Discourse'; R. S. Sugirtharajah, *Asian Biblical Hermeneutics and Postcolonialism: Contesting the Interpretations*

perform the following tasks. First, scrutiny of biblical documents for their colonial entanglements: the Bible as a collection
of documents which came out of various colonial contexts –
Egyptian, Persian, Assyrian, Hellenistic and Roman – and was
produced under the courtly supervision of Davidic and Solo-
monic dynasties needs to be investigated again. In doing this,
postcolonial reading practice will reconsider the biblical narratives, not as a series of divinely guided incidents or reports
about divine–human encounters, but as emanating from
colonial contacts. It will revalue the colonial ideology, stigmati-
zation and negative portrayals embedded in the content, plot
and characterization. It will scour the biblical pages for how
colonial intentions and assumptions informed and influenced
the production of the texts. It will attempt to resurrect lost
voices and causes which are distorted or silenced in the canon-
ized text. It will address issues such as nationalism, ethnicity,
deterritorialization and identity, which arise in the wake of
colonialism.

For an example of colonial entrenchment in a narrative,
postcolonial reading will wish to revisit the Book of Esther, in
order to unveil its ideological and cultural assumptions. Esther
comes out of a Persian colonial context, and the narrative as
such does not question the Persian tributary system which
sustains the empire, but aspires to survival or, at best, some
degree of survival within the system. Before the text can be
mined for its liberative potential, for example in the person of
Vashti, its hegemonic assumptions have to be exposed. The
Persian empire reflected in the text indicates a social formation
in which the monarch is hierarchically placed at the top and
supported by non-ruling families. Patriarchy, the inherent
feature of a feudal society, is palpable throughout the narrative.
The text narrates the luxurious living, squandering of wealth
and wasteful expenditure of the royal and wealthy families. The
pillars of the palaces were made of marble, couches were of

(Sheffield, Sheffield Academic Press, 1999); and R. S. Sugirtharajah, *The Postcolonial
Bible* (Sheffield, Sheffield Academic Press, 1998); also *Journal for the Study of the New
Testament* 73 (1999): 'Postcolonial Perspectives on the New Testament and its
Interpretation'.

gold and silver, drinks were served in golden goblets and the
wine overflowed at royal functions (Esther 1.5–9). In his careful
examination of the narrative, Mosala notes: 'This text, which is
otherwise excellent in its provision of socio-ecomomic data, is
eloquent by its silence on the conditions and struggles of the
non-kings, non-office holders, non-chiefs, non-governors and
non-queens in the Persian empire.'[13] The non-elite do not enter
the text. The text, as Mosala demonstrates, subsumes gender
questions under the nationalist and survivalist programme. It is
a patriarchal text, and it raises three questions. First, there is its
choice of a female character to achieve male objectives.
Though the narrative centres upon a woman, the hero of the
story is Mordecai. Mosala notes that 'Esther struggles but
Mordecai reaps the fruit of the struggle.'[14] Second, gender
struggle is sacrificed to the nationalist cause. In the name of the
struggle for national survival of the Jewish people, the narrative
deprivileges the question of gender oppression and exploitation.
Third, it suppresses the class issue, including cultural practices.
In particular, the feast of Purim, which is the principal cultural
benefit of Esther's revolution, is not placed in a class context.
The central thrust of the book is the revolt of Queen Vashti.
She represents the form of struggle with which, as Mosala
recommends, African woman can identify. The Book of Esther
encourages largely a strategy of assimilation, endorses conformity and has little relevance for liberative purposes, or for that
matter for the present-day diasporic communities who live in
alien contexts seeking to negotiate an identity which will both
celebrate their own ethnicities and embrace the cultural heritage of the foreign countries in which they are settled.

The second task of postcolonial criticism is to engage in
reconstructive reading of biblical texts. Postcolonial reading will
reread biblical texts from the perspective of postcolonial concerns such as liberation struggles of the past and present; it will
be sensitive to subaltern and feminine elements embedded in

---

[13] Itumeleng J. Mosala, 'The Implications of the Text of Esther for African Women's
Struggle for Liberation in South Africa', *Semeia: An Experimental Journal for Biblical
Criticism* 59 (1992), 134.

[14] Ibid., p. 136.

the texts; it will interact with and reflect on postcolonial circumstances such as hybridity, fragmentation, deterritorialization, and hyphenated, double or multiple, identities. One postcolonial concern is the unexpected amalgamation of peoples, ideas, cultures and religions. The religious landscape is so complex that reading a text through one single religious view may not yield much these days when cultural identities and religions coalesce. Postcolonial reading will, for instance, see the confrontation of Elijah and the priests of Canaan with the Phoenician god Baal at Mount Carmel, not as a straight theological conflict between two deities, Yahweh and Baal, nor as one religious community and its gods pitched against another and its gods, but as a complex issue where communities intermingle and the gods are significantly beyond their theological propensities. Mainstream and missionary scholarship tend to see the Mount Carmel episode as a clear theological conflict between two deities, one virtuous and the other evil, extrapolate it to denigrate Asian and African religions as idolatrous, superstitious and evil, and see the victory of Yahweh as proof of the superiority of the biblical God. Postcolonial reading will re-examine what the confrontation is all about.[15]

When the Israelites settled in Canaan, they incorporated a number of Canaanite theological concepts into their theological thinking. For example, it was from the Canaanite religion that Israel learnt to speak of the 'God of Heaven'. It was a Canaanite concept that was transformed into the 'hosts of heaven' (1 Kings 22.19; Isa. 6.3); the 'God of thunder' was turned into Yahweh as the one who rides in the clouds (Pss. 68.4; 104.3), and, faced with El, the highest god in the Canaanite pantheon, Yaweh was simply identified as equal to El. As there was already an identification and assimilation of Canaanite theological notions, the inevitable question is why there is this confrontation with Baal. We need to ask what Baal is and what Baal

---

[15] My reading of this episode is based on the critical work of Wielenga. See Bastian Wielenga, *It's a Long Road to Freedom: Perspectives of Biblical Theology* (Madurai, Tamilnadu Theological Seminary, 1988), pp. 151–63; Bastian Wielenga, 'The God of Israel and the Other Deities: Why So Particular?', in *Biblical Insights on Inter-Faith Dialogue: Source Material for Study and Reflection*, ed. Israel Selvanayagam (Bangalore, The Board for Theological Text-Books Programme of South Asia, 1995), pp. 51–7.

stands for. Conventionally, Baal was known as a wealth god, worshipped as a giver of fertility. But there is another side to Baal. Baal means 'owner', 'possessor' or 'to have power'. This concept is important in understanding the conflict. Baal worship was prevalent in the Northern Kingdom. Ahab married Jezebel, the daughter of the King of Tyre. Tyre at that time was developing into a dominant colonial power in the Mediterranean, with its mercantile capitalism and an economy based on money where everything has a price. In Canaanite law, land was a saleable commodity. It was from Jezebel that Ahab learnt how Canaanite rulers wielded power and expropriated land from peasants (1 Kings 21). The Northern Kingdom came under Canaanite law and Jezebel had no qualms about acquisitioning the land of Naboth. For Naboth this was unthinkable. Under Israelite law, it was an inheritance, a gift, which had to remain within the family in order to maintain equality of power and wealth; hence Naboth's plea – 'could I give the inheritance of my fathers?' The urban economy of Canaan and Tyre clashed with the rural economy of Israel where each family was living on its share of the land: 'The land shall not be sold in perpetuity, for the land is mine; and you are strangers and sojourners with me' (Lev. 25.23). The land and its fruits and its blessing belong to the people. In 1 Kings 21 we read of the prophet of Yahweh, Elijah, siding with the peasant Naboth, the victim of land acquisition, against the power of an Israelite king. It is against this background that we need to look at the line-up at Mount Carmel. If we look at the opposing sides, it becomes evident that the conflict is not as simple as we imagine. On the one side, there were Ahab, the king of Israel, and his queen Jezebel, the daughter of Ethabaal, king of Sidonians (1 Kings 16.31). On the other side was Elijah, the persecuted prophet, and a starving widow in Zarephath, which belonged to Sidon (1 Kings 17.9). Both survived the drought together, when King Ahab was more concerned about his horses (i.e. his military strength) than the well-being of his subjects. Thus, the Israelite king and the Canaanite queen face an Israelite prophet and a Canaanite widow. It is not Yahweh/Israel versus Baal/Canaan, but Yahweh the protector of the poor against rulers who exploit, the king of Israel being one of them. Viewed against this scenario, the conflict is not a straightforward clash between two gods and their adherents. It depicts a complicated picture where the oppressed, irrespective of their faith affiliations, seek alleviation and where God, too, takes sides and goes against his own people when they turn power and wealth into the ultimate purpose of life. The Mount Carmel incident also demonstrates that even an 'idolatrous' deity can possess positive aspects. According to Wielenga, 'what is true of Baal worship, namely, the rain is a blessing from God' is 'taken out of the context of wealth-worship and attributed to the God who takes the cause of the poor'.[16] This is the theological and social context of Yahweh and Baal. At a time when people think across and beyond the traditional boundaries erected by institutionalized religion, and fumble through to some understanding of faith which would incorporate common values like justice, love and truth, the Mount Carmel incident provides a paradigm of how eclectic and mixed-up are both gods and their communities.

The third task of postcolonial criticism is to interrogate both colonial and metropolitan interpretations. The aim here is to draw attention to the inescapable effects of colonization and colonial ideologies on interpretative works such as commentarial writings, and on historical and administrative records which helped to (re)inscribe colonial ideologies and consolidate the colonial presence. For instance, it will investigate a narrative segment like the tribute-money question (Matt. 22.15–22; Mark 12.13–17; Luke 20.20–6) – a narrative which depicts the rare challenge of Jesus questioning the legitimacy of the Roman presence in Palestine – and how this encounter of Jesus with the religious and political leaders of the time has been commented on in various scholarly works. Samuel Rayan, who studied a random sample of nearly twenty commentaries produced between 1857 and 1978, draws attention to two different exegetical conclusions arrived at by biblical commentators. According to Rayan, the one reached during the colonial

---

[16] Wielenga, 'The God of Israel and Other Deities', p. 54.

period was used by the commentators to advance an anti-Zealot and pro-Roman position which endorsed Caesar's rule and Jewish subjugation and, by extension, legitimized the then current colonial rule and supported the tax demands of the ruling authorities. But commentators after the dismantling of the Empire took a different approach. In the changed context, the narrative was not mined for its political overtones, but came to be seen as favouring personal fidelity and moral conscience. There was a definite shift from political issues to the personal question of conscience. The tribute-money incident was now seen by commentators as reflecting the situation after the Jewish Revolt, the destruction of the Jewish temple and the heightened tension between the early Christian movement and the Jews. In that altered context, the commentators suggested that the members of the Jewish movement were encouraged to dissociate from political and revolutionary causes and to pay their respects and taxes to the state authorities, who were appointed by God as an instrument to defeat evil. Nonetheless, both readings, the one undertaken during the Empire days and the other after its collapse, saw the payment of tax as 'both lawful and obligatory'. Rayan's study includes well-known English commentators such as H. Goodwin, B. Swete, A. Plummer and Vincent Taylor; and among the Germans it includes Oscar Cullman and E. Haenchen, whose texts were recommended reading in many Third World theological colleges even after the demise of the Empire. Collectively they were trying to say, according to Rayan, that 'the coin represented Roman organization, security of person and property, transit facilities and stable government: it is but just to pay for their maintenance'.[17] Plummer spoke for all when he commented on the narrative:

The tribute was not a gift, but a debt. Caesar gave them the inestimable benefit of stable government; were they to take it and decline to pay anything towards its maintenance? The discharge of this duty to Caesar in no way interfered with the discharge of their duty to God; indeed the one duty was included in the other.[18]

---

[17] Samuel Rayan, 'Caesar Versus God', in *Jesus Today*, ed. S. Kappen (Bombay, AICUF Publication, 1985), p. 90.
[18] A. Plummer, *The Gospel According to St Mark* (Cambridge, Cambridge University Press, 1915), p. 147.

Plummer even went on to claim that in this passage Jesus says nothing 'as to the relations between Church and state'.

I have shown elsewhere that Weitbrecht Stanton, exegeting the Matthean record of this narrative in a commentary series produced for Indian students during the colonial days (the Indian Church Commentaries), saw it as a straightforward case of fair dealing between the rulers and the ruled: 'You profit by the protection of and administration of the imperial government, and are willing to use [it to] enrich yourselves . . . You are bound therefore to give back due value in the way of taxation for what you have received.'[19]

Postcolonial reading will also investigate interpretations which contested colonial interests and concerns. It will bring to the fore how the invaded, often caricatured as abused victims or grateful beneficiaries, transcended these images and wrested interpretation from the invaders, starting a process of self-discovery, appropriation and subversion. The reading practices of William Apess, Equiano, Shembe, Ramabai and Banerjea, recounted here, are examples of such an enterprise. Although they were incorporated into colonial ideologies, nonetheless they resisted them with the very tools provided by colonialism. Such readings will also challenge the notion of a mystical, irrational, stagnant Orient pitched against a progressive, rational and secular Occident.

To conclude this section: the Christian Bible is not subjected to a postcolonial gaze in order to make the texts come alive and provide solace and comfort to those devout (or in some cases not so devout) readers who also have social and political perceptiveness. In an age when many people question traditional sources of moral authority, sacred texts – the Bible among them – may not be the only place to look for answers to abstract or existential problems. The purpose of postcolonial reading is not to invest texts with properties which no longer have relevance to our context, or with excessive and exclusive theological claims which invalidate other claims. It seeks to puncture the Christian Bible's Western protection and pretensions, and to

---

[19] Sugirtharajah, *Asian Biblical Hermeneutics and Postcolonialism*, p. 77.

help reposition it in relation to its oriental roots and Eastern heritage. The aim is not to rediscover the biblical texts as an alternative or to search in their pages for a better world, as a way of coping with the terrors of the colonial aftermath. The Bible is approached not for its intrinsic authoritativeness or distinctiveness, but because of the thematic presuppositions of postcolonialism, which are influenced by such cultural and psychological effects as hybridity and alienation triggered by colonialism.

Postcolonialism's critical procedure is an amalgam of different methods ranging from the now unfashionable form-criticism to contemporary literary methods. It is interdisciplinary in nature and pluralistic in its outlook. It is more an avenue of inquiry than a homogeneous project. One of the significant aspects of postcolonialism is its theoretical and intellectual catholicism. It thrives on inclusiveness, and it is attracted to all kinds of tools and disciplinary fields, as long as they probe injustices, produce new knowledge which problematizes well-entrenched positions and enhance the lives of the marginalized. Any theoretical work that straddles and finds its hermeneutical home in different disciplines is bound to suffer from a certain eclectic theoretical arbitrariness. Such a selective bias, though lacking coherence, is sometimes necessary for the sake of the task in hand.

In defining the task of postcoloniality, Gloria Anzaldúa points out that postcoloniality looks at power systems and disciplines ranging from government documents to anthropological compositions and asks, 'Who has the voice? Who says these are rules? Who makes the law? And if you're not part of making the laws and rules and the theories, what part do you play? . . . What reality does this disciplinary field, or this government, or this system try to crush? What reality is it trying to erase? What reality is it trying to suppress?'[20] Applying this to biblical studies, postcolonial biblical criticism poses the following ques-

---

[20] Gloria Anzaldúa in conversation with Andrea Lunsford. See Andrea A. Lunsford, 'Toward a Mestiza Rhetoric: Gloria Anzaldúa on Composition and Postcoloniality', in *Race, Rhetoric, and the Postcolonial*, ed. Gary A. Olson and Lynn Worsham (Albany, State University of New York Press, 1999), p. 62.

tions: who has the power to interpret or tell stories? To whom do the stories/texts belong? Who controls their meaning? Who decides what texts we choose? Against whom are these stories or interpretations aimed? What is their ethical effect? Who has power to access data?

LIBERATION HERMENEUTICS AND POSTCOLONIAL CRITICISM: SHALL THE TWAIN MEET?

As I pointed out in the opening paragraph of this chapter, liberation hermeneutics and postcolonial criticism should be companions in arms, fighting the good fight. For both, commitment to liberation, however modernist the project may be, still has a valid purchase, for liberation as a grand narrative provides hope for countless millions of people who daily face institutional and personal violence and oppression. Both liberation hermeneutics and postcolonial criticism take the 'Other', namely the poor, seriously; both want to dismantle hegemonic interpretations and do not hesitate to offer prescriptions and make moral judgements, while acknowledging the perils of such decisions. However, to reiterate a point made in the last chapter, the entrenchment of liberation hermeneutics within the modernistic framework acts as an inhibition, and prevents it from embracing some of the virtues of postmodernism for its liberative cause. Postcolonial critical theory, on the other hand, as an off-shoot of postmodernism, while it collaborates with it, distances itself from its errors and unsavoury aspects.

While liberation hermeneutics has successfully undermined the certitude of dominant biblical scholarship, it is triumphalistic of its own achievement. Postcolonalism, on the other hand, understands the Bible and biblical interpretation as a site of struggle over its efficacy and meanings. There is a danger in liberation hermeneutics making the Bible the ultimate adjudicator in matters related to morals and theological disputes. Postcolonialism is much more guarded in its approach to the Bible's serviceability. It sees the Bible as both a safe and an unsafe text, and as both a familiar and a distant one. Liberation hermeneutics wants to redeem the Church and its past colonial atrocities through the very book which perpetuated them. In legitimizing the Bible's role in this redemptive act, Pablo Richard states that as 'an instrument of prophetic discernment of Christianity and a radical critique of Christendom, . . . [the Bible] can regain the credibility which colonial Christianity destroyed'.[21] For him, and other liberation hermeneuts, the 'problem is not the Bible itself, but the way it has been interpreted'.[22] Postcolonialism, on the other hand, sees the Bible as both problem and solution, and its message of liberation is seen as far more indeterminate and complicated. It is seen as a text of both emancipation and enervation. Postcolonial reading advocates the emancipation of the Bible from its implication in dominant ideologies both at the level of the text and at the level of interpretation. For postcolonialism, the critical principle is not derived only from the Bible but is determined by contextual needs and other warrants. It sees the Bible as one among many liberating texts. Liberation hermeneutics could usefully avail itself of some of the insights advocated by postcolonialism without abandoning or toning down its loyalty to the poor.

In its choice of biblical paradigms, and in its preoccupation with certain favoured texts and with reading them at their face value, liberation hermeneutics fails to appreciate the historical or political ramifications such an interpretation will have for those who face displacement and uprooting in their own lands and countries. For instance, in espousing and endorsing the Exodus as the foundational text for liberation in its early days, liberation hermeneutics failed to note that its suitability as a project had limited value and force. While liberation hermeneutics claimed that the Exodus was read from the point of view of the oppressed, it did not pause to think of the plight of the victims who were at the receiving end of its liberative action, and forced to embark upon what Robert Allen Warrior calls a 'reverse Exodus' from their own promised land. We saw in the last chapter how inappropriate the narrative is for Native

---

[21] Pablo Richard, '1492: The Violence of God and Future of Christianity', *Concilium* 6 (1990), 66.
[22] Ibid., p. 66.

American, Palestinian and Aboriginal contexts. It also raises awkward theological questions as to what kind of a God is posited both by the Bible and liberation theology. God is the one who emancipates Israel, but also in the process destroys Egyptians and Canaanites. Postcolonialism reads the narrative from the Canaanite point of view and discerns the parallels between the humiliated people of biblical and contemporary times. Similarly, in reading Ruth, liberation hermeneutics sees her as the paradigmatic convert and assimilator. Her inclusion into the mainstream, assimilating its key values, was seen as an important strategy. Laura Donaldson, as a Cherokee woman, tries to reposition Ruth in the light of the specific cultural and historical predicament of an American Indian woman.[23] In the face of the constant demand for ethnic minorities to assimilate into the mainstream culture, Laura Donaldson recovers another often written-out and under-exegeted indigene character – Orpah, the sister-in-law of Ruth, who, unlike Ruth, returns to her mother's house. Donaldson's contention is that it is Orpah who signifies hope and provides emancipatory vision for Cherokee women, because it is she who embraces her own clan and culture. When read from Orpah's point of view, we see a different Ruth. Both liberation hermeneutics and postcolonialism share reading as resistance, but postcolonial critical practice sees reading and resistance as a far more complex activity.

For liberation hermeneutics, the project of liberation remains within the bounds of Christianity and its construction is informed by Christian sources. Liberation hermeneutics sees liberation as something lodged and located in biblical texts, or in ecumenical and Christian Church documents, and as something which can be extracted from these textualized records. As Marcella Althaus-Reid has pointed out, however, liberation as a concept 'obeys certain masters, a certain framework of thought which in the end regulates the available strategies for freedom,

---

[23] See Laura E. Donaldson, 'The Sign of Orpah: Reading Ruth Through Native Eyes', in *Vernacular Hermeneutics*, ed. R. S. Sugirtharajah (Sheffield, Sheffield Academic Press, 1999), pp. 20–36.

even pre-emptying [*sic*] the notion of freedom in itself'.[24] It still works with the binary notions of Christian and non-Christian and sees religious pluralism as an exception rather than a norm. Postcolonialism, on the other hand, is able to draw on a larger theological pool and is not confined to a particular religious source. Liberation for postcolonialism is not imposing a pre-existing notion, but working out its contours in responding to voices within and outside the biblical tradition.

Postcolonial space refuses to press for a particular religious stance as final and ultimate. As a point of entry, individual interpreters may have their own theological, confessional and denominational stance, but this in itself does not preclude them from inquiring into and entertaining a variety of religious truth-claims. It is the multi-disciplinary nature of the enterprise which gives postcolonialism its energy. It sees revelation as an ongoing process which embraces not only the Bible, tradition, and the Church but also other sacred texts and contemporary secular events. What postcolonialism will argue for is that the idea of liberation and its praxis must come from the collective unconscious of the people. It sees liberation not as something hidden or latent in the text, but rather as born of public consensus created in democratic dialogue between text and context.

Both liberation hermeneutics and postcolonialism endorse the Other – the poor, the marginalized – as the prime site for doing theology. The former's view of the poor, however, is largely a restrictive one, confined to the economically disadvantaged. Where postcolonialism differs is that it recognizes a plurality of oppressions. Unlike liberation hermeneutics, post-colonialism does not perceive the Other as a homogenous category, but acknowledges multiple identities based upon class, sex, ethnicity and gender. In their preferential option, there is a tendency in liberation hermeneutics to romanticize the poor. For instance, when exegeting the Gospel account of the Widow's Mite (Mark 12.41–4), José Cárdenas Pallares, the

---

[24] Marcella Althaus-Reid, 'The Hermeneutics of Transgression', in *Liberation Theologies on Shifting Grounds: A Clash of Socio-Economic and Cultural Paradigms*, ed. G. de Schrijver (Leuven, Leuven University Press, 1998), p. 268.

Mexican who wrote a commentary on Mark from the liberation perspective, falls victim to liberal interpretation when he sees in the widow an exemplar of ideal piety. Her piety and sacrifice are differentiated from the barrenness of the scribal faith or the facile and pretentious offering of the rich:

In contrast with the sterility of official religion, which gets along on miracles and money alone (Mk. 11.12–22), the poor widow demonstrates true faith in God (Mk. 11.22–4). Her strength and her security are God (12.44). The interpretation Jesus and the first Christians make of this poor person's behaviour is an absolute and utter reversal of values, a contradiction of everything that motivates a classless society. For this poor person, and as for the poor Jesus and the poor primitive communities, what counts is God.[25]

Ultimately, in the name of liberation, what is offered to the poor is an old-fashioned evangelical exhortation to faith in God and trust in God's faithfulness. Postcolonialism reads the Gospel incident from the point of view of the widow and sees it not as an approval of her action but as an exposure of abuse by the temple treasury authorities. If one sees it from the widow's angle, Jesus was not applauding her action but making an assault upon an institution which generated poverty in Israel. This is evidenced by the judgement prefigured in Jesus' condemnation of an institution which destroys the poor and costs very little to the rich. Postcolonial reading will not see the widow as being singled out by Jesus as a model for piety but as a poor widow who was manipulated and swindled by the system into parting with the little she had.

Linked with the poor is the idea in liberation hermeneutics of the poor as the new people of God. That a recent volume on dalit, burakumin and aborigines has the title, *God, Christ and God's People in Asia*, is an indication of such a claim. The identification and correspondence between the biblical people of God and the current oppressed is a concept needing much more careful articulation.

---

[25] José Cárdenas Pallares, *A Poor Man Called Jesus: Reflections on the Gospel of Mark*, tr. Robert R. Barr (Maryknoll, NY, Orbis Books, 1986), pp. 57–8.

Religion and liberation

Liberation hermeneutics has to reconcile its position with the theology of religions, with religious pluralism and the religiosity of popular religions. It still operates within the Judaeo-Christian notion of what religion is. One of the reasons for its failure to get to grips with religions, according to Aloysius Pieris, is that liberation theology reels under the captivity of two 'Karls' of dialectical disposition – Karl Barth and Karl Marx. In his view, Marx's dialectical materialism failed to perceive the potentiality for revolution in religion, and Barth's dialectical theology failed to acknowledge that there was revelation in religion.[26] Though liberation theology has taken the poor seriously, as we noted in the previous chapter, it has hitherto dismissed the religious agency of the poor, expressed through mystical visions and dreams, healings and exorcisms, veneration of saints and relics, and through feasts, fasts and religious processions. In their study of liberation theology's attitude to African religions and cultures, Sathler and Nascimento conclude that liberation theology tends to maintain the purity of the Christian gospel and frown upon the liberative potentiality of the indigenous religions. They have demonstrated that even a person like Leonardo Boff, who pleaded for syncretism, maintained an offensive position towards Afro-Brazilian religious practices: 'He reduces their social elements to psychopathologies and acknowledges their members as underdeveloped subjects that need a true, universal, psychic, social, and religious salvation which can be given only in the Catholic Church. So he comes close to the orthodoxy.'[27] Pablo Richard himself, an advocate of indigenous reading of the Bible, eventually sees the Bible as adjudicator in matters related to Indian religions and cultures. 'The indigenous people must construct a new hermeneutic to decolonize the interpretation', writes Richard, but in the final

---

[26] Aloysius Pieris, *An Asian Theology of Liberation* (Edinburgh, T. & T. Clark, 1988), p. 91.

[27] Josué Sathler and Amós Nascimento, 'Black Masks on White Faces: Liberation Theology and the Quest for Syncretism in the Brazilian Context', in *Liberation Theologies, Postmodernity, and the Americas*, ed. David Bastone et al. (London, Routledge, 1997), p. 114.

analysis, the Bible is 'an instrument, a criterion, a canon, for discerning the presence and reevaluation of God in indigenous culture and religion.'[28] There is no concession to the religious claims of other faith traditions, only an apology for Christian truth. Postcolonialism, on the other hand represents the contemporary restlessness concerning religious pluralism, the validity of different confessional traditions, and the empowerment of repressed voices through visual, oral and aural means. It is distinctly postmodernistic, since it has argued from the start for a pluralistic outlook and has encouraged the possibility of alternative ways of thinking, valuing and acting. It is sceptical about the monopolistic and prescriptive nature of Christianity.

Liberation hermeneutics and postcolonialism share mutual agendas and goals, and hope for and work towards an alternative to the present arrangement. If liberation hermeneutics could eschew its homogenization of the poor, incessant biblicism and hostility to religious pluralism that plagues its interpretative focus, it should be able to join forces with postcolonial thinking to fathom and fashion a different world from the one in which we live.

SOME DECK-CLEARING EXERCISES

Since the emergence of postcolonial criticism, questions have been constantly asked about its relation to other and allied critical forces, and also about some of its own critical practices. In the following section, let me try to deal with some of the frequently asked questions.

Postmodernism and postcolonialism

Both postmodernism and postcolonialism embody an important impulse, namely to intervene and interrogate accepted knowledges and to destabilize their complacencies.[29] But what

---

[28] Richard, '1492: The Violence of God and Future of Christianity', p. 66.
[29] For literature on how these two interpretative currents overlap and seek different paths, see Ian Adam and Helen Tiffin, *Past the Last Post: Theorizing Post-Colonialism and Post-Modernism* (Hemel Hempstead, Harvester Wheatsheaf, 1993); Linda Hutcheon, 'The Post always Rings Twice: the Postmodern and Postcolonial', *Textual Practice* 8:2 (1994), 205–38; Quayson, *Postcolonialism*, pp. 132–55.

distinguishes typically postmodern discourse from postcolonialism is postmodernism's scepticism regarding history, its implicit privileging of current Western cultural norms, its lack of any political agenda and its mischievous misreading of texts. Unlike postmodernism, which sees the end of grand narratives, postcolonialism views liberation as a meta-story which still has to play out its full potential. Modernity itself is often regarded by postmodernists as an anachronism, but postcolonialism sees the less perverted forms of modernization as a very appealing and applicable option for Third World people, particularly as a vehicle of economic liberation. In its veneration of plurality, and its fear of replicating the modernistic sin of prescriptive and hegemonic tendencies, postmodernism is shy of making hard ethical and moral decisions. By contrast, postcolonial criticism argues for ethical practice even though it is suspicious of its universal applicability. Here I agree with Ato Quayson's plea for a proactive ethical involvement, notwithstanding the risk and danger involved in such an enterprise:

Recognizing that there is much destitution, poverty and sheer despair in the world, it seems to me increasingly imperative that the risk of appearing prescriptive is worth taking if one is not to surrender completely to a debilitating anomie brought on by the apprehension of persistent social tragedies. Those who lose their limbs to landmines, are displaced through refugee crises or merely subsist in the intermittent but regularly frustrated hope that the world can become a better place, cannot wait for complete moral certitude before they take action to improve their existence. It is partly in the implicit (and often real) alliance with those who, to appropriate a phrase from Julian Murphet, 'keep running all the time simply to keep pace with events' that we ought to take courage to make ethical judgements even in the full knowledge that we may be proved wrong. To this larger picture, and in service of this larger affirmation we ought to commit our critical enterprises.[30]

Is it right to subject past documents to current notions of racism, sexism, and so forth?

Historians are often impatient if twentieth-century concerns are imported into ancient materials. Any attempt to read past

---

[30] Quayson, *Postcolonialism*, p. 155.

documents from postcolonial and feminist perspectives is frowned upon. The other objection is that, as most of the interpreters are dead and unable to respond, there is no point in dragging them into the present debate. Talal Asad aptly puts the reasons for engaging with the past:

The objection could only be made by readers who haven't understood what is involved in belonging to a living tradition. Criticisms of the past are morally relevant only when that past still informs the present – when contemporaries invoke the authority of founding ancestors against each other. In criticizing the dead, one is therefore questioning what they have authorized in the living. (To reject everything that preceding generations have authorized is, of course, to abandon the tradition as a whole, to call for a severance of all links between the living and the dead.)[31]

The real question is, as Gayatri Spivak puts it, 'why structures of patriarchal domination should be unquestionably recorded'. She goes on to say that 'historical sanctions for collective action toward social justice can only be developed if people outside of the discipline question the standards of "objectivity" preserved as such by the hegemonic tradition'.[32] Another point is that, if these documents reflect the cultural and historical reality of the time and are historical phenomena, we should not claim any universal validity or contemporary relevance for them, be they biblical or Shakespearean texts, and should leave them at that. More to the point, we revisit these texts not to be judgemental but to readjust our perceptions and prejudices and to inform our present knowledge, which often accepts discriminatory practices as the norm.

Finally, on the question of investigating past histories and personalities, it is worth recalling the words of E. P. Thompson:

Such judgement must itself be under historical controls. The judgement must be appropriate to the materials. It is pointless to complain that the bourgeoisie have not been communitarians, or that the Levellers did not introduce an anarchosyndicalist society. What we may do, rather, is identify with certain values which past actors

---

[31] Talal Asad, 'A Comment on Translation, Critique, and Subversion', in *Between Languages and Cultures: Translation and Cross-Cultural Texts*, ed. Anuradha Dingwaney and Carol Maier (Delhi, Oxford University Press, 1996), p. 328.

[32] Spivak, *A Critique of Postcolonial Reason*, p. 301.

upheld, and reject others. We may give our vote for Winstanley and for Swift; we may vote against Walpole and Sir Edwin Chadwick.

Our vote will change nothing. And yet, in another sense, it may change everything. For we are saying that these values, and not those other values, are the ones which make this history meaningful *to us*, and these are the values which we intend to enlarge and sustain in our own present. If we succeed, then we reach back into history and endow it with our own meanings: we shake Swift by the hand. We endorse in our present the values of Winstanley, and ensure the low and ruthless kind of opportunism which distinguished the politics of Walpole is abhorred.[33]

Is everything postcolonial?

Increasingly one hears today that, since most countries have gone through some kind of colonial experience, everything is postcolonial. There is a tendency to smooth out the different colonial experiences. Thus, the nineteenth-century British imperialists are equated with the tenth-century Mongols who had the largest-ever land empire, and the American invasion of Grenada is treated as equal to that of the Indonesian occupation of East Timor. It is this kind of thinking which would like to present British colonialism in Hong Kong as a benevolent intrusion, and Chinese nationalism as native backwardness. Such a position, according to Rey Chow, flattens out past injustices and plays into the hands of global capitalism, which views past injustices as irksome and dispensable. For some postcolonials, whom Chow terms postmodern hybridites, there is not much difference between the new globalism and cosmopolitanism. Such claims blur and obliterate complex histories, emphasizing the 'post' in the postcolonial, and reading it as 'after' and 'over with' rather than putting the emphasis on the colonial. The meaning of 'post' here is not 'after' but, rather, it designates a space of cultural contest and change. Postcolonialism is not about a particular epoch. It is about a set of measures undertaken to infuse a new sense of destiny.[34]

---

[33] I located this quotation in Jeff Guy, *The Heretic: A Study of the Life of John William Colenso 1814–1883* (Johannesburg, Raven Press, 1983), p. 355.

[34] Rey Chow, *Ethics after Idealism: Theory-Culture-Ethnicity-Reading* (Bloomington, Indiana University Press, 1998), pp. 155–6.

Perils of pluralizing colonialism

While acknowledging historical specificities and varieties of colonialism, one should also address the perils and hazards of pluralizing it. The counter-measure is not to undermine the variety of colonialisms. Preoccupation with specificities can, in the words of Barker, Hume and Iverson, become 'another version of the empiricist fallacy in which all attempts to theorize are answered by the supposedly irrefutable case of a counter-example'.[35] There are valid reasons for holding on to a general concept. As Spivak notes in another context, one has to 'posit a great narrative in order to be able to critique it'.[36] Meyda Yeğenoğlu's proposal is to see colonialism as a *'complexity within such a unity'*.[37] She writes: 'Thus to understand the complexity of the unity of colonialism and colonial discourse we need to conceive of it as a network of codes, imageries, signs, and representations which serve as a reference system and function as a regulatory principle of a discursive regime that we can label as colonial.'[38]

Who can engage in postcolonial discourse?

One hears two types of stories. The first is perpetuated by the former colonized who insist on the experience of oppression as a vital ingredient for holding on to a particular theoretical position. Their routine argument – 'you don't know what it was like, because it never happened to you, and therefore you have no right to speak' – does not allow room for a sober assessment. The colonial archives record instances of a missionary or a colonial civil servant, to the annoyance of the establishment,

---

[35] Francis Barker, Peter Hulme and Margaret Iversen, 'Introduction', in *Colonial Discourse / Postcolonial Theory*, ed. Francis Barker, Peter Hulme and Margaret Iversen (Manchester, Manchester University Press, 1994), pp. 10–11.

[36] Gayatri Chakravorty Spivak, 'Neocolonialism and the Secret Agent (Interviewed by Robert Young)', *The Oxford Literary Review* 13:1–2 (1991), 222.

[37] Meyda Yeğenoğlu, *Colonial Fantasies: Towards a Feminist Reading of Orientalism* (Cambridge, Cambridge University Press, 1998), p. 38.

[38] Ibid., p. 38.

taking up the cause of the victims. There have been numbers of righteous non-Jews, and anti-apartheid non-blacks who spoke out for what was right, irrespective of who they were. It would be lamentable to resort to personal experience as a hermeneutical trump card. In that case, one would have to be a Jew to resist anti-Semitism, a gay to support homosexual rights, and poor in order to advocate welfare reforms. If one took this to its logical conclusion, then only animals could do animal theology and only trees could talk about deforestation. Personal experience, cultural affinities and ideological closeness, important though they are, are poor surrogates for understanding and accountability in hermeneutics. Sensing and feeling what is right is sufficient. One does not need to have lived it. To espouse a cause or plead for something because it concerns only you is far less impressive than championing it simply because it is fair.

The second type of story comes from those mainstream intellectuals who wish to restrict the discipline to the former colonial victims, and to declare it a no-go area for First World people. This is a skilful way of restricting the discipline and ghettoizing it. Segregation and setting up 'we' against 'them' are part of the colonial grand design. The point of postcolonial study is not only to question the unfairness meted out to certain groups of people and to their histories and cultures, but to study the involvement and incorporation of European and American institutional processes which facilitated, legitimatized and perpetuated such inequalities. The Chinese cultural critic, Phebe Shih Chao, basing her argument on Fanon, charts similar processes which the colonizer and colonized undergo. The colonized passes through stages, from imitation of the master to the desire to return to his or her roots and through to being an awakener of his or her people. Similarly, the colonizer, in his turn, moves from being a willing participant in colonialism to a feeling of remorse and finally to seeking to rectify past misdeeds and misperceptions. These processes may not coincide, and need not go hand in hand. Since both the colonized and the colonizer are inextricably involved and have a stake in unravelling race, gender and ethnicity, the whole exercise becomes pedagogically and critically ineffective if the field is restricted to one group of people.[39]

Finally, some of the hermeneutical and praxiological agendas that postcolonialism seeks to pursue coincide with other liberative movements such as feminism. Though there is this shared intellectual and vocational mission, postcolonialism differs significantly from these critical undertakings in two ways. It combats the West's textualizing defamation of the colonized and redresses cultural and political catastrophes caused by Western civilization. The other difference is that, unlike the dominant theoretical categories, postcolonialism did not begin its career as an answer to the West's intellectual and psychological dilemmas, but as meeting the needs of the colonized other. Interestingly, it is by them and about them, but has tremendous hermeneutical consequences for the West.

CONSEQUENCES, CONCERNS AND CAUTIONS

Like it or not, postcolonialism as a critical category will continue to exercise influence at least for some time to come, both in academic discourse and in general usage, since it signals an important new starting point and a significant shift. In its name significant work has already been done: the marginals and the natives have been rescued without fantasizing and investing them with a venerable status; colonial configurations have been unmasked; and established ideas and conventional discourse about representations set in place by colonialism have been dislodged. But this does not mean that everything is fine and that better days are here. The temptation is to be mesmerized by the recent kudos accorded by the academy, to turn gamekeeper and superintend and police the discourses of subaltern groups. It is important to employ the postcolonial discourse with caution and suspicion, and to use it as an oppositional tool.

In spite of ambiguities, postcolonialism is a serviceable category because it conveys the historical phenomenon of European

---

[39] Phebe Shih Chao, 'Reading *The Letter* in a Postcolonial World', in *Visions of the East: Orientalism in Film*, ed. Matthew Bernstein and Gaylyn Studlar (London, I. B. Tauris Publishers, 1997), pp. 292–3.

subjugation and colonialism and its attendant features, namely the rearrangement of power and the inter-mix of cultures within particular geographical locations. It is a convenient tool to unmask the past textual production of colonialism and to dislodge its legitimizing strategies. Positively, it provides a location for other voices, histories and experiences to be heard. The category is also useful in creating awareness of the colonial legacy as it continues to maintain a hold on people, communities and culture. It is also useful in signifying changing relations among these people, cultures and communities in the postmodern world. More to the point, postcolonial space helps us to break free from the interpretative cages into which some of us are corralled. Simply because a person is from the Third World, he or she is forced, enticed, encouraged and, in some cases, volunteered to speak from the limited confines of nationalism, ethnicity and religious enclosures. As Arthur Ashe said in another context, carrying our ethnicity has become for some of us a second full-time job. Postcolonial space frees us from the nationalistic mode of analysing and firm commitment to cultural ghettos. There are no more frontiers to be guarded and defended. Postcolonial criticism encourages one to be highly eclectic and to embrace every tool as long as it promotes just causes.

Unlike other critical categories which are in vogue today, postcolonialism's original incarnation was in the form of imaginative literature, in the writings of Indians, Africans and Latin Americans. Theoretical fine-tuning followed later. In an era which is so paranoid about getting theoretical procedures correct, postcolonial critics may be enticed into spending their energy in a search for finer theoretical excellence and, in doing so, losing their ability to trigger a new wave of imaginative hermeneutical renditions. If we persist in this we will forfeit its appeal and momentum, and are bound to become redundant. Such a pursuit would then be seen as an escapist activity, with inventive hermeneutical productions giving way to theoretical purity. The concern Segundo raised about Latin American liberation theologians long ago may also become true of postcolonial critics:

[M]any Latin American theologians, under this banner, which made them fashionable in the international market, if not fully appreciated in their particular churches, engaged in relentless and quite useless battle with their European and North American peers comparing methods and theological loci. As a result, twenty years later, Latin American liberation theology is more a repetitive apology for itself than a constructive theological discourse.[40]

The ravages and marks of colonialism will never be totally erased. As history has shown, old forms will be replaced with new. A case in point is the current globalization which is taking over the universalism which ruled the roost in the old days. In the light of this, postcolonialism has a continual role in reconciling the past with the present. Until some sort of an end to colonialism is reached, if ever that is possible, postcolonial criticism has a role to play. It must be persistently vigilant, but more to the point, it must also be critical of its own parameters. Any theory or discourse that does not have within itself an inbuilt mechanism for its own deconstruction will become a potent tool for theological and ideological propaganda. This applies to postcolonial theory as to any other.

Most of the postcolonial critics, for a variety of reasons, have made the academy their home. We may not be in an ideal position to represent the indigenes or the natives. But we can engage in what Edward Said has urged the interpreters to do – to speak truth to the powerful. In his 1993 Reith Lectures, Said said: 'Speaking the truth to power is no Panglossian idealism: it is carefully weighing the alternatives, picking the right one, and then intelligently representing it where it can do the most good and cause the right change.'[41] Tainted though we may be by our links with the academy, nonetheless we can still be spokespersons for the dalits, the burakumins, the aborigines and countless oppressed national minorities and women; we can write about and represent them, so that their condition may be

---

[40] Luis Juan Segundo, *Signs of the Times: Theological Reflections*, tr. Robert R. Barr (Maryknoll, NY, Orbis Books, 1993), pp. 75–6.
[41] Edward W. Said, *Representations of the Intellectual: The 1993 Reith Lectures* (London, Vintage, 1994), p. 75.

better known, their memories kept alive, their condition alleviated and their fractured lives reconciled. By doing so, we can offer counter-information and check the negative and stereotypical images emanating from powerful and authoritative sources. The task of the postcolonial critic is not limited to speaking truth to the powerful, but includes also speaking to the poor about the powerful, especially about the enormous power wielded by the media, multinationals and the institutional Church.

The success of postcolonialism depends on its engagement with more than one constituency. It should be able to move freely within the academy and in the world outside. It should involve both intellectual and popular discourse. Postcolonial theory, as it is practised in certain circles, has been perceived to be too complex and esoteric to have much influence outside the academy. While the academic community has produced incisive critiques of Orientalism, the popular media, especially the ecumenical and denominational press, continue to orientalize in their voracious portrayals of an exotic/demonic version of India/Africa through food, famine, films, and so forth. One of the uses of postcolonial theory is to make readers and audiences aware of the nature of representation.

If postcolonial theory helps us to familiarize ourselves with the by-lanes and pathways of Dickensian London, but acts as a diversion and fails to take note of today's inner cities and Third World problems, then the theory will not be worth employing. Textual reclamations and resistant reading practices will make sense only if they address the questions people face today. Ultimately, the question is not whether our reading practice is seen as colonial or postcolonial, modern or postmodern. Its usefulness will not be judged by its ability to offer a critique of the complex heritage that colonial occupation produced. Its critical relevance will be apparent when it has a bearing on the issues that cause concern to our people, such as housing, education, homeland, healthcare, social security and the justice system. Its worth will be appraised in the light of the vital role it can play when the time comes for deciding these issues which affect people, rather than whether its theoretical base is modern or non-modern, colonial or anti-colonial. The task of postcolonialism is ensuring that the needs and aspirations of the exploited are catered to, rather than being merely an interesting and engaging avenue of inquiry.

Afterword

Let me bring this volume to a conclusion by making a few obvious observations. First, it is clear from the interpretative practices narrated here that reading is not a simple activity. A hundred years ago, faced with similarly bewildering reading and textual practices, Richard G. Moulton urged his readers to cultivate the simple habit of reading:

We have done almost everything that is possible with these Hebrew and Greek writings. We have overlaid them, clause by clause, with exhaustive commentaries; we have translated them, revised the trans-lations, and quarrelled over revisions; we have discussed authenticity and inspiration, and suggested textual history with the aid of coloured type; we have mechanically divided the whole into chapters and verses, and sought texts to memorise and quote; we have epitomised into handbooks and extracted school lessons; we have recast from the feminist point of view, and even from the standpoint of the next century. There is yet one thing left to do with the Bible: simply to read it.[1]

What is evident from these interpretations is that Moulton's noble call is not easy to follow. As long as there are texts and readers, reading will be a consciously manufactured activity. Texts are malleable and readers are manipulative. Neither the text nor the reader is a blameless partner in this venture. Either the texts seek to invade and transform the reader, thus making him or her a prey, or the reader imposes his or her power on the text. Both are involved in the manipulation and enticement of each other.

---

[1] Richard G. Moulton, *A Short Introduction to the Literature of the Bible* (London, D. C. Heath and Co., 1900), pp. iii-iv.

Secondly, what we have encountered in the preceding pages are representative samples of biblical interpretations from the Third World. As indicated in the introduction, these are not the only interpretations to arise out of the Third World. These are reflections of a people, which came out of a particular period, and do not claim to be timeless or culture-less essences. As expositions these interpretations are neither correct nor incorrect. Their crucial importance lies in their potential to challenge the received accounts, and to serve as a reminder to be vigilant when newer forms of race, class, gender and sexual hierarchies continue to be constructed.

Thirdly, these interpretations indicate that it is the needs of the present which detect and control any reading practice. Therefore, hermeneutics, far from being a disinterested recovery of ancient biblical history, is actually an unfolding of the past to meet the present concerns and preoccupations of the interpreter, and, by extension, the interests of the interpretative communities he or she represents. It is apparent that present concerns are plural. Consequently the interpretations of the past will also be plural and highly contentious. In spite of the plurality of these often conflicting interests, we continue to interpret, since we need to explain the present and also to forge a future for ourselves.

The other point worth reiterating is that we select from the past those narratives which endorse what we want from the present. These contribute to the construction of a self-image and identity to suit contemporary cultural and political needs. Texts which provide such hermeneutical sustenance are seized upon, projected back into the canon and baptized as truly biblical and truly Christian. When a narrative fails to answer the needs of the present, and if it cannot be retold to meet new demands, it will be relegated and pushed out of the interpretative frame. The unappropriated texts do not wither away but recede into the background, yielding their place to the newly chosen texts which are accorded the status of the living Word of God. Nonetheless, texts left out remain true and valid, awaiting their turn to be resurrected. No one narrative remains static or eternally valid.

Finally, the extensive use of the Bible narrated here may give
the impression that the Bible is well and safe in the Third
World, and that the entire Third World is buzzing with biblical
vision. This is a false assumption. It must be recognized that the
spiritual truth found in the Christian Scripture is one among
many theological riches available to humankind, and that the
Bible, like any other sacred text, has to stake its claim. It is still
viewed with suspicion for its entanglement with colonialism. In
most of the countries of the Third World, especially in Asia, the
Bible is read inevitably from a situation of marginality.

The question then is: what is so Third World about these
appropriations or, for that matter, what is so Indian, or African
or Latin American about them? There is a real difficulty in
defining what is so specific about Thirdworldness owing to
geographical, linguistic, religious and cultural differences and
sensibilities. We have yet to define clearly what is meant by
what is characteristically Indian or African. The question itself
engages the minds of Western interpreters only when a person
from the Third World is writing in English. Let me bring in the
Indian literary critic and academic Meenakshi Mukherjee,
since what she says about Indian writings in English is also
equally true about Third World biblical hermeneutics:

> If I were to write a novel in Marathi, I would not be called an Indian
> writer in Marathi, but simply a Marathi novelist, the epithet Marathi
> referring only to the language, not conveying the larger burden of
> culture, tradition and ethos. No one would write a doctoral disserta-
> tion on the Indianness of my Marathi novel. But when it comes to
> English fiction originating in our country, not only does the issue of
> Indianness become a favourite essentializing obsession in academic
> writings and the book review circuit, the writers themselves do not
> seem unaffected by it, the complicating factor being that English is
> not just any language it was the language of colonial rulers and
> continues even now to be the language of power and privilege. Our
> discourse on Indian novels in English tends to get congealed into
> fairly rigid and opposed positions.[2]

---

[2] Meenakshi Mukherjee, 'The Anxiety of Indianness: Our Novels in English', in
*Mapping Cultural Spaces: Postcolonial Indian Literature in English. Essays in Honour of Nissim
Ezekiel*, ed. Nilufer E. Bharucha and Vrinda Nabar (New Delhi, Vision Books, 1998),
pp. 79–80.

The earlier generation of Indian interpreters, and some of the current practitioners who employ vernacular languages, take India as given and refer to it vaguely in their articulations. They are not unduly troubled by the question of what it means to be an Indian. Krishna Pillai, Vedanaygam and Tilak, in the past, and Dayandan Francis and Sathiasatchy, in the present, are not self-consciously worried about being Indian, let alone being a Maharashtrian or a Tamil. The predominant influence on their hermeneutical activity is provided by the immediate linguistic and vernacular environment. They write in the secure knowledge of knowing their constituency, and how equipped the constituents are with the keys for decoding the oblique messages in their writings. Interpretative themes handled by some of the vernacular interpreters in chapter six are a case in point.

Behind the hunt for the authentic Indian or African lies the notion that, in spite of the long history of Western colonization, non-Western cultural productions should remain pure, original, truly indigenous and totally untainted by the impact of older and newer forms of colonialism. What a correspondent wrote in the *Liverpool Post* of 20th July 1920 epitomises such a quest:

We of the West do not want from the East poetic edifices built upon a foundation of Yeats and Shelley and Walt Whitman. We want to hear the flute of Krishna as Radha heard of it, to fall under the spell of the blue God in the lotus-heart of dreams.[3]

Such a search envisages the task of interpretation as establishment of an identity rather than as a process in which identity, context and texts constantly evolve in response to new demands. Rey Chow refers to those who yearn for the past as 'root searchers' because roots signify a nostalgic return to the past so that the plurality of the present can be reduced to 'a long-lost origin'.[4] Behind the post-imperial quest by Western interpreters for an authentic Thirdworldness there lurks a

---

[3] Cited in Indu Saraiya, 'After Rain, the Rainbow', in *Mapping Cultural Spaces: Postcolonial Indian Literature in English. Essays in Honour of Nissim Ezekiel*, ed. Nilufer E. Bharucha and Vrinda Nabar (New Delhi, Vision Books, 1998), p. 112.

[4] Rey Chow, *Ethics After Idealism: Theory-Culture-Ethnicity-Reading* (Bloomington, Indiana University Press, 1998), p. 162.

feeling of homesickness for traditional culture and values, which once they controlled and which now are not within their reach. If one wants to look for Thirdworldness in the examples recounted here, it lies in the refusal of Third World interpreters to accept reigning modes of interpretation and, in their readiness to interrogate, speak against the accepted modes and then devise an alternative set of interpretative proposals which enhances the subalterns' status.

What, then, is the next step forward? Do we replace the works of these unheard voices with accepted works of academic scholarship? The concern Edward Said raised for those who work in literary studies is equally valid for those who engage in biblical interpretation:

> Do we say: now that we have won, that we have achieved equality and independence, let us elevate ourselves, our history, our cultural or ethnic identity above that of others, uncritically giving this identity of ours centrality and coercive dominance? Do we substitute for a Eurocentric norm an Afrocentric or Islamo- or Arabo-centric one? Or, as happened so many times in the postcolonial world, do we get our independence and then return to models for education, derived lazily, adopted imitatively and uncritically, from elsewhere? In short, do we use the freedom we have fought for merely to replicate the mind-forged manacles that once enslaved us, and having put them on do we proceed to apply them to others less fortunate than ourselves?[5]

The validity of an interpretation does not depend on positing an alternative reading or supporting it with new data. Simply replacing a metropolitan reading with a subaltern one does not make the latter more legitimate than the one it tries to dislodge. Combatting one set of data with a counter set is not enough to unsettle hegemonic readings. Instead, the discursive modes through which narratives and facts are produced must also be called into question. The crucial question is not to do with one set of data replacing the other, but with which text, theory or author is relevant and meaningful to the context in which they are appropriated.

One way to bridge the gap between texts emanating from the

[5] Edward W. Said, 'Identity, Authority, and Freedom: The Potentate and the Traveler' in *The Future of Academic Freedom*, ed. Louis Menand (Chicago, The University of Chicago Press, 1996), pp. 223–4.

margins and from the centre is to engage in contrapuntal reading. This is a reading strategy advocated by Edward Said, with a view to encouraging the experiences of the exploited and exploiter to be studied together. To read contrapuntally means to be aware simultaneously of mainstream scholarship and of other scholarship which the dominant discourse tries to domesticate and speak and act against. In Said's words, we 'reread it not univocally but *contrapuntally*, with a simultaneous awareness both of the metropolitan history that is narrated and of those other histories against which (and together with which) the dominating discourse acts'.[6] Translating this into a theological discipline, it means to read Bas van Iersel's *Mark: A Reader-Response Commentary* with Kinukawa's *Women and Jesus in Mark*; Elsa Tamez's *The Amnesty of Grace* with Käsemann's commentary on Romans; *The Postcolonial Bible* with *The Postmodern Bible*; and the *New Revised Standard Version* with the *African Bible*. Such readings are undertaken, not with a view to refuting or contesting, but as a way of showing a substantial relationship between the centre and the periphery. By likening such works to each other, juxtaposing neglected texts with the mainstream, we can highlight convergences, absences and imbalances. Such a reading will reiterate that many readings are possible, and that it is preferable to highlight the diversity rather than privileging the one over the others. More importantly, such an undertaking will prevent any authoritative closure of meaning.

Finally, during the halcyon days of the Empire and of missionary enterprise, the Bible, which originated with marginal groups, was poised to inherit the earth. But like many things in contemporary life, the Bible is currently going through a crisis. For some of our recent moral questions about such issues as genetic engineering and cloning, the Bible may not be the right place to look for answers. The book which controlled the fabric of Western society and fuelled its imagination has now almost lost its grip. It is no longer possible to trace in its pages the missionary motive and missionary expansion. Sustained historical investigation has put an end to such an exegetical

---

[6] Edward W. Said, *Culture and Imperialism* (London, Chatto & Windus, 1993), p. 59.

enterprise. Moreover, the many inadequate and harmful ways in which its texts have been summoned to support slavery, the subjugation of women and violation of the environment make it still a suspicious document, although a resistant reading on the part of the blacks, feminists and liberationists may offset such a view. The missionaries' hope that the Christian Bible would eventually replace other peoples' sacred stories and writings has not happened. There is an increased acknowledgement that no one scripture conveys the full divine–human experience. These texts coalesce, coexist and interact with one another. One way for the Bible to gain its respectability in a post-missionary and postcolonial context is to shed its Western protection and its imperialistic intentions and to find its place where it began its life, in West Asia. Its future role may depend on rediscovering its oriental roots and becoming one of the sacred books of the East. Such a relocation may not be a bad idea. It could produce a different effect both on the text and on those who read it.

Select bibliography

BIBLICAL HERMENEUTICS

Aland, Kurt and Aland, Barbara, *The Text of the New Testament: An Introduction to the Critical Editions and to the Theory and Practice of Modern Textual Criticism* (Grand Rapids, MT, William B. Eerdmans, 1987).

Althaus-Reid, Marcella, 'The Hermeneutics of Transgression', in *Liberation Theologies on Shifting Grounds: A Clash of Socio-Economic and Cultural Paradigms*, ed. G. de Schrijver (Leuven, Leuven University Press, 1998).

Arul Raja, Maria, 'Towards a Dalit Reading of the Bible: Some Hermeneutical Reflections', *Jeevadhara: A Journal of Christian Interpretation* 26:151 (1996).

'Assertion of Periphery: Some Biblical Paradigms', *Jeevadhara: A Journal of Christian Interpretation* 27:157 (1997).

'A Dialogue Between Dalits and Bible', *Journal of Dharma* 24:1 (1999).

Ateek, Naim S., 'Biblical Perspectives on the Land', in *Voices from the Margin: Interpreting the Bible in the Third World*, new edition, ed. R. S. Sugirtharajah (Maryknoll, NY, Orbis Books, 1995).

Barrett Montgomery, Helen, *The Bible and Missions* (West Medford, The Central Committee on the United Study of Foreign Missions, 1920).

The Bible and Culture Collective, *The Postmodern Bible* (New Haven, Yale University Press, 1995).

The Bible in Many Tongues (London, The Religious Tract Society, 1853).

Boff, Clodovis, 'Hermeneutics: Constitution of Theological Pertinency', in *Voices from the Margin: Interpreting the Bible in the Third World*, ed. R. S. Sugirtharajah (London, SPCK, 1991).

Boff, Leonardo, 'The New Evangelization: New Life Bursts in', *Concilium* 6 (1990).

Boyd, R. H. S., 'The Use of the Bible in Indian Christian Theology', *Indian Journal of Theology* 22:4 (1974).

Bright, Pamela, 'Biblical Ambiguity in African Exegesis', in *De Doctrina Christiana: A Classic of Western Culture*, ed. Duane W. H. Arnold and Pamela Bright (Notre Dame, IN, University of Notre Dame Press, 1995).

Bright, Pamela (ed. and tr.), *Augustine and the Bible* (Notre Dame, IN, University of Notre Dame Press, 1999).

Broomhall, Marshall, *The Bible in China* (London, The British and Foreign Bible Society, 1934).

Browne, George, *The History of the British and Foreign Bible Society: From Its Institution in 1804, to the Close of Its Jubilee in 1854* (London, Bagster and Sons, 1859), vols. I–II.

Canton, William, *The Story of the Bible Society* (London, John Murray, 1904).

A History of the British and Foreign Bible Society, Volume II (London, John Murray, 1904).

Cardenal, Ernesto, *The Gospel in Solentiname*, tr. Donald D. Walsh (Maryknoll, NY, Orbis Books, 1982), vols. I–IV.

Carr, Dhyanchand, 'A Biblical Basis for Dalit Theology', in *Indigenous People: Dalits: Dalit Issues in Today's Theological Debate*, ed. James Massey (Delhi, ISPCK, 1994).

Cavalcanti, Tereza, 'Social Location and Biblical Interpretation: Tropical Reading', in *Reading from This Place*, vol. II: *Social Location and Biblical Interpretation in Global Perspective*, ed. Fernando F. Segovia and Mary Ann Tolbert (Minneapolis, Fortress Press, 1995).

Colenso, John William, *St Paul's Epistle to the Romans: Newly Translated and Explained from a Missionary Point of View* (Cambridge, Macmillan and Co., 1861).

The Pentateuch and Book of Joshua Critically Examined (London, Longman, Green, Longman, Roberts, & Green, part I, 1862; parts II and III, 1863; part IV, 1864).

The Pentateuch and Book of Joshua Critically Examined (London, Longmans, Green & Co., part VI, 1871; part VII, 1879).

Natal Sermons: A Series of Discourses Preached in the Cathedral Church of St Peter's Maritzburg (London, N. Trubner & Co., 1866).

Natal Sermons: Second Series of Discourses Preached in the Cathedral Church of St Peter's Maritzburg (London, N. Trubner & Co., 1868).

Natal Sermons. Series III (n.p.; n.d.)

Devasahayam, V., *Doing Theology in Biblical Key* (Madras, Gurukul Lutheran Theological College and Research Institute, 1997).

Donaldson, Laura E., 'The Sign of Orpah: Reading Ruth Through Native Eyes', in *Vernacular Hermeneutics*, ed. R. S. Sugirtharajah (Sheffield, Sheffield Academic Press, 1999).

Equiano, Olaudah, *The Interesting Narrative and Other Writings* (London, Penguin, 1995).

Fison, William, *Colportage: Its History, and Relation to Home and Foreign Evangelization* (London, Wertheim, Macintosh, and Hunt, 1859).

Gamaliel, James Canjanam, *Dharma in the Hindu Scriptures and the Bible* (Delhi, ISPCK, 1999).

Glover, William B., *Evangelical Nonconformists and Higher Criticism in the Nineteenth Century* (London, Independent Press Ltd, 1954).

Gnanavaram, M., ' "Dalit Theology" and the Parable of the Good Samaritan', *Journal for the Study of the New Testament* 50 (1993).

Gutiérrez, Gustavo, *On Job: God-Talk and the Suffering of the Innocent* (Maryknoll, NY, Orbis Books, 1987).

Hall, Isaac H., 'The Syriac Translations of the New Testament', in *The Syriac New Testament Translated into English from the Peshitto Version*, tr. James Murdock (Boston, MA, Scriptural Tract Repository, 1893).

Harris, W. B., *A Commentary on the Epistle of St Paul to the Romans*, The Christian Students' Library, 33 (Madras, The Christian Literature Society, 1964).

Hawley, Susan, 'Does God Speak Miskitu? The Bible and Ethnic Identity Among Miskitu of Nicaragua', in *Ethnicity and the Bible*, ed. Mark G. Brett (Leiden, E. J. Brill, 1996).

Hendricks, Osayande Obery, 'Guerrilla Exegesis: A Post Modern Proposal for Insurgent African American Biblical Interpretation', *The Journal for the Interdenominational Theological Center* 22:1 (1994).

Hooper, J. S. M., *The Bible in India with a Chapter on Ceylon* (London, Oxford University Press, 1938).

Hudspeth, Will H., *The Bible and China* (London, The British and Foreign Bible Society, 1952).

Kilgour, R., *The Bible Throughout the World: A Survey of Scripture Translations* (London, World Dominion Press, 1939).

Kinukawa, Hisako, *Women and Jesus in Mark: A Japanese Feminist Perspective* (Maryknoll, NY, Orbis Books, 1994).

Lawton, David, *Faith, Text and History: The Bible in English* (Charlottesville, University Press of Virginia, 1990).

Lee, Archie C. C., 'The Recitation of the Past: A Cross-Textual Reading of Ps. 78 and Other Odes', *Ching Feng* 39:4 (1996).

Lee, Peter K. H., 'Two Stories of Loyalty', *Ching Feng* 32:1 (1989).

Marx, Steven, *Shakespeare and the Bible* (Oxford, Oxford University Press, 2000).

Masenya, Madipoane J., '*Ngwetsi* (Bride): The Naomi–Ruth Story from an African-South African Perspective', *Journal of Feminist Studies in Religion* 14:2 (1998).

Maurico de Barros, Saulo, 'Popular Reading of the Bible: A Liberating Method', MA dissertation (University of Birmingham, 1998).

Mesters, Carlos, *Defenseless Flower: A New Reading of the Bible*, tr. Francis McDonagh (Maryknoll, NY, Orbis Books, 1989).

Miguez-Bonino, José, 'Marxist Critical Tools: Are They Helpful in Breaking the Stranglehold of Idealist Hermeneutics?', in *Voices from the Margin: Interpreting the Bible in the Third World*, new edition, ed. R. S. Sugirtharajah (Maryknoll, NY, Orbis Books, 1995).

Mosala, Itumeleng J., 'The Implications of the Text of Esther for African Women's Struggle for Liberation in South Africa', *Semeia: An Experimental Journal for Biblical Criticism* 59 (1992).

Musopole, A. C., 'Witchcraft Terminology, the Bible, and African Christian Theology: An Exercise in Hermeneutics', *Journal of Religion in Africa* 23:4 (1993).

Nakanose, Shigeyuki, *Josiah's Passover: Sociology and the Liberating Bible* (Maryknoll, NY, Orbis Books, 1993).

Neil, W., 'The Criticism and Theological Use of the Bible, 1700–1950: Criticism of the Traditional Use by Rationalists', in *The Cambridge History of the Bible: The West from the Reformation to the Present Day*, ed. S. L. Greenslade (Cambridge, Cambridge University Press, 1963).

Norton, David, *A History of the Bible As Literature*, vol. I: *From Antiquity to 1700* (Cambridge, Cambridge University Press, 1993).

Owen, John, *The History of the Origin and First Ten Years of the British and Foreign Bible Society* (London, Trilling and Hughes, 1816), vols. I–II.

Oxtoby, Willard G., ' "Telling in Their Own Tongues": Old and Modern Bible Translations as Expressions of Ethnic Cultural Identity', *Concilium* 1 (1995).

Pallares, José Cárdenas, *A Poor Man Called Jesus: Reflections on the Gospel of Mark*, tr. Robert R. Barr (Maryknoll, NY, Orbis Books, 1986).

Pattel-Gray, Anne, 'Dreaming: An Aboriginal Interpretation of the Bible', in *Text & Experience: Towards A Cultural Exegesis of the Bible*, ed. Daniel Smith-Christopher (Sheffield, Sheffield Academic Press, 1995).

Phillips, Godfrey E., *The Old Testament in the World Church: With Special Reference to Younger Churches* (London, Lutterworth Press, 1942).

Ploeg, J. P. M. van der, *The Christians of St Thomas in South India and Their Syriac Manuscripts* (Bangalore, Dharmaram Publications, 1983).

Plummer, A., *The Gospel According to St Mark* (Cambridge, Cambridge University Press, 1915).

Rayan, Samuel, 'Caesar Versus God', in *Jesus Today*, ed. S. Kappen (Bombay, AICUF Publication, 1985).

Records of the English Bible: The Documents Relating to the Translation and Publication of the Bible in English, 1525–1611, ed. Alfred W. Pollard (Oxford, Oxford University Press, 1911).

Richard, Pablo, '1492: The Violence of God and Future of Christianity', *Concilium* 6 (1990).

'The Hermeneutics of Liberation: A Hermeneutic of the Spirit', in *Reading from This Place*, vol. II: *Social Location and Biblical Interpretation in Global Perspective*, ed. Fernando F. Segovia and Mary Ann Tolbert (Minneapolis, Fortress Press, 1995).

'Indigenous Biblical Hermeneutics: God's Revelation in Native Religions and the Bible (After 500 Years of Domination)', in *Text & Experience: Towards a Cultural Exegesis of the Bible*, ed. Daniel Smith-Christopher (Sheffield, Sheffield Academic Press, 1995).

'Biblical Interpretation from the Perspective of Indigenous Cultures of Latin America (Mayas, Kunas, and Quechuas)', in *Ethnicity & the Bible*, ed. Mark G. Brett (Leiden, E. J. Brill, 1996).

Richardson, Alan, *The Bible in the Age of Science* (London, SCM Press, 1961).

Robinson, Maxwell R., *A Commentary on the Pastoral Epistles*, The Christian Students' Library, 27 (Madras, The Christian Literature Society, 1962).

Rogerson, John *Old Testament Criticism in the Nineteenth Century: England and Germany* (London, SPCK, 1984).

Roth, Wolfgang M. W., *Old Testament Theology*, The Christian Students' Library, 41 (Madras, The Christian Literature Society, 1968).

Sahi, Jyoti, 'Reflections on the Image of the Prodigal Son', *Indian Theological Studies* 34:1, 2, 3 (1997).

Scharper, Philip and Scharper, Sally, *The Gospel in Art by the Peasants in Solentiname* (Maryknoll, NY, Orbis Books, 1980).

Soares-Prabhu, George M., 'Two Mission Commands: An Interpretation of Matthew 28:16–20 in the light of a Buddhist Text', *Biblical Interpretation: A Journal of Contemporary Approaches* 2:31 (1995).

Standaert, Nicolas, 'The Bible in Early Seventeenth-Century China', in *Bible in Modern China: The Literary and Intellectual Impact*, ed. Irene Eber, Sze-Kar Wan and Knut Walf (Sankt Augustine, Institut Monumenta Serica, 1999).

Steinberg, Naomi, 'Israelite Tricksters: Their Analogues and Cross-Cultural Study', *Semeia: An Experimental Journal for Biblical Criticism* 42 (1988).

Sugirtharajah, R. S., 'The Bible and Its Asian Readers', *Biblical Interpretation: A Journal of Contemporary Approaches* 1:1 (1993).
The Postcolonial Bible (Sheffield, Sheffield Academic Press, 1998).
Asian Biblical Hermeneutics and Postcolonialism: Contesting the Interpretations (Sheffield, Sheffield Academic Press, 1999).
Tamez, Elsa, 'Quetzalcoatal Challenges the Christian Bible', SBL Annual Conference (San Francisco, 1992), unpublished paper.
The Amnesty of Grace: Justification by Faith from a Latin American Perspective, tr. Sharon H. Ringe (Nashville, Abingdon Press, 1993).
Thuesen, Peter J., *In Discordance with the Scriptures: American Protestant Battles Over Translating the Bible* (New York, Oxford University Press, 1999).
Tilley, Maureen A., *The Bible in Christian North Africa: The Donatist World* (Minneapolis, MN, Fortress Press, 1997).
Vaage, Leif E. (ed. and tr.), *Subversive Scriptures: Revolutionary Readings of the Christian Bible in Latin America* (Valley Forge, PA, Trinity Press International, 1997).
Wagner, Reinhold, 'The Malayalam Bible', *Indian Church History Review* 2:2 (1968).
Warrior, Robert Allen, 'Canaanites, Cowboys, and Indians', in *Voices From the Margin: Interpreting the Bible in the Third World*, new edition, ed. R. S. Sugirtharajah (Maryknoll, NY, Orbis Books, 1995).
West, Gerald O., *Contextual Bible Study* (Pietermaritzburg, Cluster Publications, 1993).
The Academy of the Poor: Towards a Dialogical Reading of the Bible (Sheffield, Sheffield Academic Press, 1999).
Westcott, Brooke Foss, *The Bible in the Church: A Popular Account of the Collection and Reception of the Holy Scriptures in the Christian Churches* (London, Macmillan and Co., 1887).
Westhelle, Vitor, 'Elements for a Typology of Latin American Theologies', in *Prejudice: Issues in Third World Theologies*, ed. Andreas Nehring (Madras, Gurukul Lutheran Theological College and Research Institute, 1996).
Wielenga, Bastian, *It's a Long Road to Freedom: Perspectives of Biblical Theology* (Madurai, Tamilnadu Theological Seminary, 1988).
'The God of Israel and the Other Deities: Why So Particular?', in *Biblical Insights on Inter-Faith Dialogue: Source Material for Study and Reflection*, ed. Israel Selvanayagam (Bangalore, The Board for Theological Text-Books Programme of South Asia, 1995).
Yeo, Khiok-Khung, *What Has Jerusalem to Do with Beijing?: Biblical Interpretation from a Chinese Perspective* (Harrisburg, PA, Trinity Press International, 1998).
Yieh, John Y. H. 'Cultural Reading of the Bible: Some Chinese

Cases', in *Text & Experience: Towards A Cultural Exegesis of the Bible*, ed. Daniel Smith-Christopher (Sheffield, Sheffield Academic Press, 1995).

Yuasa, Yuko, 'Performing Sacred Text', *Concilium* 3 (1998).

THEOLOGY

Abesamis, Carlos H., *A Third Look at Jesus: A Guidebook Along the Road Least Travelled* (Quezon City, Claretian Publications, 1999).

Abraham, Koshy, *Prajapathi: The Cosmic Christ* (Delhi, ISPCK, 1997).

Adhav, S. M., *Pandita Ramabai*, Confessing the Faith in India, no. 13 (Bangalore, The Christian Institute for Study of Religion and Society, 1979).

Appasamy, A. J., *Christianity as Bhakti Marga* (Madras, The Christian Literature Society, 1928).

What is Moksa? (Madras, The Christian Literature Society, 1931).

Banerjea, K M., *The Arian Witness: Or the Testimony of Arian Scriptures in Corroboration of Biblical History and the Rudiments of Christian Doctrine, Including Dissertations on the Original and Early Adventures of Indo-Arians* (Calcutta, Thacker, Spink & Co., 1875).

Two Essays as Supplements to the Arian Witness (Calcutta, Thacker, Spink & Co., 1880).

Bultmann, Rudolf, *Faith and Understanding* (London, SCM Press, 1969).

De Schrijver, G. (ed.), *Liberation Theologies on Shifting Grounds: A Clash of Socio-Economic and Cultural Paradigms* (Leuven, Leuven University Press, 1998).

Francis, Dayanandan, 'Brief Remarks on the Relevance of the Indian Context for Christian Reflection: A Tamil Perspective', in *Christian Contribution to Indian Philosophy*, ed. Anand Amaladass (Madras, The Christian Literature Society, 1995).

Gutiérrez, Gustavo, *A Theology of Liberation: History, Politics, and Salvation*, tr. Caridad. Inda and John Eagleson (Maryknoll, NY, Orbis Books, 1973)

A Theology of Liberation: History, Politics, and Salvation, revised edn, tr. Caridad Inda and John Eagleson (Maryknoll, NY, Orbis Books, 1988).

The Truth Shall Make You Free: Confrontations, tr. Matthew O'Connell (Maryknoll, NY, Orbis Books, 1990).

Healy, Joseph and Sybertz, Donald, *Towards an African Narrative Theology* (Maryknoll, NY, Orbis Books, 1996).

Jacob, P. S. (ed.), *The Experimental Response of N. V. Tilak*, Confessing the Faith in India Series, no. 17 (Madras, The Christian Literature Society, 1979).

Kitamori, Kazoh, *Theology of the Pain of God* (Richmond, VA, John Knox Press, 1965).

Koyama, Kosuke, 'Theological Education: Its Unities and Diversities', *Theological Education Supplement* 1:30 (1993).

Kuribayashi, Teruo, 'Recovering Jesus for Outcasts in Japan', in *Frontiers in Asian Christian Theology*, ed. R. S. Sugirtharajah (Maryknoll, NY, Orbis Books, 1994).

'Theology of Crowned with Thorns', in *God, Christ & God's People in Asia*, ed. Dhyanchand Carr (Hong Kong, CCA Theological Concerns, 1995).

Maurice, Frederick Denison, *The Religions of the World and Their Relations to Christianity* (London, Macmillan and Co., 1886).

Menchu, Rigoberta, *I. Rigoberta Menchu: An Indian Woman in Guatemala*, ed. Elisabeth Burgos-Debray, tr. Ann Wright (London, Verso, 1984).

Paul, Rajaiah D., *The Cross Over India* (London, SCM Press, 1952).

Philip, T. V., *Krishna Mohan Banerjea: Christian Apologist*, Confessing the Faith in India Series, no. 15 (Bangalore, The Christian Institute for the Study of Religion and Society, 1982).

Pieris, Aloysius, *An Asian Theology of Liberation* (Edinburgh, T. & T. Clark, 1988).

Rayan, Samuel, 'Wrestling in the Night', in *The Future of Liberation Theology: Essays in Honor of Gustavo Gutiérrez*, ed. Marc H. Ellis and Otto Maduro.(Maryknoll, NY, Orbis Books, 1989).

Sathiasatchy, 'P. A., Theological Exploration Into Ancient Tamil Poems', in *Doing Theology with the Poetic Traditions of India: Focus on Dalit and Tribal Poems*, ed. Joseph Patmury (Bangalore, PTCA/ SATHRI, 1996).

Sathler, Josué and Nascimento, Amós, 'Black Masks on White Faces: Liberation Theology and the Quest for Syncretism in the Brazilian Context', in *Liberation Theologies, Postmodernity, and the Americas*, ed. David Bastone et al. (London, Routledge, 1997).

Schreiter, Robert J., *The New Catholicity: Theology Between the Global and the Local* (Maryknoll, NY, Orbis Books, 1997).

Segundo, Juan Luis, *The Liberation of Theology*, tr. John Drury (Maryknoll, NY, Orbis Books, 1976).

Signs of the Times: Theological Reflections, tr. Robert R. Barr (Maryknoll, NY, Orbis Books, 1993).

Song, C. S., *The Tears of Lady Meng: A Parable of People's Political Theology* (Geneva, The World Council of Churches, 1981).

Treat, James (ed.), *Native and Christian: Indigenous Voices on Religious Identity in the United States and Canada* (New York, Routledge, 1996).

Vidales, R., 'Methodological Issues in Liberation Theology', in

Frontiers of Theology in Latin America, ed. Rosino Gibellini (London, SCM Press, 1980).

Wagua, Aiban, 'Present Consequences of the European Invasion of America', *Concilium* 6 (1990).

Winter, Michael, *Problems in Theology: The Atonement* (London, Geoffrey Chapman, 1994).

HISTORY: COLONIAL AND ECCLESIASTICAL

'The Acts of the Abitinian Martyrs', *Donatist Martyr Stories: The Church in Conflict in Roman North Africa. Translated with Notes and Introduction*, tr. Maureen A. Tilley (Liverpool, Liverpool University Press, 1996).

Apess, William, *A Son of the Forest and Other Writings by William Apess, a Pequot*, ed. Barry O'Connell (Amherst, University of Massachusetts Press, 1992).

   On Our Own Ground: The Complete Works of William Apess, a Pequot, ed. Barry O'Connell (Amherst, University of Massachusetts Press, 1992).

Bartlett, J. Vernon, and Carlyle, A. J., *Christianity in History: A Study of Religious Development* (London, Macmillan and Co., 1917).

Buchanan, Claudius, *Christian Researches in Asia, to Which Are Prefixed a Memoir of the Author, and an Introductory Sketch of Protestant Missions in India: With an Appendix Containing a Summary of the Subsequent Progress of Missionary Operations in the East* (London, The Society for the Promotion of Popular Instruction, 1840).

Burton, Antoinette, 'Colonial Encounters in Late-Victorian England: Pandita Ramabai at Cheltenham and Wantage', *Feminist Review* 49 (1995).

Chakravarti, Uma, *Rewriting History: The Life and Times of Pandita Ramabai* (New Delhi, Kali for Women, 1998).

Colenso, John William, *Ten Weeks in Natal: A Journal of a First Visitation Among the Colonialists* (Cambridge, Macmillan & Co., 1855).

   Bringing Forth Light: Five Tracts on Bishop Colenso's Zulu Mission, ed. Ruth Edgecombe (Pietermaritzburg, University of Natal, 1982).

Costanzo, Angelo, *Surprising Narrative: Olaudah Equiano and the Beginnings of Black Autobiography* (New York, Greenwood Press, 1987).

Dubois, Abbé J. A., *Letters on the State of Christianity in India* (New Delhi, Associated Publishing House, n.d.).

England, John C., *The Hidden History of Christianity in Asia: The Churches of the East Before 1500* (Delhi, ISPCK, 1996).

Flemming, Leslie A., 'Between Two Worlds: Self-Construction and Self-Identity in the Writings of Three Nineteenth-Century Indian

Christian Women', in *Women as Subjects: South Asian Histories*, ed. Nita Kumar (Charlottesville, University Press of Virginia, 1994).

Forrester, Duncan B., *Caste and Christianity: Attitudes and Politics on Caste of Anglo-Saxon Protestant Missions in India* (London, Curzon Press, 1980).

Foster, John, *The Church of the T'ang Dynasty* (London, SPCK, 1939).

Frend, W. H. C., *The Donatist Church: A Movement of Protest in Roman North Africa* (Oxford, Clarendon Press, 1952).

Gardner, C. E., *Life of Father Goreh* (London, Longmans, Green, and Co., 1900).

Gilmont, Jean-François, 'Protestant Reformations and Reading', in *A History of Reading in the West*, ed. Guglielmo Cavallo and Roger Chartier (London, Polity Press, 1999).

Guy, Jeff, *The Heretic: A Study of the Life of John William Colenso 1814–1883* (Johannesburg, Ravan Press, 1983).

Hall, Fielding, *A People at School* (New York, Macmillan and Co., 1906).

Hickley, Dennis, *The First Christians in China: An Outline History and Some Considerations Concerning the Nestorians in China During the Tang Dynasty* (London, The China Study Project, 1980).

Hilton, Boyd, *The Age of Atonement: The Influence of Evangelicalism on Social and Economic Thought 1785–1865* (Oxford, Clarendon Press, 1991).

Lanternari, Vittorio, 'Revolution and/or Integration in African Socio-Religious Movements', in *Religion, Rebellion, Revolution: An Interdisciplinary and Cross-Cultural Collection of Essays*, ed. Bruce Lincoln (London, Macmillan, 1985).

Legge, James, *The Nestorian Monument of Hsî-an-Fû in Shen-Hsî, China* (London, Trubner and Co., 1888).

Maclagan, Edward, *The Jesuits and the Great Mogul* (London, Burns Oates and Washbourne, 1932).

Macnicol, Nicol, *Pandita Ramabai* (London, SCM Press, 1927).

Martin, Roger H., *Evangelicals United: Ecumenical Stirrings in Pre-Victorian Britain, 1795–1830* (Metuchen, NJ, The Scarecrow Press, 1983).

Moffat, Robert, *Missionary Labours and Scenes in Southern Africa* (London, John Snow, 1842).

Moffett, Samuel Hugh, *A History of Christianity in Asia*, vol. 1: *Beginnings to 1500*, revised and corrected edition (Maryknoll, NY, Orbis Books, 1998).

Mundadan, A. M., *Indian Christians: Search for Identity and Struggle for Autonomy* (Bangalore, Dharmaram Publications, 1984).

Murphy, G. Roland, *The Saxon Savior: The Germanic Transformation of the Gospel in the Ninth-Century Heliand* (New York, Oxford University Press, 1989).

Nedungatt, George, 'The Spirituality of the Syro-Malabar Church', in *East Syrian Spirituality*, ed. Augustine Thottakkara (Bangalore, Dharmaram Publications, 1990).

Park, Mungo, *Travels in the Interior Districts of Africa: Performed Under the Direction and Patronage of the African Association in the Years 1795, 1796 and 1797* (London, W. Blumer and Co., 1810).

Phan, Peter C., *Mission and Catechesis: Alexandre de Rhodes and Inculturation in Seventeenth Century Vietnam* (Maryknoll, NY, Orbis Books, 1998).

Podipara, Placid, 'Hindu in Culture, Christian in Religion, Oriental in Worship', in *The St Thomas Christian Encyclopaedia of India*, vol. II: *Apostle Thomas, Kerala, Malabar Christianity*, ed. George Menachery (Trichur, St Thomas Christian Encyclopaedia of India, 1973).

Polo, Marco, *The Travels of Marco Polo*, tr. Ronald Latham (London, The Folio Society, 1958).

Potkay, Adam, 'Olaudah Equiano and the Art of Spiritual Autobiography', *Eighteenth-Century Studies* 27 (1994).

Raven, Susan, *Rome in Africa* (London, Routledge, 1993).

Saeki, P. Y., *The Nestorian Documents and Relics in China* (Tokyo, The Academy of Oriental Culture, 1937).

Shah, A. B., *The Letters and Correspondence of Pandita Ramabai* (Bombay, Maharashtra State Board for Literature and Culture, 1977).

Sundkler, Bengt G. M., *Bantu Prophets in South Africa* (London, Lutterworth Press, 1948).

Walvin, James, *An African's life: The Life and Times of Olaudah Equiano, 1745–1797* (London, Continuum, 2000).

Wittmann, Reinhard, 'Was There a Reading Revolution at the End of the Eighteenth Century?', in *A History of Reading in the West*, ed. Guglielmo Cavallo and Roger Chartier (London, Polity Press, 1999).

Wolffe, John, 'Rethinking the Missionary Position: Bishop Colenso of Natal', in *Religion in Victorian Britain*, vol. V: *Culture and Empire*, ed. John Wolffe (Manchester, Manchester University Press, 1997).

CRITICAL THEORIES

Adam, Ian, and Tiffin, Helen, *Past the Last Post: Theorizing Post-Colonialism and Post-Modernism* (Hemel Hempstead, Harvester Wheatsheaf, 1993).

Ananda Murthy, U. R., 'The Search for an Identity: A Kannada Writer's Viewpoint', in *Asian and Western Writers in Dialogue: New Cultural Identities*, ed. Guy Amirthanayagam (London, Macmillan, 1982).

Asad, Talal, 'A Comment on Translation, Critique, and Subversion', in *Between Languages and Cultures: Translation and Cross-Cultural Texts*, ed. Anuradha Dingwaney and Carol Maier (Delhi, Oxford University Press, 1996).

Ashcroft, Bill, Griffiths, Gareth and Tiffin, Helen, *Key Concepts in Post-Colonial Studies* (London, Routledge, 1998).

Barker, Francis, Hulme, Peter and Iversen, Margaret, 'Introduction', in *Colonial Discourse/Postcolonial Theory*, ed. Francis Barker, Peter Hulme and Margaret Iversen (Manchester, Manchester University Press, 1994).

Bhabha, Homi K., *The Location of Culture* (London, Routledge, 1994).

Chao, Phebe Shih, 'Reading *The Letter* in a Postcolonial World', in *Visions of the East: Orientalism in Film*, ed. Matthew Bernstein and Gaylyn Studlar (London, I. B. Tauris Publishers, 1997).

Chari, V. K., *Sanskrit Criticism* (Delhi, Motilal Banarsidass Publishers, 1990).

Childs, Peter and Williams, Patrick, *An Introduction to Post-Colonial Theory* (London, Prentice Hall, 1997).

Chow, Rey, *Writing Diaspora: Tactics of Intervention in Contemporary Cultural Studies* (Bloomington, Indiana University Press, 1993).

Dharmarajan, Geeta, 'Treading Euclid's Line', in *Katha Prize Stories*, vol. IV, ed. Geeta Dharmarajan (New Delhi, Katha, 1994).

Dirlik, Arif, 'Global in the Local', in *Global/Local: Cultural Production and the Transnational Imaginary*, ed. Rob Wilson and Wimal Dissanayake (Durham, NC, Duke University Press, 1996).

Gandhi, Leela, *Postcolonial Theory: A Critical Introduction* (Edinburgh, Edinburgh University Press, 1998).

Gates, Jr, Henry Louis, *The Signifying Monkey: A Theory of Afro-Afroamerican Literary Criticism* (Oxford, Oxford University Press, 1987).

Hadjor, Kofi Buenor, *Dictionary of Third World Terms* (London, Penguin Books, 1993).

Hall, Stuart, 'When Was "the Post-Colonial"? Thinking at the Limit', in *The Post-Colonial Question: Common Skies Divided Horizons*, ed. Iain Chambers and Lidia Curti (London, Routledge, 1996).

Loomba, Ania, *Colonialism/Postcolonialism* (London, Routledge, 1998).

Lunsford, Andrea A., 'Toward a Mestiza Rhetoric: Gloria Anzaldúa on Composition and Postcoloniality', in *Race, Rhetoric, and the Postcolonial*, ed. Gary A. Olson and Lynn Worsham (Albany, State University of New York Press, 1999).

Lutgendorf, Philip, *The Life of a Text: Performing the Rāmcaritmānas of Tulsidas* (Berkeley, University of California Press, 1991).

McLeod, John, *Beginning Postcolonialism* (Manchester, Manchester University Press, 2000).

Mongia, Padmini (ed.), *Contemporary Postcolonial Theory: A Reader* (London, Arnold, 1996).

Moore-Gilbert, Bart, *Postcolonial Theory: Contexts, Practices, Politics* (London, Verso, 1997).

Moore-Gilbert, Bart, Stanton, Gareth and Maley, Willy, *Postcolonial Criticism* (London, Longman, 1997).

Nandy, Ashis, *The Intimate Enemy: Loss and Recovery of Self Under Colonialism* (Delhi; Oxford, Oxford University Press, 1991).

Niranjana, Tejaswini, *Siting Translation: History, Post-Structuralism, and the Colonial Context* (Berkeley, University of California Press, 1992).

Paranjape, Makarand, 'Beyond Nativism: Towards a Contemporary Indian Tradition in Criticism', in *Nativism: Essays in Criticism*, ed. Makarand Paranjape (Delhi, Sahitya Akademi, 1997).

Quayson, Ato, *Postcolonialism: Theory, Practice or Process?* (Cambridge, Polity Press, 2000).

Said, Edward W., *Orientalism* (Harmondsworth, Penguin, 1985).

  Culture and Imperialism (London, Chatto & Windus, 1993).

  Representations of the Intellectual: The 1993 Reith Lectures (London, Vintage, 1994).

Schwarz, Henry and Sangeeta, Ray (eds.), *A Companion to Postcolonial Studies* (Oxford, Blackwell Publishers, 2000).

Seth, Sanjay, Gandhi, Leela and Dutton, Michael, 'Postcolonial Studies: A Beginning', *Postcolonial Studies: Culture, Politics, Economy* 1:1 (1998).

Spivak, Gayatri Chakravorty, *In Other Worlds: Essays in Cultural Politics* (New York, Routledge, 1988).

  The Post-Colonial Critic: Interviews, Strategies, Dialogues, ed. Sarah Harasym (New York, Routledge, 1990).

  'Neocolonialism and the Secret Agent (Interviewed by Robert Young)', *The Oxford Literary Review* 13:1–2 (1991).

  Outside in the Teaching Machine (New York, Routledge, 1993).

  A Critique of Postcolonial Reason: Toward a History of the Vanishing Present (Cambridge, MA, Harvard University Press, 1999).

Warrior, Robert Allen, *Tribal Secrets: Recovering American Indian Intellectual Traditions* (Minneapolis, University of Minnesota Press, 1996).

Yeğenoğlu, Meyda, *Colonial Fantasies: Towards a Feminist Reading of Orientalism* (Cambridge, Cambridge University Press, 1998).

Zemka, Sue, *Victorian Testaments: The Bible, Christology, and Literary Authority in Early-Nineteenth-Century British Culture* (Stanford, CA, Stanford University Press, 1997).

THE BIBLE SOCIETY REPORTS

After a Hundred Years: A Popular Illustrated Report of the British and Foreign Bible Society for the Centenary Year 1903–1904 (London, The Bible House, 1904).

Behold a Sower: A Popular Illustrated Report of the British and Foreign Bible Society for the Year 1900–1901 (London, The Bible House, 1901).

The Book Above Every Book (London, The Bible House, 1910).

The Book and the Sword: A Popular Illustrated Report of the British and Foreign Bible Society for the Year 1914–1915 (London, The Bible House, 1915).

The Book of God's Kingdom: A Popular Illustrated Report of the British and Foreign Bible Society 1901–1902 (London, The Bible House, 1902).

The Bridge Builders: A Popular Report of the British and Foreign Bible Society for the Year 1922–1923 (London, The Bible House, 1923).

Building the City: A Popular Report of the British and Foreign Bible Society 1921–1922 (London, The Bible House, 1922).

The Common Bond (London, The British and Foreign Bible Society, 1935).

For Such a Time as This: A Popular Report of the British and Foreign Bible Society for the Year 1917–1918 (London, The Bible House, 1918).

For the Healing of the Nations: A Popular Report of the British and Foreign Bible Society for the Year 1915–1916 (London, The Bible House, 1916).

A Fountain Unsealed: A Popular Report of the British and Foreign Bible Society 1910–1911 (London, The Bible House, 1911).

Goodwill Toward Men: A Popular Report of the British and Foreign Bible Society for the Year 1920–1921 (London, The Bible House, 1921).

Have Ye Never Read?: A Popular Report of the British and Foreign Bible Society 1912–1913 (London, The Bible House, 1913).

The Highway in the Wilderness: A Popular Illustrated Report of the British and Foreign Bible Society for the Year 1907–1908 (London, The Bible House, 1908).

The Immortal Story (London, The British and Foreign Bible Society, 1927).

In the Mother Tongue (London, The British and Foreign Bible Society, 1930).

In the Vulgar Tongue: A Popular Illustrated Report of the British and Foreign Bible Society 1913–1914 (London, The Bible House, 1914).

The Leaves of the Tree: A Popular Illustrated Report of the British and Foreign Bible Society for the Year 1906–1907 (London, The Bible House, 1907).

Like Unto Leaven: A Popular Illustrated Report of the British and Foreign Bible Society for the Year 1923–1924 (London, The Bible House, 1924).

More Golden Than Gold: A Popular Illustrated Report of the British and Foreign Bible Society 1911–1912 (London, The Bible House, 1912).

Our Heritage (London, The British and Foreign Bible Society, 1934).

Rebuilding on the Rock: A Popular Report of the British and Foreign Bible Society for the Year 1918–1919 (London, The Bible House, 1919).

Seed Corn for the World: A Popular Report of the British and Foreign Bible Society for the Year 1904–1905 (London, The Bible House, 1905).

Tell the World (London, The British and Foreign Bible Society, 1933).

The Word Among the Nations: A Popular Illustrated Report of the British and Foreign Bible Society for the Year 1908–1909 (London, The Bible House, 1909).

Index of biblical references

Index of names and subjects

300